4/10/17 - pink highlighting
+ pen underlining JB

Chicano Politics:
Readings

Edited by
F. Chris Garcia
University of New Mexico

MSS Information Corporation
655 Madison Avenue, New York, N.Y. 10021

This is a custom-made book of readings prepared for the courses taught by the editor, as well as for related courses and for college and university libraries. For information about our program, please write to:

MSS INFORMATION CORPORATION
655 Madison Avenue
New York, New York 10021

MSS wishes to express its appreciation to the authors of the articles in this collection for their cooperation in making their work available in this format.

Library of Congress Cataloging in Publication Data

Garcia, F   Chris, comp.
    Chicano politics.

    1. Mexican Americans--Politics and suffrage--
Addresses, essays, lectures. I. Title.
E184.M5G36   323.1'16'82073   72-11569
ISBN 0-8422-5076-X
ISBN 0-8422-0274-9 (pbk)

CONTENTS

PREFACE

The last few years have witnessed a great change in the relationships of Chicanos to the American political system. This at one time "invisible minority" has become a significant political and social force in this country's affairs.

Unfortunately, the current impact of the Chicano movement has not yet been proportionately reflected in the writings of scholars and social observers. Thus, even though the Chicano movement has been gathering momentum for the past several years, and Americans of Mexican-Spanish descent have been involved in American politics for over a century, a person interested in closely examining this situation immediately confronts the problem of inadequate reading materials. For example, there is at present no textbook on the subject of Chicano politics, nor even another collection of readings on the topic.

The selections in this work are organized in the following manner: Parts I through III examine the historical, sociological, psychological and institutional foundations for Chicano politics; these are followed by selections which illustrate the various major styles and strategies of politics, those of traditional "accommodation" politics (Part IV) and the less conventional alternatives of separatism and radicalism (Part V).

I would like to express my sincere appreciation to the authors and publishers who permitted their articles to be included in this volume.

F. Chris Garcia
January 1, 1973
University of New Mexico

PART I

THE SOCIO-HISTORICAL BASE

A MINORITY NOBODY KNOWS

BY HELEN ROWAN

THERE are some five million Americans of Mexican descent or birth. About four and a half million live in five Southwestern states: Arizona, California, Colorado, New Mexico, and Texas. Between them, California and Texas account for 82 percent of the Southwest's total, with California holding the edge.

Census statistics and other studies show the Mexican-Americans in the Southwest to be worse off in every respect than the nonwhites (Negroes, Indians, and Orientals), not to mention the dominant Anglos (everybody else). They are poorer, their housing is more crowded and more dilapidated, their unemployment rate is higher, their average educational level is lower (two years below nonwhite, four below Anglo).

What is extraordinary about the situation is not so much that it exists as that it is so little known. In California, Mexican-Americans outnumber Negroes by almost two to one, but probably not one Californian in ten thousand knows that simple fact. It is an easy one to overlook if you measure a minority's importance by the obvious signs: poverty programs, education, and job-training activities geared to its situation, the elected and appointed officials it can number, the attention directed to it by the press, politicians, and even textbooks, and the help given it by do-good organizations. By all these measures, the Mexican-Americans have been slighted.

The Johnson Administration is beginning to pay them some attention, though in a fitful and nervous manner. Mexican-Americans have been demanding such baubles as jobs, federal appointments, and Great Society programs tailored to their needs.

THE ATLANTIC MONTHLY, 1967, Vol. 219, No. 6, pp. 47-52.

8

Since they justifiably consider themselves to be the nation's best-kept secret, they would like some national visibility, preferably through the lens of a White House Conference focused on their many problems. This the Administration has been loath to give them, though it has tried to appease them for a couple of years by holding out the possibility of such a meeting. Still, there are signs that the *federales* are thinking of some programs specifically designed for Mexican-Americans. While their first needs are the same as those of a lot of other people — money and jobs — there are certain issues which clearly affect them in a special way.

The Mexican-American birthrate is 50 percent higher than that of the general population; the community's average age is already ten years younger than that of the total population. The school dropout rate is higher than that of any other group, and very few of those who do graduate from high school move on to college. Even in California, with its vaunted and supposedly inclusive system of higher education, only about 2 percent of the four-year college enrollment is Mexican-American, while Mexican-Americans constitute about 10 percent of the total population and a much higher percentage of the school-age population. Delinquency and drug addiction rates are high. Residential segregation is increasing. As far as jobs go, the old devil, overt discrimination, has been largely replaced by the new devil, automation, and by more subtle "cultural discrimination" in the form of tests which penalize the Mexican-American first as a student and then as a prospective employee. Finally, there are signs of increasing family change. In the Spanish-speaking ghetto of east Los Angeles, for instance, 26 percent of all children under eighteen are not living with both parents (the figure is only 13 percent for Los Angeles as a whole). This is a particularly serious development for the Mexican-American community, which springs from a culture in which the family is the strongest of all institutions.

If they think of them at all, Easterners are likely to think of Mexican-Americans in terms of wetbacks who cross the border to fester in farm shacks for the miserly wages paid to migratory workers. In fact, Mexican-Americans are heavily urbanized. Almost 80 percent in the Southwest live in cities and towns, a proportion fully as high as the Anglo concentration and considerably higher than the nonwhite. For every Mexican-American picking fruit in California's Central Valley there are scores working as hod carriers and busboys in Los Angeles. For every stereotypical migrant who follows the crops, there are dozens crowded into the *colonias* and *barrios* that cling to the fringes of innumerable Southwest towns. The recent urbanization of such a group, given its low educational level and other characteristics, must represent social, economic, educational — and potentially political — significance of a high order.

But the Mexican-Americans' few successes in bringing themselves to national attention have had to do with the farm-labor issue, which is appropriate yet somewhat ironic. The farm workers, with an average annual income of about $1500 and generally unspeakable living and working conditions, are worse off than anybody else. In the past two years, Cesar Chavez managed to organize and sustain a successful strike of grape pickers. The strike was dramatic, colorful, and immensely appealing, and it drew the support of activist Anglos from all over. Pilgrimages to the Central Valley were undertaken by Bobby Kennedy and youngsters from SNCC, by correspondents of the New York *Times* and television crews from national networks. Bay area liberals who had never set foot in San Francisco's Mission District or in east San Jose made the 550-mile round trip to Delano, the strike headquarters, carrying money, food, and clothing. And many middle-of-the-road Californians did not eat so much as one grape for months, so as not to risk patronizing a struck vineyard.

The condition of the farm workers is obvious and desperate. But Chavez himself is said to have urged urban leaders not to allow the farm-labor issue to deflect their attention from the more complex problems of the *barrios*, which are bound to grow worse as the ghettos continue to receive steady influxes of Mexican immigrants (almost a thousand a week) and displaced domestic farm workers.

East Los Angeles is one of those areas that Eastern eyes would never recognize as being poor. The low dwellings (though there may be as many as three on a tiny lot) have yards around them, and flowers, and on smogless days the nearby mountains stand out beautifully. There is a color that is heightened by the leftover symbols of other peoples for whom the area earlier served as a port of entry: Orientals, Italians, and then Russian Jews. Mexicatessens offer kosher *burritos* and Okie *frijoles*, and Winchell's Do-Nut House features a Taco Fiesta. Youngsters cruise around in beat-up cars for which they buy gas by the quarter's worth. An "Operator Wanted" sign in a curtained storefront window signifies that yet another small sweatshop has opened where the illiterate (and perhaps illegal) immigrant or school dropout may find a few days' work sewing blouses or shirts.

Following the riots in nearby Watts, a special census was made of that area and east L.A. What attention the survey got was mainly directed to the part on Watts, but those who read the rest of the report could find that in east L.A., too, between 1960 and 1965 real income slipped by 8 to 10 percent, housing deteriorated, home ownership declined.

O<small>F THE</small> two courses that Mexican-Americans might follow to bring themselves helpful attention, one they have been unable to take and the other they have been unwilling to take. They have not been able to organize into an effective political bloc, and they have not been willing to riot and burn. One federal official describes them as "the most disorganized ethnic group in the country." The federal establishment, according to some officials, is so desperate to find a real leader to treat with that it would even welcome the emergence of a Mexican-American Stokely Carmichael.

There are good reasons for the Mexican-Americans' lack of political clout, but they escape anyone who tries to understand the Mexican-American experience in terms of other ethnic groups. Ernesto Galarza, a distinguished scholar and writer, points out that historically Mexican-Americans have not been seen as a great constitutional and moral issue, as were the Negroes, nor as an ordinary immigrant group to be acculturated or assimilated. They have been looked on simply as an ever replenishing supply of cheap and docile labor.

The Mexican-Americans do have in common with the Negroes a long history of discrimination, but they were never enslaved and no war was ever fought over them, though one was fought over their land. Harsh as the discrimination was, including lynchings and segregation in schools and other public facilities, it was spotty (you could get into a swimming pool if you weren't too swarthy) and varied from place to place and from time to time.

The somewhat nebulous quality of the discrimination — and the concomitant fact that a lucky Mexican-American could "make it" into the middle class — helps explain why the Mexican-Americans

11

have not yet produced the spontaneous leadership or found the unifying force of the civil rights movement. And the very institutions which might have been expected to recognize the condition and champion the cause of the Mexican-Americans — the Roman Catholic Church, labor, the Democratic Party, liberal groups, educational institutions, and the Eastern philanthropic and press establishment — have been by and large deaf, dumb, and blind on the subject. "For the Mexican-American," says a college professor, "there are no liberals."

This is not literally true, of course. Some individuals such as Carey McWilliams have for years written and spoken vigorously on the problem, and twenty years ago Fred Ross, supported by Saul Alinsky's Industrial Areas Foundation, began community organization efforts in Mexican-American sections of California. Other individuals and groups have done effective work on a small scale, and a few priests (though often at the cost of being silenced or sent away by their superiors) have been fairly militant spokesmen for the Mexican-Americans.

But there has been no wide-scale involvement. The white liberals who at one time helped to lead and to bankroll the Negro movement had few Anglo counterparts working with and speaking out on behalf of the Mexican-Americans. Many Southwestern Anglos supported the Negro movement, however, and even some Mexican-American college students confessed to me that they became active in the Negro cause before they caught on that there was work to be done closer to home.

The lack of outside interest and help (spelled m-o-n-e-y), combined with the fact that until recently the group was overwhelmingly rural and had very few educated members, has given the Mexican-Americans of today very little political leverage. Social, fraternal, and thinly disguised political organizations appear and disappear with startling rapidity, but there has never been a Mexican-American equivalent of the NAACP or Urban League, let alone SNCC or CORE. Even the sturdiest and longest-lived of the organizations have very little in the way of paid staffs. If you want to see the head of some group, you phone his place of business or his house, because it is quite likely that there isn't any headquarters. There is no effective clearinghouse or information center, and communications within the community are weak — among the leaders, and also between them and the poverty-stricken of town and country.

Chavez is the most authentic leader in the traditional sense: a charismatic man sprung from a rural proletariat whose understanding and loyalty he commands. What is questionable is whether the basis of his appeal — a combination of religious pageantry, evocation of the heroes of the Mexican Revolution, and nonviolent civil rights techniques — could successfully be transferred from the fields to the city streets.

"There are dozens of Chavezes hidden in the *barrios*," a city spokesman said sadly, but presumably these buried Chavezes will have to find new ways to rally the new urban proletariat. For whatever the culture of the *barrios* may be, it is certainly a hybrid one, neither classical Mexican nor traditional Anglo urban.

"It's always my parents telling me to be proud I'm Mexican and the school telling me to be American," a junior high school student cried out. For the city youngsters (50 percent of the Mexican-American population is under twenty), the goodies offered by the industrialized society are all too visible and unavailable. "The thing to do is learn how the *gringos* keep you down," they say. And the residents of the *barrios* are sophisticated enough to recognize that it is the future they have to fear more than the present.

"They are teaching my boy nothing in that school, *nothing*," a mother said to me with a despair that is impossible to convey in writing. "What will happen to him? What will he do?"

Considering their numbers in California (now estimated at nearly two million), the Mexican-Americans have a singular dearth of elected representation. There is one congressman of Mexican descent, Edward R. Roybal, a Democrat from Los Angeles. No Mexican-American sits in either house of the California legislature, or on the city council, or elected board of education in L.A. Roybal became the first of his community since 1881 to serve on the city council when he was elected in 1949, but when he left for Congress in 1962 his seat was contested by four Mexican-Americans and one Negro, with the result one might expect.

What the Mexican-Americans have lacked in elective political muscle they have tried to make up for by extracting promises and appointments from Anglo politicians. Here again they are handicapped: the Democrats have taken them for granted (traditionally, about 90 percent of the relatively

13

small registration votes Democratic), and the Republicans haven't bothered much until recently. Most Mexican-Americans agree that Democratic Governor Pat Brown did more for the group than any previous governor. Still, it wasn't enough.

During the last campaign the Reagan forces made some successful overtures to the community, and the Republicans made some electoral inroads, notably around Los Angeles, but the Democrats believe that overall they managed to hold on to about 75 percent of the Mexican-American vote. The defections in California and the rest of the Southwest, however, apparently worried the Democrats (they hastily appointed a Mexican-American to the National Committee), and they should be worried; while they may have no place else to go now, the Mexican-Americans are looking around. A mutually satisfactory political marriage will not easily be achieved. The one thing that Anglos and Mexican-Americans do most certainly for each other is to provide inexhaustible sources of frustration. The Anglo litany of complaints about Mexican-American political behavior, to abbreviate it drastically, runs like this:

They can't get organized, they can't agree among themselves, there aren't any real leaders, and the so-called leaders can't deliver. ("They'd come to us with talk about 400,000 votes," one of Governor Brown's campaign managers said aggrievedly, "but some of those guys couldn't deliver their own families.") The community is uninvolved, and it is difficult to find out what it wants. An assistant to a southern California congressman says that when he sends out invitations to a meeting with the congressman — say 250 to the Negro community and 250 to the Mexican-American — about 150 Negroes usually turn up, and about 30 Mexican-Americans. "And the first question, sometimes the only question, they ask is: 'How many Mexican-Americans on your staff?' If it was 100 percent it still wouldn't be enough," he adds glumly.

This leads to another Anglo complaint: that many Mexican-Americans view the American political process with an eye to appointments and that politics for them becomes a superficial numbers game, with little attention paid either to the potential importance of the jobs or the ability and effectiveness of the appointees.

Finally, Anglos complain that many Mexican-American spokesmen prefer to compete among themselves for elective or appointive jobs instead of working out ways and means for achieving at least a show of unity, a drive for a cause. All too often four or five Mexican-Americans insist on running for an office, thus dividing the vote.

Beyond the Anglo politicos, who have special and self-centered interests in view, others who are highly sympathetic and have no political axes to grind are appalled by the amount and ferocity of infighting that goes on and the fact that it is so often caused not by ideological but by purely personal differences. So strong is the role of *personalismo* in Mexican-American politics that, as one sympathetic observer commented: "They wouldn't even vote to establish a postal system unless they knew who would be the mailman on the block."

Although there is much evidence to support these complaints, they do not take into account a number of relevant factors, including the Anglo role in perpetuating disunity and ineffectiveness within the group, whether intentionally or heedlessly. The Anglo politicians who criticize the lack of Mexican-American political organization make the very decisions that render such organization nearly impossible. In California, the Democrats, apparently thinking they knew a safe thing when they saw it, gerrymandered the Spanish surname sections of Los Angeles and San Francisco so as to make Spanish-speaking voters the pivotal but never the controlling factors in their various districts. This makes it difficult for Mexican-Americans to vote as a bloc and cuts off incipient leadership.

While the Democrats complain that they have to deal with leaders who have no followers, they have not financed the kind of block-to-block canvassing and voter registration that would produce organized constituencies. In search of votes, they woo the heads of the Mexican-American organizations and other community leaders in the hope that the leaders can exert personal influence over the community; it has to be personal, since the organizations themselves lack the money or manpower to organize real constituencies.

In making appointments, too, Anglos seem to set up situations which inevitably cause trouble in and for the Mexican-American community. Because they want to get the maximum political mileage from the few appointments they are willing to make, Anglo officials undertake elaborate though clandestine efforts to procure the perfect all-purpose Mexican-American, then assert that no man can be found to meet the wildly unrealistic qualifications established for the job.

15

Anglo officials make incessant demands for unity among Mexican-Americans, the implication being that the Anglos are unable to do anything until they can discern an unmistakably clear picture of exactly what the community wants. While there are real frustrations involved in dealing with a group as fragmented as the Mexican-Americans, there is also real cynicism involved in the way so many Anglo officials in positions of power at all levels seize on the condition as an excuse to do nothing. It should not be necessary to identify genuine leaders or take a poll of the grass roots to guess, for instance, that no group "wants" to have urban renewal accomplished at the price of its own removal (in at least one border town the Mexican-Americans were renewed right over into Mexico); that no community "wants" to be slashed into chunks by hideous freeways (as has happened in east Los Angeles); that few people "want" their children to attend a school run by someone who could remark, as the former principal of an east Los Angeles high school did in the presence of an Anglo friend of mine, "We couldn't run this school without the dropout rate. They don't belong here anyway — they belong in the fields."

The truth is that the endless jockeying, delaying, rumormongering, and playing of the cat-and-mouse game simply elicit and intensify the very kind of behavior the Anglos deplore: dissension and a flying off in all directions. The entire protracted handling of the on-again, off-again White House Conference is a perfect case in point.

In the fall of 1965, some Mexican-Americans, having heard of plans for a major civil rights conference in Washington, asked to be included. They were given to understand, in writing, that a separate conference would be held for Mexican-Americans or possibly all Spanish-speaking Americans. From then on there were unanswered telegrams from this group, unanswered letters from that one, understandings and misunderstandings, and joint attempts by the leaders of Mexican-American groups to apply pressure. A year ago the President had a few spokesmen to dinner and left them with the impression that there would be a conference. Others of a group that considered itself the prime negotiating committee were not invited. Their exclusion, of course, strained relations among the Mexican-Americans as well as between them and the *federales*.

No more was heard of the much-wanted conference until late October of 1966, when high officials of the Administration found time, despite, or because of, the imminence of the elections, to meet with about sixty Mexican-American spokesmen in "preplanning" discussions of the real conference. Since then official silence has been accompanied by comic-opera goings-on. A small group with Labor Department leadership and the use of White House stationery — but with offices in neither place — is known to be "doing something" about Mexican-Americans and other Spanish-speaking Americans. A receptionist answers its phone "National Conference" but is unable to say on what, or where, or when, or for whom any conferring is being or is going to be done. So rumors fly, consternation and frustration increase among the Mexican-Americans, and much of their attention, time, and energy, and that of a number of federal officials, is diverted from the real problems, which continue to grow more malignant.

THE school systems of the Southwest have totally failed the Mexican-American community," says Dr. Miguel Montes of California's state board of education. The cold statistics alone make his case.

What is striking is that so little has been done or said until recently, despite the fact that a few educators such as Dr. George Sanchez of the University of Texas have for years been urging bilingual instruction, a revision of the curriculum and textbooks to appeal to the interests and to strengthen the sense of cultural identity of Mexican-American students, decent counseling and guidance, and teacher training that might produce instructors capable of reaching and educating Mexican-American children.

In most of the states, among them California, it is against the law to use any language but English as the medium of instruction, though the law is openly flouted by the few teachers who can speak Spanish. The psychological and educational implications of such a policy are clear. By denying the child the right to speak his own language (in some places children are still punished for speaking Spanish even on the playground), the system is telling him, in effect, that his language, his culture, and by extension he himself, are inferior. And he rapidly becomes truly inferior in achievement, since the teachers must perforce water down the subject matter, such as arithmetic or social studies, for use as a vehicle for teaching English rather than

17

the subject itself.

Counseling in the schools is notoriously bad, and constitutes a special source of bitterness for the Mexican-Americans who have survived it — that is, defied it. "Realistic" counselors say, in effect: college costs too much; besides, you couldn't make it anyway; besides, you couldn't get a good job when you finished. Congressman Roybal was advised to become an electrician on the strength of an A in his ninth-grade algebra class (he was lucky to get into algebra; "general math" is usually considered sufficient). Julian Nava, a young professor at San Fernando Valley State College with a Ph.D. in history from Harvard, was advised to take, and did take, body and fender courses in high school in east Los Angeles. There are plenty of current stories of this sort.

The inadequacy of ability tests when applied to many groups is also notorious; the question is how, when the fact is so well known, school officials can summon the arrogance to brand young children as mentally deficient when it is the tests and the schools that are deficient. In California, Negro and Mexican-American children are overwhelmingly overrepresented proportionally in classes for the "mentally retarded." A former education official (an angry Anglo) told me of visiting a school in the San Joaquin Valley where he saw records listing one child as having an I.Q. of 46. Wanting to learn more about how such a mental basket case could function at all, he inquired around and found that the child, a boy of eleven, has a paper route, takes care of his four younger brothers and sisters after school, and prepares the evening meal for the family. He also speaks no English.

Many Anglo educators claim that they cannot make headway against the problems of language, culture, and parents. The stereotype has it that Mexican-Americans are not interested in having their children get an education, though every bit of evidence I found suggested just the reverse. In fact, many Mexican-American adults have an entirely unwarranted respect for the wisdom of teachers and principals, which is one reason why they have allowed their children to be pushed around for so long. There are problems, but they are by no means insurmountable. Actually, they have been used as a mask, and not a very effective one at that, for the real attitudes of the Anglo community at large.

"The schools are the places where Anglos and Mexican-Americans come to learn and act out the roles they will later play," says Theodore W. Parsons, an anthropologist at the University of California. He recently spent months studying the schools in a California town where the population is about 57 percent Mexican-American; practices similar to the ones he observed there are followed in many schools all over the feudal Southwest. The children — Anglos are called "Americans" and Mexican-Americans are called "Mexicans" — are conditioned for their respective roles in the adult world from their first day in school to their final one, when at graduation the Mexicans march in last and sit at the back of the platform. "This makes for a better-looking stage," a teacher explained to Parsons, adding that it allows the Americans, who have all the parts in the program, to get to the front more easily.

"Once we did let a Mexican girl give a little talk of some kind," Parsons was told, "and all she did was mumble around. She had quite an accent, too. Afterwards we had several complaints from other parents, so we haven't done anything like that since. That was about twelve years ago."

THE Negro revolution has stimulated, but by its great drama has also obscured, already existing ferment within the Mexican-American community. Spokesmen have had increasingly stormy sessions (and nonsessions — the walkout is becoming something of a fad) with federal, state, and local officials.

Many Anglos seem to dismiss the volubly expressed anger of Mexican-American leaders as not being "representative" of the feelings of the masses, but it is foolish to do so. No Mexican-American I know of has ever threatened that blood will run in the streets if conditions continue to grow worse, but thoughtful spokesmen acknowledge that no one can predict what outlet the growing hostility will find, a hostility that may be the more malignant because it has been so long suppressed.

"Man, if east L.A. ever blows, it will *really* blow," one said, and Herman Gallegos of San Francisco, a highly responsible leader, reports that some Mexican-Americans decline to join picket lines or other peaceful demonstrations because they fear they could not remain nonviolent. There is undeniable resentment of not only Anglos but Negroes: "If they don't move over, they're going to find footprints on their backs," one temperate Mexican-American said. He and other sophisticated Mexican-Americans realize that it is not the Negroes' "fault" that they are getting a little bit more of not enough, but there is the dangerous tension that always exists when poor people are set to scrambling for the few crumbs tossed out by the affluent society.

The fuel that could set off a Watts-type explosion is present in ample supply. Perhaps one day it will be ignited by some incident. Or perhaps the youthful population will simply retreat into increasing withdrawal, alienation, and addiction.

There is also, of course, a third possibility: that Anglos will give up their cynical game of divide and rule, listen to the growing number of articulate Mexican-American spokesmen as they define the community's problems, and allow Mexican-Americans the tools they can use to carry themselves into the mainstream of American life.

Ralph Guzmán

The Function of Anglo-American Racism in the Political Development of *Chicanos*

THE SOUTHWEST is a region that differs from the eastern seaboard geographically and sociologically. The conditions of social contact between those who held political power and those who did not were not the same. Thus the political socialization of minority groups like the *Chicanos*[1] followed paths that were only vaguely reminiscent of the Irish experience and that of other European immigrants who came to the East Coast.

Why the *Chicano* experience should differ so drastically from that of the European immigrants is explored in this essay. My thesis is that historical conditions of social contact between a group-in-power and a group-out-of-power, generate a number of attitudes, assumptions, judgments, and stereotypes—one of the other, that have a *major* influence upon both. These, I argue, are part of the political socialization of a people. To understand the political development of *Chicanos* in the Southwest, one must analyze two kinds of ideologies. One is the aggregation of articulated views, judgments, and presuppositions about ethnic groups that have been held by the dominant society—the Anglo view. For convenience, these are labeled *Anglo group ideologies*. The other is the aggregation of perceptions of the larger society by the minority and its internal self-appraisal, labeled

CALIFORNIA HISTORICAL QUARTERLY, 1971, Vol. 50,
No. 1, pp. 321-337.

Chicano group ideologies—the *Chicano* view. My focus here is on Anglo group ideologies.

Contrary to an assumption popular in the East, the Southwest and Far West do not have a tradition of racial tolerance. The historical conditions of social contact between *Chicanos* and the larger Southwest society bear ample testimony to the opposite. A relevant contrast between this region and the rest of the United States is the different origin of the "foreigners." Historically, the Southwestern "foreigners" were mainly American Indians and *Chicanos*. There were few blacks. After some time, people of recent European origin penetrated the Southwest. Many had already become "Americanized" elsewhere in the United States and they embraced the Anglo-Saxon notion of the subordinate position of Orientals, *Chicanos*, and Indians with great zeal. Thus, racial ideologies prevailing elsewhere in the nation found ready acceptance in the Southwest—only the targets were different.

The American obsession with race has indeed had a powerful influence on the *Chicano* people. This influence has differed in intensity from place to place as well as over time. In Texas, prevailing views of race have a Southern tinge, with blacks, as the reference population. In California racial views reflect the North, the South, and other regions of the country.

One of the effects of the majority's racial ideologies has been the social, political and economic suppression of *Chicanos*. Politics has been one of the main arenas of competition in which *Chicanos* have long been unable to act with maximum effectiveness. This failure, often attributed to political apathy, in fact seems to reflect clear knowledge of Anglo institutional repression. Apathy implies a choice not to act while knowing that action is possible. In the past much of the reluctance of *Chicanos* to compete in politics reflected their belief that such action was not possible. *Chicanos* did not vote, not because voting was an Anglo thing, but because Anglos forbade *Chicano* involvement at the polls. American society imposed clear restrictions based on law and custom. These were enforced with violence and terror.

The political socialization of a minority group is retarded when the host society is perceived to be, or is indeed, hostile. By comparison, cultural factors, such as the often cited *individualism* of *Chicanos*, language deficiencies, and the apathy usually associated with poverty, have probably been of secondary importance. Fear has been a strong inhibiting factor in the world of the exploited: fear of the society that controls him, fear of his ethnic brothers, and often fear of himself. Fear stunts the political growth of any group and it also damages its educational and economic development. In the case of the *Chicanos*, some of their political development was, in fact, effectively reduced through self-stereotypes which often duplicated the majority's perjorative views of the *Chicano* minority. The Anglo judgment that *Chicanos* are emotional can provide a convenient excuse for political and social failure. Similarly, transference of the opinion that *Chicanos* do not work hard from the economic sector to the political arena severely limits the *Chicano* community's opportunities to acquire meaningful political power. Both majority views establish the parameters for self-fulfilling prophecies.

The discussion of majority ideologies in the Southwest is divided in the following pages into decades so as to allow judgments on the varying degrees to which they inhibited *Chicano* political growth. Decades have been selected for this purpose without any claim that the society's articulated views really changed with the passage of each 10-year period. Evidently, majority views of the *Chicanos* were formed throughout the entire period of social contact that began in the early years of the nineteenth century.[2] In large measure, the stereotypes formed during this period conformed to nativistic themes, emphasizing foreign-ness, hinting at radicalism, and at the unacceptability of Catholicism. Almost always *Chicanos* were assumed to represent a different religion and a different race. These themes somtimes led to sympathetic concern, but increasingly, with the wave of immigration that accompanied the Mexican revolution, they led to expressions of alarm.

In 1912 a sociology student from the University of Southern California conducted a study of *Chicanos* living in Los Angeles that was published in a Methodist mission magazine. Although his orientation was sympathetic, the student faithfully reproduced the view of *Chicanos* held in the dominant society of that time. His writings appeared at a time when border raids by Francisco (Pancho) Villa were common topics of conversation.

It is generally estimated that there are from 20,000 to 40,000 Mexicans within the city boundaries. . . . Economic reasons [are] of great influence in causing them to come to the United States. . . . Very few of the Mexicans are naturalized, due in the main to their ignorance of the possibility and somewhat to their prejudice against Americans and American customs. . . . The Mexican laborer is generally regarded as *less efficient* than other labor. . . . The chief fault found with the Mexican laborer is his *irregularity and uncertainty.* Much of this is caused by drunkenness. . . .

The Mexican *plane of living is probably the lowest* of any race in the City. . . . There is general antipathy for the Mexicans, and they are looked down upon by all races. The Mexicans meet this attitude with one of haughty indifference. . . . The social life of the Mexicans is meager in the extreme.

The Mexicans furnish more than their proportion of *criminals.* . . . These people are non-moral rather than immoral, but their conditions are immoral from the viewpoint of Christian civilization and are a perpetual challenge to us to improve them. . . . The small children attend public school. . . . but as soon as it is possible for them to do so, they *quit school and go to work.* The small children are very bright, quick, attentive and responsive, but, after reaching the fifth grade, they become slow and dull. A general cause of this mental condition is more or less irregular attendance, due to home conditions. The problems presented by this *race of ignorant, illiterate and non-moral people, complicated by their low plane of living, their tendency to crime, and their bad housing conditions,* are serious in the extreme and urgently demand the attention of all Christian reformers and social workers. . . . [Emphases added][3]

The document focuses attention on the reality component in the stereotyped view of *Chicanos.* Though admittedly using primitive research techniques, the above generalizations represent the student's attempt at systematic exploration of reality; official statistics are cited, interviews conducted, and some direct observations are made. In the political arena, on the other hand, ethnic stereotypes are based on a process of abstraction which—unlike the attempt at objectivity even in this primitive empirical research—often selects, exaggerates, and preserves observations without continuous check on "reality." (Congressional hearings and similar investigations may be exceptions.) Once established as conventional categories, ethnic stereotypes, at least latently, incorporate a plan of action toward the ethnic group. As already indicated, the minority often inadvertently "cooperates" with the majority in perpetuating the stereotype. For example, accommodative minority leaders may find it convenient to relate to the dominant system in conventional terms, and "special concessions" may be made to the ethnic group based on its stereotyped characteristics. In this regard, the stereotype may become in part a self-fulfilling prophecy, insofar as its preservation establishes a universe of discourse within which *both* majority and minority can interact.

Thus, the statements made in this document were like—and yet unlike—statements made about *Chicanos* in the ensuing years. I turn to a detailed account of the period of the twenties.

Nativist feeling was at a high pitch in the 1920's. Concern over the preservation of the "American stock" was the subject of extensive public debate. In the Southwest, the debate took the form of fears that the region might be mongrelized by "Mexicans." Samuel J. Holmes, a professor of zoology at the University of California, argued that *Chicanos* like the African slaves of an earlier era, represented a problem that might not end for centuries.[4] Similar warnings about the "danger of building up in this state a large mongrel population" were issued in Texas.[5] Apprehension that the American stock would be diluted by *Chicanos* was expressed by Robert F. Foerster, a Princeton professor of economics, in these words:

It is a deplorable fact that numerous, intelligent and enterprising one hundred per cent Americans, to say nothing of other brands, are busy helping along this insiduous elimination of their own breed in favor of the progeny of Mexican peons who will continue to afflict us with an embarrassing race problem.[6]

24

The relative racial qualifications of the *Chicano* people were a subject of extensive discussion, often centering on the concept of the *mestizo* or the mixed race. Hybrids produced by the union of distant stocks might tend to be "superior to the poorer strain and inferior to the better strain."[7] On this basis, the exemption of Western Hemisphere immigrants from the national quota system of 1924 was debated on the floor of both the U.S. Senate and the House of Representatives, but an amendment to include them in the system was soundly defeated. The issue was reopened in the years 1926 to 1930 when public debate focused for the first time directly on immigration from Mexico. Again, however, no action was taken. In the main, the insistence of Southwest agricultural employers that they needed Mexican labor, combined with foreign policy considerations, was sufficient to ward off attempts to legislate a curtailment of Mexican immigration. But the Congressional debate revealed again the then current preoccupation with race. Congressman John Box of Texas, who sponsored a bill in 1926 to include the Western Hemisphere countries under the quota law, stated that Mexican immigrants were "illiterate, unclean, peonized masses" who stemmed from "a mixture of Mediterranean-blooded Spanish peasants with low grade Indians who did not fight to extinction but submitted and multiplied as serfs."[8] Likewise, Senator John B. Kendrick observed "that of all the alien races they [the *Chicanos*] amalgamate the least with the white man; they live entirely in a separate way." But he added that they were really an orderly people in our country.[9]

In Texas, the dominant society tended to equate *Chicanos* with blacks, and notions of racial inferiority were easily transferred from one group to the other. The African strains that some *Chicano* people reflected were attributed to 19th century runaway slaves from Texas and Louisiana who settled in the state of Veracruz. It was reported that the Indian women of Veracruz like the "liveliness and good humor" of the persecuted blacks "better than the quieter ways of their own countrymen."[10] The fact that a few *Chicanos* were, indeed, descendants of black slaves from the South helped to validate the tendency to equate all *Chicanos* or at least the darker ones with black Americans.

Interestingly, the hopeful notion of the melting pot, so commonly applied to European immigrants in the 1920's was seldom invoked with respect to *Chicanos*. It was generally assumed that the latter represented a separate race with such foreign ideas and habits, social standards, and historical traditions that they were disqualified from membership in American society. To one writer *Chicanos* were an underprivileged and unassimilable group of people that threatened to "lessen the racial homogeneity of our population."[11]

Not all articulated views were so negative. For example, one writer stressed the *Chicano* population did produce good citizens when they were paid a living and a stable wage.[12] Another believed that the *Chicano* was a *peon* (a peasant) who was not such a bad fellow even though he was "hopelessly more alien to the United States than any European."[13] Still another observer concluded that the *Chicanos* were confused in their own minds as to whether they were or were not Amricans.[14]

Because the *Chicano* was not seen as being assimilable and because he was not a black, it was suggested that he might represent a third separate group. The notion of a "third race" was also upheld by some Mexican intellectuals during this period. For example, Enrique Santibañez, the Mexican Consul General in San Antonio, Texas, said:

Judging the bronze race by its color and remembering that the Anglo-Saxon was not mixed with the colored races one must conclude that future generations of Mexicans, living in the United States, will live apart from the larger society, which is basically white and nordic, for as long as we can see. In other words, Mexicans will never be an integral part of the spiritual life of the American people. . . .

Consequently, the United States will never be a harmonious social unit as it was when it was founded. Instead the United States will be a society divided into three parts: white, bronze, and black.[15]

Pressure from the white people to keep *Chicanos* on the same level as the black was resisted by the *Chicano* people, according to Handman. Pressure of this type, Handman predicted, would someday cause bitterness, animosity, and conflict. Interestingly, he intimated that *Chicanos* would revolt against the larger society before the blacks did. In this respect Handman's comment is noteworthy.

The Negro-white situation is difficult enough, but it is simple. The Negro has his place in the scheme of things. He is disfranchised and he accepts it—for how long I do not know—but he accepts it. He is limited in his educational opportunities and in his occupational field, and he accepts that also. But the Mexican is theoretically limited neither in his educational opportunities nor in his occupational field. Neither is he disfranchised.[16]

Enough has been said to suggest that, reflecting a general trend in American Society, the core of the Southwest ideology between 1920 and 1930 in regard to *Chicanos* was clearly racial. However, the thrust of this concern was not *how Chicanos* could be brought into the larger community. It was instead focused on differentiation, on characteristics that served to rationalize the social exclusion of the group. Differentiation was made using social referents familiar to the majority; namely black people and American Indians. Majority group ideologies in the 1920's, of course, greatly deterred the political socialization of *Chicanos*. With the possible exception of the League of United Latin American Citizens (LULAC), a middle class group with important links in the larger society, *Chicanos* appeared to offer no significant resistance to this condition. Yet they were not silent and they did not accept the ideological judgments of the larger society. Reaction came on the *barrio* level in neighborhood *platicas* (conversations) and only sporadically from organized *Chicano* groups. The attempted formation of a Federation of Mexican Laborers' Unions and the strike of cantaloupe pickers in California's Imperial Valley in the late 1930's is one example of organized *Chicano* reaction. However, both of these episodes tended to confirm the Anglo view that *Chicano* organizations were susceptible to foreign ideologies that threatened the American social order. The violent Imperial Valley strike, a precursor of labor strife, served notice that *Chicanos* could be effective revolutionaries, proving themselves to be considerably less docile than was commonly believed.[17]

Anglo preoccupation with race in the 1930's centered on the masses of Mexicans who had poured into the United States in the previous decade and who continued to cross the border without formal immigration. These illegals were called "wet" Mexicans because they often waded or swam across the Rio Grande. They entered the United States, it was charged, to "become the fathers of born-on-the-soil offspring, whose right to American citizenship cannot be denied."[18] The prolific birth rate of these people was seen as a threat to American society. *Chicano* children were considered a hybrid race of inferior quality. "Their white strain," one observer said, "may be 1/16, 1/32, or 1/64. The rest may be Amerind (American Indian), Negro, or a mixture of the two."[19]

With the growth of the feminist movement in the United States, attention turned to the plight of the *Chicano* woman who was believed to be completely submissive to the whims and wishes of the male. According to this notion, the freedom that American women enjoyed was incomprehensible and bewildering to *Chicanas*. To the militant feminists, *Chicanas* were stark reminders of an archaic social system where the males possessed absolute authority. Unfamiliar with the English language and long conditioned to a life of personal sacrifice, *Chicanas* apparently were not recruited by the feminist movement of this era. However, a few middle class *Chicanas* became involved in prototypical protest movements.[20]

The empathy and chagrin of the American woman was expressed by Ruth Allen who wrote:

Uncomplainingly, she labors in the field for months at a time and receives as a reward from the head of the family, some gew-gaw from the five and ten cent store, or at best, a new dress. The supremacy of the male is seldom disputed. First her father, then her husband, or, if she becomes a widow, her son, receive her unquestioning service.[21]

As the *Chicano* people became more evident in or near large urban centers, the majority's attention turned to the problem of crime. *Chicanos* were considered a people with substantial and perhaps irradicable criminal proclivities. There was an assumption of criminality particularly in confrontations between school, police, and social welfare officials. The young with their stylishly long hair, bizarre dress habits, and reputed drug habits were the special targets of an irate majority group. The belief that all *Chicanos* had deeply imbedded criminal tendencies was not easily disproved when the jails were almost always crowded with *Chicano* inmates.

The judgment of criminality and the numbers who were actually in prison combined to cement the view that *Chicanos* were, in fact, dangerous to the social order. In California, for example, a state prison report claimed that sixty per cent of the violations of prison laws and rules were caused by *Chicano* prisoners who refused to conform. One writer noted that California has "as many Mexican prisoners as the entire prison population of two American states."[22]

Another significant ideology during the 1930's was the view that *Chicanos* were a docile, unintelligent people who were susceptible to communism. This view was stressed as the Anglo fear of communism increased. Bogardus, a sociologist, warned that "A Christmas basket for one day in the year and poverty for 365 days . . . [was] poor philanthropy . . . to keep the Mexican from becoming a bolshevist."[23] Communist recruitment in *Chicano barrios* during the 1930's remains as another unwritten chapter in the history of these people. For example, the International Workers of the World and other radical groups entered *Chicano* neighborhoods in massive efforts to recruit members. Their limited success in recruiting bore strange fruit in the 1950's when the federal government arrested and deported scores of *Chicanos* who had joined the IWW during this earlier period.

As the Southwest became engulfed in the Great Depression, protection of native labor and the reduction of welfare expenses were Anglo concerns. In an attempt to resolve both needs, *Chicanos*, whatever the legality of their presence in the United States, were rounded up and forcibly removed from the United States. This episode of extreme Anglo hostility represents still another little known chapter in the history of the *Chicanos*.

During the 1930's interactions between *Chicanos* and the larger society became varied, and so did mutual perceptions. The conditions of social contact which were previously rural and caste-like in quality altered slightly. A few (very few) obtained membership in traditional labor unions. Others attended meetings of organizations like the IWW. The era of the New Deal, with its stress on social reforms, helped to change a few majority group attitudes toward *Chicanos* but not in a substantial manner. Still, on the whole, the caste-like relationship that typified life in the rural areas was modified. An unsteady foundation, the beginning of the urban phase of the *Chicano* people's political socialization had been established.

World War II increased the urbanization of *Chicano* population; but urban institutions were ill prepared to cope with the *Chicano* people. Both public and private agencies saw *Chicanos* as problems, and rarely as potential contributors to society. School systems established special schools and police agencies made special efforts to discover the inner workings of the *Chicano* mind. An example of law enforcement research in this area can be seen in a 1942 report to the Los Angeles County Grand Jury by a member of the Sheriff's Department from the same county. In the early 1940's juvenile disorders involving *Chicanos* had increased. The Los Angeles County Sheriff's Department assigned Ed Duran Ayres to make a study. His analysis included the conclusion that all *Chicanos* were biologically inferior and disposed to violence. Officer Ayres said that *Chicanos* were unlikely to respect the American tradition of a fair fight because of their peculiar genetic make-up. The Ayres report states in part:

The caucasian, especially the Anglo-Saxon, when engaged in fighting, particularly among youths, resorts to fisticuffs and may at times kick each other, which is considered unsportive, but this Mexican element considers all that to be a sign of weakness, and all he knows and feels is a desire to use a knife or some lethal weapon. In other words, his desire is to kill, or at least let blood. That is why it is difficult for the Anglo-Saxon to understand the psychology of the Indian or even the Latin, and it is just as difficult for the Indian or the Latin to understand the psychology of the Anglo-Saxon or those from Northern Europe.[24]

The Chief of the Los Angeles Police Department wrote a letter to the foreman of the Grand Jury endorsing the Ayres findings:

Lieutenant Ayres of the Sheriff's Department, gave an intelligent statement of the psychology of the Mexican people, particularly the youths. He stated many of the contributing factors that caused the gang activities.[25]

A year later, in June, 1943, the Los Angeles zoot-suit riots began. The riots were widely reported, and they brought *Chicanos* before the nation much more forcefully than had the meager ethnic writings of the past. The riots were violent upheavals. The participants were, on the one hand, young *Chicanos*—teenagers and young adults—called *pachucos* by the *Chicano* bourgeoisie. Armed forces personnel and white civilians of all ages represented the other side.[26] Sporadic fighting in bars, theatres, streetcars, and the public streets continued for five days.

Newspaper accounts were, in large part, unfavorable to the *Chicanos*. There were racial overtones in the reporting and much of what officer Ayres had written provided a basis for hasty journalism. The good guys were Anglos and members of the armed forces and the bad guys were *Chicanos*. On a purely impressionistic level, there was something quite natural about these confrontations; *Chicanos* and Anglo-Americans squared off against each other as they had for generations, only this time the battle-ground was the city of Los Angeles instead of the agricultural fields and the mining camps of the past. *Chicanos* objected to the role of the news-papers but there was little that they could do. Daily newspapers published stories in which armed forces personnel were always cleared of wrong-doing.

A number of well-known public figures addressed themselves to the issue of race. Eleanor Roosevelt suggested that the riots could be traced to long-standing discrimination against *Chicanos*. She expressed concern for the welfare of *Chicanos* living in California and in states along the border. In Los Angeles, authorities denied Mrs. Roosevelt's allegations, and so did the California State Chamber of Commerce.[27] Earl Warren, then Governor of the State, argued that "this isn't a Mexican problem, this is an American problem. It is one of juvenile delinquency . . ."[28] There is no question that the riots had serious social consequences. On the one hand, they added one more bitter experience to the history of the *Chicano* people; on the other, then convinced many members of the larger society that *Chicanos* were not assimilable.

Significantly, sources for this period are generally letters, official docu-ments, and newspaper accounts. Serious scholarly analysis of these events is scarce. In an article for the *American Journal of Sociology* Turner and Surace did a content analysis of newspaper articles that appeared during this period.[29] Yet newspapers and other literature remain as principal sources.

The *Christian Century* magazine noted that news pictures supported the conclusion that these were race riots. Overt hostility was clearly directed at *Chicanos* because "no white wearers of these bizarre clothes [zoot-suits] were disturbed" and because "hundreds of Mexicans and Negroes who were not wearing zoot-suits were attacked."[30]

It is, of course, difficult to link the overt behavior of Anglo mobs to Anglo ideology. It is similarly quite a task to show empirically that *Chicano* street corner societies based their actions on a minority ideology. Never-theless, substantive assumptions of social roles were involved on both sides of the conflict. On one side, second generation *Chicano* youths refused the subservient social roles that American institutions demanded for them. They fought the larger society without strategies, without internal com-munications, and almost, it seemed, with suicidal recklessness. For young *Chicanos* the zoot-suit riots were not unlike a pogrom; the street battles involved "us" and "them" explicitly and without gentle protocol. On the other side, equally young Anglos from many parts of the United States, a terribly frightened mass of confused, uprooted draftees with over-blown notions of Americanism found ideal conditions for the displacement of pressured frustrations in the foreign-looking *Chicano* neighborhoods. With only a slight mental adjustment, the *Chicano* could even look Japanese. For *Chicanos*, the sounds of hate and the acts of violence were not unfamiliar—they were deeply rooted in the folklore, the ballads and the legends of *la raza*. Uniformed or not, the Anglos were, as always, the enemy.

Turner and Surace saw a conflict of ideologies within the majority group. Some *Chicanos* were associated with romantic Olvera Street (an important tourist attraction), and other romantic images. Others were linked with a rising tide of juvenile vandalism and deviant social behavior. In order to resolve this contradiction, and to provide a more explicit moral justification for racial discrimination, an unambiguous, unfavorable symbol was needed. The two sociologists suggested that the zoot-suit label had connotations of sex crimes, draft-dodging, gang warfare, and other unsavory images. The zoot-suit label which technically applied across ethnic and class lines to all wearers of the garb, was simply equated to *Chicanos*. Thus *Chicanos*, whatever their clothing preferences, were beaten, arrested and otherwise humiliated by non-discriminating members of the larger society.[31]

The conditions of social contact between *Chicanos* and the larger society were altered by the demographic change from rural to urban but they were not improved. Greater social mobility—meaning freedom to live where they chose, eat at restaurants they could afford, visit public facilities that offered comfort and rest—was not forthcoming for all *Chicanos*.

The ground rules of American society in the cities were often even more explicit than they were in the agrarian areas. Signs on house porches and in employment agencies advised *Chicanos* in Spanish and in English that they were not welcome. When written signs were missing the silent language of the doorman, the foreman, the school principal, and others, made it apparent that social ingress was not possible.

The state of Texas to this day provides the best examples of social exclusion. For example, in 1945 a U.S. Senate Subcommittee on Education learned that *Chicanos* from McCarney, Texas, traveled forty-five miles to Fort Stockton for a haircut because Anglo barbers would not cut *Chicano* hair and *Chicanos* could not legally become barbers in McCarney.[32] Other witnesses reported that they could not use a public street to celebrate a Fourth of July because the holiday was "for white people only."[33] In a Texas restaurant a *Chicano* customer, asked to identify his race, answered "Misanthrope" and was promptly served.

The war years forced *Chicanos* to interact widely and intensely with the larger society. Change had to take place because *Chicanos* and other disadvantaged groups were needed in the defense factories and in the battlefields. The competence of *Chicanos* as semi-skilled workers modified some stereotype attitudes. At one Los Angeles area aircraft company an enterprising *Chicano* rose from the position of custodian to a high administrative post "mostly on nerve and need."[34]

On the battle front, the fighting qualities of *Chicano* servicemen serving in integrated units similarly influenced majority group reservations about their loyalty. While the war years did not completely reverse majority views of the past, they did bring about increased social interaction between *Chicanos* and non-*Chicanos*. For *Chicanos*, the war years became another important stage in their urban political socialization. The war experience and post-war developments, such as the educational opportunities offered to *Chicanos* through the G.I. Bill of Rights, helped *Chicanos* to see American society more clearly.

The majority's views of *Chicano* political behavior have, of course, a very direct bearing on the political participation of *Chicanos*. These views have been a part of the Anglo ideologies as far back as the early years of this century. Among the most important are (1) that *Chicanos* in general are submissive and, therefore not capable of effective political activity; (2) that *Chicanos* are deeply imbued with foreign values and, therefore, cannot understand the American political system; and (3) that *Chicanos* cannot achieve ethnic unity. These views have more or less persisted to the present day.

It was often said that *Chicanos* had values that were not consonant with the American value system. In politics, for example, *Chicanos* were not expected to understand cherished beliefs about the rights of man, freedom of religion, and other constitutional guarantees. *Chicanos* were considered products of a semi-feudal, colonial social system where the poor obeyed the dictates of benevolent employers. *Chicano* women, Anglo ideologues argued, were shamefully mistreated by their husbands. Finally, it was argued that Roman Catholics, particularly primitive Roman Catholics, could not possibly practice religious freedom.

The assumption of submissiveness carried with it the belief that *Chicanos* were not interested in the acquisition of political power. It was held that members of this minority were accustomed to the commands of priests and labor *patrones*. Consequently, personal initiative was not a well developed trait. People without personal initiative, it was rationalized, could not aspire to the control of political institutions.

The conclusion that *Chicanos* were irrevocably Catholic and eternally foreign was a powerful and pervasive conclusion. The Roman Catholic Church was, indeed, foreign and totally overwhelming. Fear existed that *Chicanos* would react according to the direction of the Church once they acquired political power. Traditional Anglo mistrust of the Roman Catholic Church found a new target in the *Chicano* group. In Los Angeles, civic meetings held in parish halls reinforced the belief that priests and nuns guarded the political life of their impressionable but devout parishioners. The truth is that the Roman Catholic Church, operated by Anglo nuns and priests, did exercise substantial political control over devout *Chicanos*.

Well-meaning individuals who were willing to help the *Chicano* people during the early post-war years were openly skeptical about the ability of these people to organize effectively. Liberal democrats in particular were doubtful. In Los Angeles they greeted the first mass registration of *Chicano* voters in the country with aplomb. While viewing the figures that reported great success, a liberal Democrat said, "So they're registered, will they vote?"

Ideologies are often inconsistent. For example, in the 1930's a view diametrically opposed to the assumption of an incurable ethnic disunity existed. *Chicanos* were considered to be group-minded, and thus there was apprehension that they might develop a Tammany Hall type of organization. Evidence for this fear of *Chicano* bloc voting and machine politics came from experience in the state of New Mexico. Ethnic politics in that state proved to some observers that *Chicanos* practiced a religious-ethnic solidarity even within the political system. Only one party, the Democrats or the Republicans, received the votes of the *Chicanos* according to one Anglo scholar. He indicated that New Mexico's *Chicano* population would accept whatever political party their leaders designated. As a consequence, recruitment of *Chicano* voters by *non-Chicano* outsiders was considered difficult. "This is something our Anglos . . . find extremely irritating," a writer commented.[35] New Mexico, then, where the political involvement of the *Chicanos* was extremely high (when one compares that state with the rest of the Southwest), justified an ideological conclusion that was out of phase with judgments about disunity made in other regions.

Why the Anglo majority would appear to emphasize ethnic unity in New Mexico while underscoring disunity elsewhere is not difficult to understand when region and time are considered. The *Chicano* population was deeply rooted in New Mexico when American political institutions were imposed. The state's institutions were already in *Chicano* hands, and group mindedness and religious-ethnic solidarity was indeed a reality. New Mexicans reacted negatively to outsiders—the conquering Anglos who seized their land with the force of arms. Nevertheless, in terms of time, New Mexico *Chicanos* had a head start of a few generations over *Chicanos* from other states, particularly those who came later in the 20th century. *Chicanos* in New Mexico represented an original population as opposed to the immigrant population from Mexico that followed. New Mexicans appeared to interact with American society *as a group* with a solidarity that distinguished them sharply from *Chicanos* living elsewhere.

Still another image of *Chicanos* was that as a group they were easily controlled. While this notion appealed to many members of the dominant Anglo society, it tended to repel others. In the 1920's and 1930's, fear was expressed that *Chicanos* would not vote for the "vested interests" in agriculture and industry on which they depended and that rural landlords, in particular, would be able to herd them to the polls with "banners flying."[36] On the other hand, it was said that the group was also easy prey for demagogues. "Socialism, the I.W.W. and Communism find a ready soil for their seed among the Mexicans in our country," said one writer who deplored *Chicano* "*gullibility*."[37]

Thus, the apprehensions of Anglo society militated against political activity by *Chicanos*. Adding to the Anglo majority's fears was a feeling of uncertainty, ambivalence, and frustration with regard to *Chicano* leadership. Until World War II it was commonly believed that the group was devoid of responsible leaders who could stimulate a sense of collective commitment—part of an Anglo ideology that *Chicanos* were quiescent and satisfied with life at it was. Typical of this view was an Anglo businessman's statement that *Chicanos* were a contented and leaderless people "who did not, in the last analysis, know what they wanted. They are like children."[38] Finally, *Chicanos* were considered to be even more handicapped because socially mobile *Chicanos*, the economic achievers, tended to forsake life in the *barrio*, thus depriving lower class *Chicanos* of an articulate middle class.[39]

Anglo expectations concerning *Chicano* leadership have always had a significant impact on the political participation of this minority. This impact became even greater after World War II when growing urbanization and the return of *Chicano* veterans who did maintain their contact with people living in the *barrio* increased the political potential of the group. The importance of Anglo ideologies stems partly from the fact that the validation of *Chicano* leaders has often come not from the minority itself but from Anglo society—a condition that parallels the political history of other ethnic or racial groups in this country and has only recently been modified in the case of blacks who prefer self-determination. Thus, Anglos would urge *Chicanos* to find and develop leaders, with the implicit understanding that these would be "acceptable"; or they would express distrust of individuals who represented themselves as *Chicano* spokesmen. It was the political power structure of the dominant Anglo society that ultimately decided who were legitimate *Chicano* leaders. The problem of the validation of *Chicano* leadership has continued to this day.

The aggregated views, judgments, and presuppositions about the *Chicano* minority held by the larger Anglo society have been described. To recapitulate, they constitute constellations of ideologies that differ from one place to another and from one historical period to the next. In order to clarify what is meant by majority ideologies, the notion of conditions of social contact between the minority and the majority was re-examined in terms of other American ethnic groups. In each instance it was shown that social contact between the minority and the majority generated mutual views that usually hampered and only occassionally assisted the minority group to grow politically. Conditions of social contact on the eastern seaboard were different from those that existed in the Southwest; the ethnic actors were different and so were their reasons for being in this social order. *Chicanos* initially by-passed the well-known process of urban political socialization. While there were few political machines in the Southwest, fear that they might become common in *Chicano* areas was expressed. This fear, and other social expressions concerning *Chicanos*, impinged upon their political experience. They grew politically within an oppressive, racist environment that clearly restricted social opportunity. Within this context of explicit and implicit social discrimination and economic exploration, *Chicanos* created counter-ideologies that contained judgments of the Anglo social order. The contents of those counter-ideologies and their function in the increased political consciousness of *Chicanos* remains to be examined.

NOTES

1. The term *Chicano*, once used almost exclusively by poor, lower class Mexicans who struggled for economic survival in the crowded *barrios* of the Southwest, was also avoided by the Mexican bourgeoisie who lived in more comfortable surroundings. Today, the term has been re-enforced, particularly by the young descendants of both economic classes. It reflects the central thesis of this paper: that American racism in the Southwest limited and attempted to destroy the political development of a people whose major crime was grinding poverty. The term Mexican is used here only to refer to citizens of Mexico or in order to make clear a particular point requiring the use of that term. Otherwise *Chicano* is used throughout the essay.

2. See Cecil Robinson, *With the Ears of Strangers* (Tucson, 1965).

3. *El Mexicano* (November-December, 1913), 1; (January, 1914), 1; and (April, 1914), 2.

4. Kenneth Roberts, "The Docile Mexican," *Saturday Evening Post*, CC (February 18, 1928), 165.

5. William E. Garnett, "Immediate and Pressing Race Problems of Texas," *Proceedings of the Southwestern Political and Social Science Association* (Austin, 1925), 35-36.

6. Samuel J. Holmes, "Perils of Mexican Invasion," *North American Review*, CCXXVII (1929), 622.

7. Robert F. Forester, *The Racial Problems Involved in Immigration from Latin America and the West Indies to the United States* (Washington, D.C., 1925), 330-331.

8. For details and documentation see Ronald Wyse, "The Position of Mexicans in the Immigration and Nationality Laws," in Leo Grebler, *Mexican Immigration to the United States: The Record and its Implications* ("Mexican American Study Project," Advance Report 2, University of California, Los Angeles, 1966), D-9 to D-11.

9. See U.S. Congress, Senate, *Restriction of Western Hemisphere Immigration,* 1928, Hearings, 71.

10. Kenneth Roberts, "Wet and Other Mexicans," *Saturday Evening Post,* (February 4, 1928), 11.

11. Frederick Simpich, "The Little Brown Brother Treks North," *Independent,* CXVI (February 27, 1926), 239.

12. "Let it be said that there is no doubt as to the ultimate ability of the Mexicans to become a good citizen. Pay him a living and stable wage which will enable him to raise his family to the American standard, and put him in an American community which opens its schools and other friendly agencies to him, and he soon surprises and silences his detractors." Charles A. Tomson, "What of the Bracero?" *Survey,* LIV (June 1, 1925), 292.

13. Richard Lee Strout, "A Fence for the Rio Grande," *Independent,* CXX (June 2, 1928), 520.

14. Helen W. Walker, "Mexican Immigrants and American Citizenship," *Sociology and Social Research, 1928-1929,* XIII (1929), 470.

15. Translated from Enrique Santibañez, *Ensayo acerca de la imigracion Mexicana en los Estados Unidos* (San Antonio, 1930) 95.

16. Max Sylvanus Handman, "The Mexican Immigrant in Texas," *Proceedings National Conference of Social Work,* LIII (1926), 338.

17. See *Mexicans in California,* Report of Governor C.C. Young's Mexican Fact-Finding Committee (San Francisco, 1930), 171. Discussion of this point can also be found in Leo Grebler, *Mexican Immigration,* 24.

18. C. M. Goethe, "Peons Need Not Apply," *World's Work,* LIX (November, 1930), 47.

19. *Ibid.*

20. Middle class *Chicanas,* or at least women who could read and write the English language and who had an economic base, led some of the protests of the *barrio* in the 1930's. They would storm the court house, the offices of the social workers, or would bar the path of investigating officials while shouting and gesturing in a most "un-Mexican" manner. Their little-known role suggests still another area deserving intensive historical analysis.

21. Ruth Allen, "Mexican Peon Women in Texas," *Sociology and Social Research,* XVI (November-December 1931), 131.

22. Goethe, "Peons Need Not Apply," 48.

23. Emory Bogardus, *The Mexican in the United States* (Los Angeles, 1934), 48.

24. Letter written by Ed Duran Ayres to E. W. Oliver, Foreman, Los Angeles County Grand Jury, 1942, 2. Copy on file with the UCLA Mexican American Study Project.

25. C. B. Horrall, Letter to Foreman Oliver, on file with the UCLA Mexican American Study Project.

26. The garments that these young people wore were called "drapes," "zoots," and were synonymous with *Chicanos.* A newspaper explanation of the history and use of zoot suits includes the observation that "many a young Mexicin in a zoot suit

works hard and takes his money home to mamacita for frijoles refritos, . . ." Timothy Turner, "Zuit Suits Still Parade Here Despite OPA Ban," *Los Angeles Times,* March 22, 1943, sec. II, 8.

27. Fletcher Bowron, then Mayor of Los Angeles, told newspaper reporters that, "Nothing that has occurred can be construed as due to prejudice against Mexicans or discrimination against young men of any race. Neither is there a foundation for anyone to say that attacks or arrests have been directed toward members of minority groups." *Los Angeles Daily News,* June 10, 1943, 3.

28. *Los Angeles Examiner,* June 17, 1943, Sec. 1, 1.

29. The use of the term *Mexican* in newspapers is carefully traced by these two scholars over a ten and one-half year period. The use of the symbol, they say, led to overt hostility on the part of members of the majority group who were, inadvertently, goaded to act against the *Chicanos.* For further details about this hypothesis see Ralph H. Turner and Samuel J. Surace, "Zoot Suiters and Mexicans: Symbols in Crowd Behavior," *The American Journal of Sociology,* LXII (July 1956), 14-20. See also comments by Neil J. Smelser, *Theory of Collective Behavior* (London, 1962), 105-106.

30. "Portent of Storm," *Christian Century,* LX (June, 1943), 735.

31. This discussion rests heavily on the article by Ralph H. Turner and Samuel J. Surace.

32. Statement of Alonzo S. Perales, Chairman, Committee of One Hundred, Director General, League of Loyal Americans, San Antonio, Texas, U.S. Congress Senate, Subcommittee of the Committee on Education and Labor, Hearings, Fair Employment Practice Act on S.101, S.459, 79th Congress, 1945, 150.

33. *Ibid.*

34. Mr. Paul Zamudio (pseudonym) was first a janitor, then an interpreter, and eventually a high ranking officer in the company.

35. The ideological conclusion that *Chicanos* represented a threat is well documented by Mary H. Austin, "Mexicans and New Mexico," *Survey Graphic,* LXVI (May, 1931), 143.

36. See Kenneth L. Roberts, "Wet and Other Mexicans," 12.

37. Thomas Brown, "The Challenge of Mexican Immigration," *The Missionary Review of the World,* L (September, 1927), 193.

38. Frances Jerome Woods, *Mexican Ethnic Leadership in San Antonio, Texas* (Washington, D.C., 1949), 23-24, 49.

39. Leonard Broom and Eshref Shevky, "Mexicans in the United States," *Sociology and Social Research,* XXXVI (1951-1952), 54.

OZZIE G. SIMMONS

The Mutual Images and Expectations
of Anglo-Americans and Mexican-Americans

A NUMBER of psychological and sociological studies have treated ethnic and racial stereotypes as they appear publicly in the mass media and also as held privately by individuals.[1] The present paper is based on data collected for a study of a number of aspects of the relations between Anglo-Americans and Mexican-Americans in a South Texas community, and is concerned with the principal assumptions and expectations that Anglo- and Mexican-Americans hold of one another; how they see each other; the extent to which these pictures are realistic; and the implications of their intergroup relations and cultural differences for the fulfillment of their mutual expectations.[2]

The Community

The community studied (here called "Border City") is in South Texas, about 250 miles south of San Antonio. Driving south from San Antonio, one passes over vast expanses of brushland and grazing country, then suddenly comes upon acres of citrus groves, farmlands rich with vegetables and cotton, and long rows of palm trees. This is the "Magic Valley," an oasis in the semidesert region of South Texas. The Missouri Pacific Railroad (paralleled by Highway 83, locally called "The longest street in the world") bisects twelve major towns and cities of the Lower Rio Grande Valley between Brownsville, near the Gulf of Mexico, and Rio Grande City, 103 miles to the west.

Based on an address at the annual meeting of the Mexican Christian Institute at San Antonio in 1958.

Border City is neither the largest nor the smallest of these cities, and is physically and culturally much like the rest. Its first building was constructed in 1905. By 1920 it had 5,331 inhabitants, and at the time of our study these had increased to an estimated 17,500. The completion of the St. Louis, Brownsville, and Mexico Railroad in 1904 considerably facilitated Anglo-American immigration to the Valley. Before this the Valley had been inhabited largely by Mexican ranchers, who maintained large haciendas in the traditional Mexican style based on peonage. Most of these haciendas are now divided into large or small tracts that are owned by Anglo-Americans, who obtained them through purchase or less legitimate means. The position of the old Mexican-American landowning families has steadily deteriorated, and today these families, with a few exceptions, are completely overshadowed by the Anglo-Americans, who have taken over their social and economic position in the community.

The Anglo-American immigration into the Valley was paralleled by that of the Mexicans from across the border, who were attracted by the seemingly greater opportunities for farm labor created by the introduction of irrigation and the subsequent agricultural expansion. Actually, there had been a small but steady flow of Mexican immigration into South Texas that long antedated the Anglo-American immigration. [3] At present, Mexican-Americans probably constitute about two-fifths of the total population of the Valley.

In Border City, Mexican-Americans comprise about 56 percent of the population. The southwestern part of the city, adjoining and sometimes infiltrating the business and industrial areas, is variously referred to as "Mexiquita," "Mexican-town," and "Little Mexico" by the city's Anglo-Americans, and as the *colonia* by the Mexican-Americans. With few exceptions, the *colonia* is inhabited only by Mexican-Americans, most of whom live in close proximity to one another in indifferently constructed houses on tiny lots. The north side of the city, which lies across the railroad tracks, is inhabited almost completely by Anglo-Americans. Its appearance is in sharp contrast to that of the *colonia* in that it is strictly residential and displays much better housing.

In the occupational hierarchy of Border City, the top level (the growers, packers, canners, businessmen, and professionals) is overwhelmingly Anglo-American. In the middle group (the white-collar occupations) Mexicans are prominent only where their bilingualism makes them useful, for example, as clerks and salesmen. The bottom level (farm laborers, shed and cannery workers, and domestic servants) is overwhelmingly Mexican-American.

These conditions result from a number of factors, some quite distinct from the reception accorded Mexican-Americans by Anglo-Americans. Many Mexican-Americans are still recent immigrants and are thus relatively unfamiliar with Anglo-American culture and urban living, or else persist in their tendency to live apart and maintain their own institutions whenever possible. Among their disadvantages, however, the negative attitudes and discriminatory practices of the Anglo-American group must be counted. It is only fair to say, with the late Ruth Tuck, that much of what Mexican-Americans have suffered at Anglo-American hands has not been perpetrated deliberately but through indifference, that it has been done not with the fist but with the elbow.[4] The average social and economic status of the Mexican-American group has been improving, and many are moving upward. This is partly owing to increasing acceptance by the Anglo-American group, but chiefly to the efforts of the Mexican-Americans themselves.

Anglo-American Assumptions and Expectations

Robert Lynd writes of the dualism in the principal assumptions that guide Americans in conducting their everyday life and identifies the attempt to "live by contrasting rules of the game" as a characteristic aspect of our culture.[5] This pattern of moral compromise, symptomatic of what is likely to be only vaguely a conscious moral conflict, is evident in Anglo-American assumptions and expectations with regard to Mexican-Americans, which appear both in the moral principles that define what intergroup relations ought to be, and in the popular notions held by Anglo-Americans as to what Mexican-Americans are "really" like. In the first case there is a response to the "American creed," which embodies ideals of the essential dignity of the individual and of certain inalienable rights to freedom, justice, and equal opportunity. Accordingly, Anglo-Americans believe that Mexican-Americans must be accorded full acceptance and equal status in the larger society. When their orientation to these ideals is uppermost, Anglo-Americans believe that the assimilation of Mexican-Americans is only a matter of time, contingent solely on the full incorporation of Anglo-American values and ways of life.

These expectations regarding the assimilation of the Mexican are most clearly expressed in the notion of the "high type" of Mexican. It is based on three criteria: occupational achievement and wealth (the Anglo-American's own principal criteria of status) and command of Anglo-American ways. Mexican-Americans who can so qualify are acceptable for membership in the service clubs and a few other Anglo-American organizations and for limited social intercourse. They may even intermarry without being penalized or ostracized. Both in their achievements in business and agriculture and in wealth, they compare favorably with middle class Anglo Americans, and they manifest a high command of the latter's ways. This view of the "high type" of Mexican reflects the Anglo-American assumption that Mexicans are assimilable; it does not necessarily insure a full acceptance of even the "high type" of Mexican or that his acceptance will be consistent.

The assumption that Mexican-Americans will be ultimately assimilated was not uniformly shared by all the Anglo-Americans who were our informants in Border City. Regardless of whether they expressed adherence to this ideal, however, most Anglo-Americans expressed the contrasting assumption that Mexican-Americans are essentially inferior. Thus the same people may hold assumptions and expectations that are contradictory, although expressed at different times and in different situations. As in the case of their adherence to the ideal of assimilability, not all Anglo-Americans hold the same assumptions and expectations with respect to the inferiority of Mexican-Americans; and even those who agree vary in the intensity of their beliefs. Some do not believe in the Mexican's inferiority at all; some are relatively moderate or sceptical, while others express extreme views with considerable emotional intensity.

Despite this variation, the Anglo-Americans' principal assumptions and expectations emphasize the Mexicans' presumed inferiority. In its most characteristic pattern, such inferiority is held to be self-evident. As one Anglo-American woman put it, "Mexicans are inferior because they are so typically and naturally Mexican." Since they are so obviously inferior, their present subordinate status is appropriate and is really their own fault. There is a ready identification between Mexicans and menial labor, buttressed by an image of the Mexican worker as improvident, undependable, irresponsible, childlike, and indolent. If Mexicans are fit for only the humblest labor, there is nothing abnormal about the fact that most Mexican workers are at the bottom of the occupational pyramid, and the fact that most Mexicans are unskilled workers is sufficient proof that they belong in that category.

Associated with the assumption of Mexican inferiority is that of the homogeneity of this group—that is, all Mexicans are alike. Anglo-Americans may classify Mexicans as being of "high type" and "low type" and at the same time maintain that "a Mexican is a Mexican."

41

Both notions serve a purpose, depending on the situation. The assumption that all Mexicans are alike buttresses the assumption of inferiority by making it convenient to ignore the fact of the existence of a substantial number of Mexican-Americans who represent all levels of business and professional achievement. Such people are considered exceptions to the rule.

Anglo-American Images of Mexican-Americans

To employ Gordon Allport's definition, a stereotype is an exaggerated belief associated with a category, and its function is to justify conduct in relation to that category.[6] Some of the Anglo-American images of the Mexican have no ascertainable basis in fact, while others have at least a kernel of truth. Although some components of these images derive from behavior patterns that are characteristic of some Mexican-Americans in some situations, few if any of the popular generalizations about them are valid as stated, and none is demonstrably true of all. Some of the images of Mexican-Americans are specific to a particular area of intergroup relations, such as the image of the Mexican-American's attributes as a worker. Another is specific to politics and describes Mexicans as ready to give their votes to whoever will pay for them or provide free barbecues and beer.[7] Let us consider a few of the stereotypical beliefs that are widely used on general principles to justify Anglo-American practices of exclusion and subordination.

One such general belief accuses Mexican-Americans of being unclean. The examples given of this supposed characteristic most frequently refer to a lack of personal cleanliness and environmental hygiene and to a high incidence of skin ailments ascribed to a lack of hygienic practices. Indeed, there are few immigrant groups, regardless of their ethnic background, to whom this defect has not been attributed by the host society, as well as others prominent in stereotypes of the Mexican. It has often been observed that for middle-class Americans cleanliness is not simply a matter of keeping clean but is also an index to the morals and virtues of the individual. It is largely true that Mexicans tend to be much more casual in hygienic practices than Anglo-Americans. Moreover, their labor in the field, the packing sheds, and the towns is rarely clean work, and it is possible that many Anglo-Americans base their conclusions on what they observe in such situations. There is no evidence of a higher incidence of skin ailments among Mexicans than among Anglo-Americans. The belief that Mexicans are unclean is useful for rationalizing the Anglo-American practice of excluding Mexicans from any situation that involves close or allegedly close contact with Anglo-Americans, as in residence, and the common use of swimming pools and other recreational facilities.

Drunkenness and criminality are a pair of traits that have appeared regularly in the sterotypes applied to immigrant groups. They have a prominent place in Anglo-American images of Mexicans. If Mexicans are inveterate drunkards and have criminal tendencies, a justification is provided for excluding them from full participation in the life of the community. It is true that drinking is a popular activity among Mexican-Americans and that total abstinence is rare, except among some Protestant Mexican-Americans. Drinking varies, however, from the occasional consumption of a bottle of beer to the heavy drinking of more potent beverages, so that the frequency of drinking and drunkenness is far from being evenly distributed among Mexican-Americans. Actually, this pattern is equally applicable to the Anglo-American group. The ample patronage of bars in the Anglo-American part of Border City, and the drinking behavior exhibited by Anglo-Americans when they cross the river to Mexico indicate that Mexicans have no monopoly on drinking or drunkenness. It is true that the number of arrests for drunkenness in Border City is greater among Mexicans, but this is probably because Mexicans are more vulnerable to arrest. The court records in Border City show little difference in the contributions made to delinquency and crime by Anglo- and Mexican-Americans.

Another cluster of images in the Anglo-American stereotype portrays Mexican-Americans as deceitful and of a "low" morality, as mysterious, unpredictable, and hostile to Anglo-Americans. It is quite possible that Mexicans resort to a number of devices in their relations with Anglo-Americans, particularly in relations with employers, to compensate for their disadvantages, which may be construed by Anglo-Americans as evidence of deceitfulness. The whole nature of the dominant-subordinate relationship does not make for frankness on the part of Mexicans or encourage them to face up directly to Anglo-Americans in most intergroup contacts. As to the charge of immorality, one need only recognize the strong sense of loyalty and obligation that Mexicans feel in their familial and interpersonal relations to know that the charge is baseless. The claim that Mexicans are mysterious and deceitful may in part reflect Anglo-American reactions to actual differences in culture and personality, but like the other beliefs considered here, is highly exaggerated. The imputation of hostility to Mexicans, which is manifested in a reluctance to enter the *colonia,* particularly at night, may have its kernel of truth, but appears to be largely a projection of the Anglo-American's own feelings.

All three of these images can serve to justify exclusion and discrimination: if Mexicans are deceitful and immoral, they do not have to be accorded equal status and justice; if they are mysterious and unpredictable, there is no point in treating them as one would a fellow Anglo-American; and if they are hostile and dangerous, it is best that they live apart in colonies of their own.

Not all Anglo-American images of the Mexican are unfavorable. Among those usually meant to be complimentary are the beliefs that all Mexicans are musical and always ready for a fiesta, that they are very "romantic" rather than "realistic" (which may have unfavorable overtones as well), and that they love flowers and can grow them under the most adverse conditions. Although each of these beliefs may have a modicum of truth, it may be noted that they tend to reinforce Anglo-American images of Mexicans as childlike and irresponsible, and thus they support the notion that Mexicans are capable only of subordinate status.

Mexican-American Assumptions, Expectations, and Images

Mexican-Americans are as likely to hold contradictory assumptions and distorted images as are Anglo-Americans. Their principal assumptions, however, must reflect those of Anglo-Americans—that is, Mexicans must take into account the Anglo-Americans' conflict as to their potential equality and present inferiority, since they are the object of such imputations. Similarly, their images of Anglo-Americans are not derived wholly independently, but to some extent must reflect their own subordinate status. Consequently, their stereotypes of Anglo-Americans are much less elaborate, in part because Mexicans feel no need of justifying the present intergroup relation, in part because the very nature of their dependent position forces them to view the relation more realistically than Anglo-Americans do. For the same reasons, they need not hold to their beliefs about Anglo-Americans with the rigidity and intensity so often characteristic of the latter.

Any discussion of these assumptions and expectations requires some mention of the class distinctions within the Mexican-American group.[8] Its middle class, though small as compared with the lower class, is powerful within the group and performs the critical role of intermediary in negotiations with the Anglo-American group. Middle-class status is based on education and occupation, family background, readiness to serve the interests of the group, on wealth, and the degree of acculturation, or command of Anglo-American ways. Anglo-Americans recognize Mexican class distinctions (although not very accurately) in their notions of the "high type" and "low type" of Mexicans.

In general, lower-class Mexicans do not regard the disabilities of their status as being nearly as severe as do middle-class Mexican-Americans. This is primarily a reflection of the insulation between the Anglo-American world and that of the Mexican lower class. Most Mexicans, regardless of class, are keenly aware of Anglo-American attitudes and practices with regard to their group, but lower-class Mexicans do not conceive of participation in the larger society as necessary nor do they regard Anglo-American practices of exclusion as affecting them directly. Their principal reaction has been to maintain their isolation, and thus they have not been particularly concerned with improving their status by acquiring Anglo-American ways, a course more characteristic of the middle-class Mexican.

Mexican-American assumptions and expectations regarding Anglo-Americans must be qualified, then, as being more characteristic of middle- than of lower-class Mexican-Americans. Mexicans, like Anglo-Americans, are subject to conflicts in their ideals, not only because of irrational thinking on their part but also because of Anglo-American inconsistencies between ideal and practice. As for ideals expressing democratic values, Mexican expectations are for obvious reasons the counterpart of the Anglo-Americans'—that Mexican-Americans should be accorded full acceptance and equal opportunity. They feel a considerable ambivalence, however, as to the Anglo-American expectation that the only way to achieve this goal is by a full incorporation of Anglo-American values and ways of life, for this implies the ultimate loss of their cultural identity as Mexicans. On the one hand, they favor the acquisition of Anglo-American culture and the eventual remaking of the Mexican in the Anglo-American image; but on the other hand, they are not so sure that Anglo-American acceptance is worth such a price. When they are concerned with this dilemma, Mexicans advocate a fusion with Anglo-American culture in which the "best" of the Mexican ways, as they view it, would be retained along with the incorporation of the "best" of the Anglo-American ways, rather than a one-sided exchange in which all that is distinctively Mexican would be lost.

A few examples will illustrate the point of view expressed in the phrase, "the best of both ways." A premium is placed on speaking good, unaccented English, but the retention of good Spanish is valued just as highly as "a mark of culture that should not be abandoned." Similarly, there is an emphasis on the incorporation of behavior patterns that are considered characteristically Anglo-American and that will promote "getting ahead," but not to the point at which the drive for power and wealth would become completely dominant, as is believed to be the case with Anglo-Americans.

Mexican ambivalence about becoming Anglo-American or achieving a fusion of the "best" of both cultures is compounded by their ambivalence about another issue, that of equality versus inferiority. That Anglo-Americans are dominant in the society and seem to monopolize its accomplishments and rewards leads Mexicans at times to draw the same conclusion that Anglo-Americans do, namely, that Mexicans are inferior. This questioning of their own sense of worth exists in all classes of the Mexican-American group, although with varying intensity, and plays a substantial part in every adjustment to intergroup relations. There is a pronounced tendency to concede the superiority of Anglo-American ways and consequently to define Mexican ways as undesirable, inferior, and disreputable. The tendency to believe in his own inferiority is counterbalanced, however, by the Mexican's fierce racial pride, which sets the tone of Mexican demands and strivings for equal status, even though these may slip into feelings of inferiority.

The images Mexicans have of Anglo-Americans may not be so elaborate or so emotionally charged as the images that Anglo-Americans have of Mexicans, but they are nevertheless stereotypes, overgeneralized, and exaggerated, although used primarily for defensive rather than justificatory purposes. Mexican images of Anglo-Americans are sometimes favorable, particularly when they identify such traits as initiative, ambition, and industriousness as being peculiarly Anglo-American. Unfavorable images are prominent, however, and, although they may be hostile, they never impute inferiority to Anglo-Americans. Most of the Mexican stereotypes evaluate Anglo-Americans on the basis of their attitudes toward Mexican-Americans. For example, one such classification provides a two-fold typology. The first type, the "majority," includes those who are cold, unkind, mercenary, and exploitative. The second type, the "minority," consists of those who are friendly, warm, just, and unprejudiced. For the most part, Mexican images of Anglo-Americans reflect the latter's patterns of exclusion and assumptions of superiority, as experienced by Mexican-Americans. Thus Anglo-Americans are pictured as stolid, phlegmatic, cold-hearted, and distant. They are also said to be braggarts, conceited, inconstant, and insincere.

Intergroup Relations, Mutual Expectations, and Cultural Differences

A number of students of intergroup relations assert that research in this area has yet to demonstrate any relation between stereotypical beliefs and intergroup behavior; indeed, some insist that under certain conditions ethnic attitudes and discrimination can vary independently.[9] Arnold M. Rose, for example, concludes that "from a heuristic standpoint it may be desirable to assume that patterns of intergroup relations, on the one hand, and attitudes of prejudice and stereotyping, on the other hand, are fairly unrelated phenomena although they have reciprocal influences on each other . . ."[10] In the present study, no systematic attempt was made to investigate the relation between the stereotypical beliefs of particular individuals and their actual intergroup behavior; but the study did yield much evidence that both images which justify group separatism and separateness itself are characteristic aspects of intergroup relations in Border City. One of the principal findings is that in those situations in which contact between Anglo-Amercans and Mexicans is voluntary (such as residence, education, recreation, religious worship, and social intercourse) the characteristic pattern is separateness rather than common participation. Wherever intergroup contact is necessary, as in occupational activities and the performance of commercial and professional services, it is held to the minimum sufficient to accomplish the purpose of the contact.[11] The extent of this separateness is not constant for all members of the two groups, since it tends to be less severe between Anglo-Americans and those Mexicans they define as of a "high type." Nevertheless, the evidence reveals a high degree of compatibility between beliefs and practices in Border City's intergroup relations, although the data have nothing to offer for the identification of direct relationships.

In any case, the separateness that characterizes intergroup relations cannot be attributed solely to the exclusion practices of the Anglo-American group. Mexicans have tended to remain separate by choice as well as by necessity. Like many other ethnic groups, they have often found this the easier course, since they need not strain to learn another language or to change their ways and manners. The isolation practices of the Mexican group are as relevant to an understanding of intergroup relations as are the exclusion practices of the Anglo-Americans.

This should not, however, obscure the fact that to a wide extent the majority of Mexican-Americans share the patterns of living of Anglo-American society; many of their ways are already identical. Regardless of the degree of their insulation from the larger society, the demands of life in the United States have required basic modifications of the Mexicans' cultural tradition. In material culture, Mexicans are hardly to be distinguished from Anglo-Americans, and there have been basic changes in medical beliefs and practices and in the customs regarding godparenthood. Mexicans have acquired English in varying degrees, and their Spanish has become noticeably Anglicized. Although the original organization of the family has persisted, major changes have occurred in patterns of traditional authority, as well as in child training and courtship practices. Still, it is the exceedingly rare Mexican-American, no matter how acculturated he may be to the dominant society, who does not in some degree retain the more subtle characteristics of his Mexican heritage, particularly in his conception of time and in other fundamental value orientations, as well as in his modes of participation in interpersonal relations.[12] Many of the most acculturated Mexican-Americans have attempted to exemplify what they regard as "the best of both ways." They have become largely Anglo-American in their way of living, but they still retain fluent Spanish and a knowledge of their traditional culture, and they maintain an identification with their own heritage while participating in Anglo-American culture. Nevertheless, this sort of achievement still seems a long way off for many Mexican-Americans who regard it as desirable.

A predominant Anglo-American expectation is that the Mexicans will be eventually assimilated into the larger society; but this is contingent upon Mexicans' becoming just like Anglo-Americans. The Mexican counterpart to this expectation is only partially complementary. Mexicans want to be full members of the larger society, but they do not want to give up their cultural heritage. There is even less complementarity of expectation with regard to the present conduct of intergroup relations. Anglo-Americans believe they are justified in withholding equal access to the rewards of full acceptance as long as Mexicans remain "different," particularly since they interpret the differences (both those which have some basis in reality and those which have none) as evidence of inferiority. Mexicans, on the other hand, while not always certain that they are not inferior, clearly want equal opportunity and full acceptance now, not in some dim future, and they do not believe that their differences (either presumed or real) from Anglo-Americans offer any justification for the denial of opportunity and acceptance. Moreover, they do not find that acculturation is rewarded in any clear and regular way by progressive acceptance.

It is probable that both Anglo-Americans and Mexicans will have to modify their beliefs and practices if they are to realize more nearly their expectations of each other. Mutual stereotyping, as well as the exclusion practices of Anglo-Americans and the isolation practices of Mexicans, maintains the separateness of the two groups, and separateness is a massive barrier to the realization of their expectations. The process of acculturation is presently going on among Mexican-Americans and will continue, regardless of whether changes in Anglo-Mexican relations occur. Unless Mexican-Americans can validate their increasing command of Anglo-American ways by a free participation in the larger society, however, such acculturation is not likely to accelerate its present leisurely pace, nor will it lead to eventual assimilation. The *colonia* is a relatively safe place in which new cultural acquisitions may be tried out, and thus it has its positive functions; but by the same token it is only in intergroup contacts with Anglo-Americans that acculturation is validated, that the Mexican's level of acculturation is tested, and that the distance he must yet travel to assimilation is measured.[13]

Conclusions

There are major inconsistencies in the assumptions that Anglo-Americans and Mexican-Americans hold about one another. Anglo-Americans assume that Mexican-Americans are their potential, if not actual, peers, but at the same time assume they are their inferiors. The beliefs that presumably demonstrate the Mexican-Americans' inferiority tend to place them outside the accepted moral order and framework of Anglo-American society by attributing to them undesirable characteristics that make it "reasonable" to treat them differently from their fellow Anglo-Americans. Thus the negative images provide not only a rationalized definition of the intergroup relation that makes it palatable for Anglo-Americans, but also a substantial support for maintaining the relation as it is. The assumptions of Mexican-Americans about Anglo-Americans are similarly inconsistent, and their images of Anglo-Americans are predominantly negative, although these are primarily defensive rather than justificatory. The mutual expectations of the two groups contrast sharply with the ideal of a complementarity of expectations, in that Anglo-Americans expect Mexicans to become just like themselves, if they are to be accorded equal status in the larger society, whereas Mexican-Americans want full acceptance, regardless of the extent to which they give up their own ways and acquire those of the dominant group.

Anglo-Americans and Mexicans may decide to stay apart because they are different, but cultural differences provide no moral justification for one group to deny to the other equal opportunity and the rewards of the larger society. If the full acceptance of Mexicans by Anglo-Americans is contingent upon the disappearance of cultural differences, it will not be accorded in the foreseeable future. In our American society, we have often seriously underestimated the strength and tenacity of early cultural conditioning. We have expected newcomers to change their customs and values to conform to American ways as quickly as possible, without an adequate appreciation of the strains imposed by this process. An understanding of the nature of culture and of its interrelations with personality can make us more realistic about the rate at which cultural change can proceed and about the gains and costs for the individual who is subject to the experiences of acculturation. In viewing cultural differences primarily as disabilities, we neglect their positive aspects. Mexican-American culture represents the most constructive and effective means Mexican-Americans have yet been able to develop for coping with their changed natural and social environment. They will further exchange old ways for new only if these appear to be more meaningful and rewarding than the old, and then only if they are given full opportunity to acquire the new ways and to use them.

REFERENCES

1 See John Harding, Bernard Kutner, Harold Proshansky, and Isidor Chein, "Prejudice and Ethnic Relations," in Gardner Lindzey (ed.), Handbook of Social Psychology (Cambridge, Addison-Wesley Publishing Company, 1954), vol. 2, pp. 1021-1061; and Otto Klineberg, Tensions Affecting International Understanding, New York, Social Science Research Council, 1950, Bulletin 62.

2 The term "Anglo-American", as is common in the Southwest, refers to all residents of Border City who do not identify themselves as Spanish-speaking and of Mexican descent. The Anglo-Americans of Border City have emigrated there from all parts of the United States and represent a wide variety of regional and ethnic backgrounds. The terms "Mexican-American" and "Mexican," as used here, refer to all residents of Border City who are Spanish-speaking and of Mexican descent. The term "Spanish-speaking" is perhaps less objectionable to many people, but for present purposes is even less specific than Mexican or Mexican-American, since it also refers to ethnic groups that would have no sense of identification with the group under consideration here.

3 For the historical background of the Valley, see Frank C. Pierce, *A Brief History of the Lower Rio Grande Valley*, Menasha, George Banta Publishing Company, 1917; Paul S. Taylor, *An American-Mexican Frontier*, Chapel Hill, University of North Carolina Press, 1934; and Florence J. Scott, *Historical Heritage of the Lower Rio Grande*, San Antonio, The Naylor Company, 1937.

4 Ruth D. Tuck, *Not with the Fist*, New York, Harcourt Brace and Company, 1946.

5 Robert S. Lynd, *Knowledge for What?* Princeton, Princeton University Press, 1948.

6 Gordon W. Allport, *The Nature of Prejudice*, Cambridge, Addison-Wesley Publishing Company, 1954.

7 For an analysis of Mexican-American value orientations and behavior in the occupational and political spheres, see Ozzie G. Simmons, Anglo-Americans and Mexican-Americans in South Texas: A Study in Dominant-Subordinate Group Relations (unpublished doctoral dissertation, Harvard University, 1952).

8 See *ibid.*, for a discussion of the Anglo-American and Mexican class structures.

9 Robert K. Merton, "Discrimination and the American Creed," in R. M. MacIver (ed.), *Discrimination and National Welfare* (New York, Harper and Brothers, 1949), pp. 99-128; John Harding, Bernard Kutner, Harold Proshansky, and Isidor Chein, *op. cit.*; Arnold M. Rose, "Intergroup Relations vs. Prejudice: Pertinent Theory for the Study of Social Change," *Social Problems*, 1956, *4*: 173-176; Robin M. Williams, Jr., "Racial and Cultural Relations," in Joseph B. Gittler (ed.), *Review of Sociology: Analysis of a Decade* (New York, John Wiley and Sons, 1957), pp. 423-464.

10 Rose, *op. cit.*

11 Simmons, *op. cit.*

12 For cultural differences and similarities between Anglo-Americans and Mexicans, see Simmons, *op. cit.*; Tuck, *op. cit.*; Lyle Saunders, *Cultural Difference and Medical Care*, New York, Russell Sage Foundation, 1954; Munro S. Edmonson, *Los Manitos: A Study of Institutional Values* (New Orleans, Middle American Research Institute, Tulane University, 1957, Publication 25), pp. 1-72; and Margaret Clark, *Health in the Mexican-American Culture*, Berkeley, University of California Press, 1959.

13 See Leonard Broom and John I. Kitsuse, "The Validation of Acculturation: A Condition to Ethnic Assimilation," *American Anthropologist*, 1955, *57*: 44-48.

PART II

THE INDIVIDUAL BASE

Toward an Operational Definition of the Mexican American

Fernando Peñalosa

THE SOCIOLOGICAL STUDY of the Mexican American, until very recently almost the exclusive province of Anglo sociologists, is about to be launched into a new period of development that should certainly produce more fruitful, more realistic, and more relevant data and conclusions than have previously been forthcoming. Before we move into this new period, however, we would be well advised to map out somewhat more carefully the population we are going to study. In developing a relatively new field it is not so nportant to attempt to produce immediately the right answers as it is to ask the right questions. If we ask simple questions we may get simple and probably misleading answers, particularly since our subject is not at all simple, but exceedingly complex. Mexican Americans may constitute one of the most heterogeneous ethnic groups ever to be studied by sociologists. With reference to the scholarly study of the Mexican American we would be well advised to stop trying to find the "typical" or "true," and seek rather to establish the range of variation. Generalizations extrapolated from the community in which a Chicano writer happened to grow up or which an Anglo sociologist or anthropologist happened to have studied can be particularly misleading.

It is furthermore essential that we avoid simplistic either-or types of questions, such as, are Chicanos a people or not?, do they have a distinctive culture or not?, or is there such a thing existentially as the Mexican American community or not? Realistically we are

AZTLAN, 1970, Vol. 1, pp. 1-12.

handicapped in attempting to answer these types of inquiries in which the alternatives are already implicitly limited by the question itself. A much more productive approach might be rather to consider prefixing our questions with a phrase such as "to what oxtont . . ." so that wo ask to what extent do Mexican Americans constitute a stratum, possess a distinct subculture, etc.

Scholars, both Chicano and Anglo, have furthermore spent countless hours debating the question of the correct name for our group, and then attempting to define the entity for which the supposedly correct name stands. Perhaps the time has come to move beyond terminological and definitional polemics to an examination of some of the dimensions along which we might explore our subject in an attempt better to understand its character.[1]

The method of procedure in this paper will be as follows. A series of questions will be asked about the Mexican American population. An attempt will be made to answer each one, based on the writer's admittedly limited perception of the current state of knowledge, and to point out some possible lines of future research along that dimension. *Some* day, when we have approximately adequate answers to the questions posed, we *may* have a more or less acceptable operational definition of the Mexican American. By way of overview, these are the questions which will be discussed:

1. To what extent do Mexican Americans constitute a separate racial entity?

2. To what extent do Mexican Americans conceive of themselves as belonging to a separate ethnic group?

3. To what extent do Mexican Americans have a separate or distinct culture?

4. To what extent do Mexican Americans constitute an identifiable stratum in society?

5. To what extent is it realistic to speak of Mexican American communities?

6. To what extent are differences in historical antecedents reflected among Mexican Americans?

7. To what extent are regional socio economic differences significant among Mexican Americans?[2]

Let us then direct our attention to each of these questions in turn.

To what extent do Mexican Americans constitute a separate racial entity?

A goodly number of Mexican Americans and others are confused as to the biological nature of this particular group. An Anglo-American may carelessly divide people into whites, Negroes, and Mexicans, or a Chicano may assertively speak of "La Raza."[3] The recently increasing use of the term "brown" similarly represents pride in the group's presumed racial distinctiveness, analogous not only to the Negroes' newly-found blackness but also to "La Raza Cósmica" of José Vasconcelos. Although most Mexican Americans are of mixed Spanish, Indian (both Southwestern and Mexican), and Negro descent, a large proportion are not physically distinct from the majority American population hence the group as a whole cannot be characterized in terms of race.[4] "Race" is essentially furthermore a nineteenth century notion which is rapidly becoming obsolete in physical anthropology and related disciplines. In any case biological differences as such are no concern of the sociologist; only the ways in which notions of race influence people's behavior concern him. The topic of our discussion is therefore what social scientists refer to as socially supposed races. Regardless of whatever mythology may be involved, however, if the majority group considers Mexican Americans as a race, and insists therefore on continuing to treat them in a discriminatory fashion, then the consequences are nonetheless real: not only the deprivation and segregation, but as the progress of the Chicano movement has shown, racial pride. Not all the consequences of racism are necessarily negative.

Some historical perspective is needed here. With reference to color discrimination it was noted by Manuel Gamio that in the 1920's dark-skinned Mexicans suffered about the same type of discrimination as Negroes, but that medium complected Mexicans were able to use second-class public facilities. Even light-brown skinned Mexicans were excluded from high-class facilities, while "white" Mexicans might be freely admitted, especially if they spoke fluent English.[5] To what extent is such a type of scale still applied in public facilities or in other areas of public and private life, and what social factors affect its application? Furthermore we might well examine the extent to which differences in physical appearances are socially significant to Mexican Americans themselves. The fact that we live in a racist society where the primary factor affecting a person's status and life chances has always been the color of his skin, means that it is unrealistic to attempt to sweep an unpleasant situation under the carpet and pretend it does not exist.

To what extent do Mexican Americans conceive of themselves as belonging to a separate ethnic group?

Tentatively at least we might characterize an ethnic group as a sub-population which shares a common ancestry and which is distinguished by a way of life or culture which is significantly different in one or more respects from what of the majority of the population, which regards it as an out-group. Do Mexican Americans conceive of themselves in this manner? If they thus conceive of themselves, what is the degree of separateness perceived? It depends of course on whom you ask. But it may be hypothesized that answers would probably fall along a spectrum or continuum, of which it is not too difficult to identify three principal segments: those at the extremes, and one at or near the center.

These segments can be characterized according to varying self-conceptions and variations in self-identity. At one extreme are those who acknowledge the fact of their Mexican descent but for whom this fact constitutes neither a particularly positive nor a particularly negative value, because it plays a very unimportant part in their lives and their self-conception. At or near the middle of this putative continuum are those for whom being of Mexican ancestry is something of which they are constantly conscious and which looms importantly as part of their self-conception. Their Mexican descent may constitute for them a positive value, a negative value, or more generally an ambiguous blend of the two. At the other end of the continuum are those who are not only acutely aware of their Mexican identity and descent but are committed to the defense of Mexican American subcultural values, and strive to work actively for the betterment of their people. Tentatively I would like to suggest, without any implication as to their "correctness," that the terms "Americans of Mexican ancestry," "Mexican-Americans," and "Chicanos," are sometimes used for those who closely resemble the three types suggested.

Research is needed to determine whether indeed such a continuum can be identified, and if so, what are the proportions of persons falling at various points along its length, and with what other social indices these positions are associated. Sample surveys would seem to be one of the most direct ways of attacking this problem.[5]

To what extent do Mexican Americans have a separate or distinct culture?

Mexican American culture or subculture whatever its precise nature, composition and structure, if such are even determinable, appears to be a product of multiple origins, as one would expect in light of its history. The focus of its synthesis and emergence is of course the barrio and it is here and not toward Mexico where we must focus our primary attention. At the same time we should not minimize differences between the way of life of Chicanos residing inside and of those residing outside the barrio.

Tentatively it may be suggested that the chief sources of Mexican American culture are four in number. First, there is the initially overriding but subsequently attenuated influence of what is usually called "traditional" Mexican culture, the way of life brought by most of the immigrants from Mexico during several centuries.[7]

Secondly there is the initially weak but subsequently growing influence of the surrounding majority American culture. Mexican Americans are subject to approximately the same educational system and mass media of communication as are other Americans and participate to varying extents in the economic, social, intellectual and religious life of the broader society. A careful comparison of the way of life of persons of Mexican descent in the United States with those of Mexico will help substantiate the notion that the former are first and foremost "Americans," and only secondary "Mexican Americans."

A third source of influence upon Mexican American culture is class influence. The fact that the bulk of the Mexican American population has been concentrated at the lower socio-economic levels of the society means that some aspects of Mexican American culture may have their source in behavior characteristic generally of lower-class people regardless of ethnic group. Thus, for example, the alleged relatively high crime rate (at least for certain types of crimes) among Mexican Americans can perhaps best be explained in terms of social class rather than ethnicity, as well as in terms of the relative youth of the group as a whole and differential law enforcement practices. Apart from the question of Anglo discrimination, insensitivity and incompetence, Mexican American problems in education seem to be as much class problems as they are cultural problems. Educational studies comparing lower class Chicano students with middle class Anglos are as methodologically faulty as they are socially pernicious. Neither must it be forgotten that class discrimination is as real in this country as racial or ethnic discrimination.

The fourth source of influence on Mexican American culture results from the minority status of its bearers. The term "minority" is not properly a numerical concept, (Chicanos outnumber Anglos in East Los Angeles) but rather a term suggesting that the group has less than its share of political, economic and social power vis-à-vis the majority population and hence suffers from educational, social, occupational and other economic disadvantages mediated through the processes of prejudice, discrimination and segregation. Inasmuch as the concept of culture basically refers to the sum-total of techniques a people has in coping with and adapting to its physical and social environment, there have been developed some special cultural responses among Mexican Americans to their minority status, as occurs among members of other minority groups. These responses may be viewed as very important components of the admittedly heterogeneous and ill-defined Chicano subculture. An obvious example of this sort of trait is the Chicano Movement itself, which is both a response to the majority culture and society, and an outstanding component of Chicano culture itself. But even here the matter gets complicated, for it is necessary to recognize that the Movement has borrowed at least some of its goals, values, techniques and strategies from both the black and Anglo civil rights Movements.

It is suggested therefore that Mexican American culture is a multidimensional phenomenon and must be studied in terms of these four dimensions at least (there may be more), as well as in terms of its historical, regional, and ecological variants. It is highly unlikely that all the various strands will ever be completely unravelled and laid out neatly side by side for us to see, but neither must we lose sight of the heterogeneous origins of Mexican American culture, the nature of the varying continuing influences on it, and its continuously changing nature, as we seek to ascertain its differential dispersal, influence, and persistence among persons of Mexican descent in this country.

To what extent do Mexican Americans constitute an identifiable stratum in society?

A number of social scientists who have studied the relations between Mexican Americans and Anglo Americans in the Southwest have described these relations as being "caste-like."[8] That is, the nature of interethnic relations was said to bear some resemblance to the relations between castes in India and elsewhere. In the United States the situation which undoubtedly most closely resembles a color caste system is the traditional pattern of race relations in the South, with its supposedly superordinate white caste and subordinate Negro caste.

Although Mexican-Anglo relations have never been as rigid as black-white relations there may still have been a resemblance, particularly in certain communities, strong enough to characterize them as "semi-caste," "quasi-caste," or "caste-like." That is, there would be manifested a strong degree of segregation, blocking of entrance to certain occupations, political impotence, ritual avoidance, and taboos on intermarriage stemming from notions of "racial" or "color" differences. Intermarriage is an important criterion, for marriage implies social equality between partners. The idea that Mexicans and Mexican Americans are not whites was certainly more prevalent before the World War II period, or at least people expressed the idea more frequently without worrying whether or not anyone might take offense. The current situation in this regard is unclear.[9] It may be that the continuing low rate of intermarriage, the tacit or explicit superior-inferior nature of ethnic relations, and the concentration of Mexican Americans in certain jobs and their virtual exclusion from others, means that Mexican-Anglo relations still approximate semi-caste, although increasingly less so.

If Anglo-Mexican relations appear to be moving away from a caste basis to a class basis, and the evidence is definitely pointing in this direction, the internal stratification of the Mexican American population looms increasingly more important. With a few exceptions, our knowledge of Mexican American stratification has had to depend so far primarily on the rather impressionistic accounts of a handful of Anglo social scientists. We know that, generally speaking, Mexican American rural populations have less differentiated social class structures than the urban ones, that is, the status spread is greater in the city than in the country. We know some of the variables associated with socioeconomic status and self and community perception. Much more we do not know.

Impressionistic accounts and reworking of U.S. Census data in the manner of the UCLA Mexican American Study Project have not been enough. Careful original sample surveys to study the interrelations of "objective" stratification variables as well as the study of the "subjective" perceptions by Chicanos of their own internal stratification systems are urgently needed. Only thus will the myth of the class homogeneity of the Mexican American population be thoroughly discredited and its heterogeneity adequately documented.

To what extent is it realistic to speak of Mexican American communities?

One badly neglected area of research is the extent to which Mexican Americans have a feeling of belonging to an identifiable Mexican American community and the extent to which their participation in its organizations and other community activities enable us to identify leadership roles and a social structure as well as a body of sentiment. Regional and ecological considerations are of primary importance here. Degree of community feeling and participation undoubtedly varies as among such places as East Los Angeles, Pomona, Tucson, Chicago, or Hidalgo County, Texas, to mention but a few. It varies between those who live in the barrio and those who live outside. Rural-urban differences are likewise significant. Rural Mexican Americans were never able to establish true communities in California, for example, because of Anglo pressures and because of the migratory work patterns of most of the people, according to Ernesto Galarza.[10] The range and variation of "communityness" must be empirically studied, not assumed a priori, both within populations and among a sample of different locales reflecting the differential impact of relevant regional and ecological variables.

To what extent are differences in historical antecedents reflected among Mexican Americans?

To a certain extent this question foreshadows the succeeding one inasmuch as the principal regional variations have emerged because of different historical antecedents, and hence it is possible to separate analytically but not empirically the geographical and historical dimensions.

The Mexican American population in the United States from 1848 down to the present has been continually expanded and renewed by immigration both legal and illegal from Mexico, a continually changing Mexico. Mexican immigrants who came for example, before the Revolution, during the Revolution, shortly after the Revolution, and more recently, each came from a somewhat different Mexico. Those coming in at the present time as permanent residents come for the most part from a Mexico vastly more industrialized, urbanized, modernized and educated than the Mexico of our fathers or grandfathers. How well have immigrants from different periods of Mexico's history, and their children, fared in the United States? What have been the differential rates of mobility and/or assimilation? We should also raise questions about generational differences, and with reference to the differential composition of Mexican American local populations in terms of their historical antecedents. How are these kinds of differences associated with significant social indices, rates of acculturation, and self-perception and self-identity variables?

To what extent are regional socio economic differences significant among Mexican Americans?

A number of Mexican American regional subcultures can probably be identified. The historical and geographical factors affecting the emergence of these sub varieties are of crucial importance in understanding their present nature. It is important to realize, for example, that the Hispanos of New Mexico and Colorado evolved their culture in isolated mountain villages fairly remote from Anglo civilization; that the Texas-Mexicans are not only concentrated along the border but are also located geographically in the South with its unique tradition of discrimination and prejudice; whereas the Chicanos of Southern California have been caught up in a changing situation of rapid urban growth.

In all areas of the Southwest, the shift from rural to urban has been a highly significant trend. The overwhelming majority of Southwestern Mexican Americans now live in urban areas. These Mexican American urban settlements have grown primarily through migration from the countryside, so that the bulk of the adult residents of those communities have not yet completely adjusted to urban life. The kinds of problems they face therefore are quite different from those they had to face in the small towns and rural areas from which they came. Simple agricultural skills are no longer enough for the security of employment. The kinds of job opportunities available are primarily of an industrial nature and increasingly require a high degree of either manual dexterity or intellectual skills or both. The needs of automation are furthermore constantly raising the level of skills required in order to compete successfully in the job market. So the urban Mexican American is pushed further and further away from pre-industrial skills, habits, and attitudes and directly into the modern industrial social order with all its complexities and problems.

At the opposite extreme, Mexican Americans in such a place as rural Texas score the lowest on all the social measures. It is in this area where the permanent residences of many migratory agricultural laborers are concentrated. There is perhaps less social differentiation of Mexican Americans here than in any other area of the Southwest, and the most vigorous preservation of so-called traditional Mexican rural culture.

The Spanish Americans, Hispanos, "Manitos," or "mejicanos," are the descendants of the original racially mixed but Europeanized settlers of New Mexico and southern Colorado, when this area was under Spanish rule, but administered and colonized from Mexico. Traditionally most of the Hispanos lived in isolated rural areas and were economically and socially handicapped. In recent years they have become increasingly urbanized as many have been forced off their lands by the more competitive Anglo farmers, or as mines were closed. Many Hispanos left New Mexico and Colorado during the World War II and post-war periods. Many came and continue to come to Southern California and other areas of high urbanization. Here we have another case of attempting to unravel the strands, as Chicano urban populations are increasing in heterogeneity with reference to interstate geographical origins. The sociological study of the Mexican American should include both the *systematic* comparative examination of regional variants of the admittedly hard to define and identify Chicano culture and community (and *not* just a series of monographic reports, each one on a separate community), as well as the way in which these differences are being gradually obliterated in the urban milieu."

In summary, seven questions were posed with reference to the Chicano population, some tentative answers were given, and some areas for future research indicated. It is not the writer's intention to imply that a series of adequately documented answers to these questions would constitute the corpus of Chicano sociology. There are a number of other extremely important unmentioned questions and topics which are obviously part of such a sociology, such as those relating to family life, value systems, power relations, bilingualism, educational questions, and many others. Rather, the explicit intention and hope is that the answers to these questions will help in the formulation of a sociological definition of our subject population before we tackle the multitude of difficult intellectual and social questions which lie ahead of us.

References

1. The terms "Mexican American" and "Chicano" are used here for convenience as equivalent and interchangeable, without any implication of their "correctness" or of the "correctness" of any other term or terms that might have been used in their place.

2. The careful reader will have detected that the writer's philosophical bias is strongly nominalistic, that is, that he conceives of "culture," "community," "ethnic group," etc., not as "things," but rather as labels which refer to abstractions conjured up by the social scientist or others as a convenience in handling the data they are trying to understand. For example, the latest issue of *El Chicano*, a newspaper published in San Bernardino, carries the headline "Mexican Community Demands Dismissal of Judge Chargin." This is a figure of speech, of course, inasmuch as if the community is indeed an abstraction, it cannot demand anything; only individuals or organized groups can demand.

3. Readers of this journal are undoubtedly acquainted with the fact that throughout the Spanish-speaking world Columbus Day is referred to as "El Día de la Raza," the word "raza" in this context referring to all persons of Hispanic culture, as it does in the motto of the National Autonomous University of Mexico: "Por mi raza hablará el espíritu." Nevertheless, in matters social, words mean what their users *want* them to mean.

4. Cf. Marcus Goldstein, *Demographic and Bodily Changes in Descendants of Mexican Immigrants.* Austin: Institute of Latin American Studies, University of Texas, 1943, and Gonzalo Aguirre Beltrán, *La Población Negra de México 1519-1810* (México, D. F.: Ediciones Fuente Cultural, 1946).

5. Manuel Gamio, *Mexican Immigration to the United States* (Chicago: University of Chicago Press, 1930), p. 53.

6. The writer is currently carrying out a random-sample survey of the Mexican American population of San Bernardino, California, with reference to internal social stratification, self-identification, and perception of community and subculture. Hopefully the results will throw some light on these questions.

7. The pitfalls of stereotyping in this area are very great, as so ably pointed out by Octavio I. Romano-V., "The Anthropology and Sociology of the Mexican Americans," *El Grito,* II (Fall, 1968), 13-26.

8. Walter Goldschmidt, *As You Sow* (New York: Harcourt, Brace and Co., 1947), p. 59; Paul Schuster Taylor, *An American-Mexican Frontier, Nueces County, Texas* (Chapel Hill: The University of North Carolina Press, 1934); Ruth D. Tuck, *Not With the Fist: Mexican-Americans in a Southwest City* (New York: Harcourt, Brace and Co., 1946), p. 44; Thomas E. Lasswell, "Status Stratification in a Selected Community," unpublished Ph.D. dissertation, University of Southern California, 1953; Robert B. Rogers, "Perception of the Power Structure by Social Class in a California Community," unpublished Ph.D. dissertation, University of Southern California, 1962; James B. Watson and Julián Samora, "Subordinate Leadership in a Bi-cultural Community," *American Sociological Review,* 19 (August 1954), pp. 413-421; Ozzie Simmons, "Americans and Mexican Americans in South Texas," unpublished Ph.D. dissertation, Harvard University, 1952; William H. Madsen, *The Mexican-Americans of South Texas* (New York: Holt, Rinehart & Winston, 1964).

It may be argued that since the authors of all these studies are Anglos they may have had a slanted view of the situation, yet it should be understood they are reporting Anglo residents' perceptions of the social barriers they themselves have set up.

9. After the 1930 Census, in which Mexicans were listed as a separate "race," persons of Mexican descent were subsequently put back into the "white" category largely because the Mexican American leaders of that time insisted Mexicans were "white." Similarly the Chicano population is substantially the same as the 1950 and 1960 Census category "White persons of Spanish surname." Understandably therefore the recent emphasis on "brown" and "La Raza" has some Anglos confused. With reference to the possible relevance of the caste model, it should be pointed out that the nature of the discrimination against Chicanos has been primarily social rather than legal, as has been the case for blacks in the South.

10. Lecture in the University of California Extension Series "The Mexican American in Transition," Ontario, California, Spring, 1967.

11. One of the findings of the writer's "Spanish-surname" sample survey of Pomona was that in every case in which a household contained a "Spanish American" adult, that person was married to a "Mexican American." It may be hypothesized on the basis of this admittedly flimsy evidence that in urban Southern California Hispanos are more likely to marry children or grandchildren of Mexican immigrants than they are Hispanos because there are no real barriers between the two groups and the statistical odds are therefore against the endogamy of the smaller group. To what extent this may be true of other areas of the country it would be hazardous to guess.

PART III

THE ORGANIZATIONAL BASE

Mexican American Community Political Organization*

"The Key to Chicano Political Power"

Miguel David Tirado

A COMMON ASSUMPTION of much of the past study of the Mexican American minority has been the belief that this ethnic group is politically apathetic and complacent with respect to participation in community organizations. Such eminent scholars as William D'Antonio and William Form, for example, have concluded that "the Spanish-name community has developed relatively few voluntary organizations. . . ." They argue that this phenomenon is a consequence of the group's low socio economic level and its low levels of internal social integration. This view is also shared by some Mexican Americans concerned with the question of political organization in the Mexican American community. In a letter to the Chairman of the Equal Employment Opportunity Commission, a former Executive Director of the National G. I. Forum, Ed. Idar Jr., argued that "over the centuries, by culture, by history, and even by his own religious convictions, the Mexican American has been 'brainwashed' into a sense of futility, docility, and resignation." "For these reasons, and others," he concludes, "the Mexican American has suffered from lack of leadership."[2]

The intent of this article is first to evaluate these assumptions of Mexican American apathy in the context of community political organization by briefly reviewing the history of Mexican American organizational behavior particularly in the State of California since

Ethnic Tenacity: A Reader in Mexican American Studies; Ralph Guzman: Editor; Palo Alto: *Cummings Publishing Company;* 1970

AZTLAN, 1970, Vol. 1, pp. 53-78.

the beginning of the mass Mexican migration to this country around 1910. Particular attention will next be given to questioning the assumption of D'Antonio, Form, and others that "unlike ethnic groups in northern and eastern cities, the Spanish surname population had not formed clubs which could serve their political interests."[3] A counter hypothesis, in turn, will be offered which suggests that many Mexican American community organizations, although not manifesting the traditional attributes of a politically-oriented body, have served a vital function in advancing the political interests of the Mexican American minority, and may therefore be referred to as community political organizations.

The third objective of this essay is to scrutinize the nature of some of those Mexican American community political organizations which have grown faster and persevered longer than others in order to isolate those ingredients which tend to promote stability and vitality in a Mexican American political organization. It is no secret that Mexican American organizational efforts in the past have been characterized by their general inability to create politically-concerned community organizations which can continue to thrive once the issue of crisis motivating their original formation has passed. Yet, as Saul Alinsky notes in the following quote, the need for permanent politically concerned bodies in the community is crucial if the minority is to permanently improve its political and economic status relative to the dominant groups in society.

> Recruits without organization, however, are meaningless. That's the basic plague of the civil rights struggle. No one can distinguish between a movement and an organization. You have a march and a lot of speeches, then it pisses out—that's a movement. The operation was a success but the patient died. An organization keeps on growing, keeps on making trouble, keeps on chipping away to get what it wants.[4]

Hopefully the ensuing historical analysis of past Mexican American efforts at community organization will offer some clues on how the current growing political ferment in the Mexican American community can be oriented toward fomenting a solid organizational foundation upon which to establish a constant source of political influence.

1900--1940

Some of the earliest organizations formed by the Mexican community in the United States were mutual benefit and protective associations whose functions were similar to those served by the mutual aid societies set up by earlier immigrant groups to this

69

country. By pooling their meager resources the Mexican immigrants learned they could provide each other with low cost funeral and insurance benefits, low interest loans and other forms of economic assistance. As Paul Taylor notes, these same mutual aid societies called "mutualistas" also provided "a forum for discussion and a means of organizing the social life of the community."[5]

It was in this capacity that several of these early Mexican "mutualistas" assumed a degree of political awareness and concern for social action. One of the best examples of this was the *Alianza Hispanoamericana* and the early activities of its "founder lodge" organized toward the end of the last century in Tucson, Arizona. As Manuel Gamio indicates, "its aims were very clearly political" since its objective was to replace the Texans in control of Tucson politics at the time with native Tucson residents of Mexican descent.[6] After succeeding in this endeavor, it subsequently assumed a primarily mutual aid function with some 275 lodges throughout the Southwest.

Another early example of how many of the Mexican "mutualistas" evolving during the first twenty years of this century took a real interest in social action is the Lázaro Cárdenas Society organized by members of the Los Angeles Mexican community soon after World War I. In addition to providing low rate insurance benefits for the community, Richard Thurston notes that "it also held meetings to discuss and take action on community issues such as the lack of school buses and of other facilities."[7] Recognizing that the municipal facilities available to them were inferior to those found elsewhere in the city, these Mexicans also realized that community organization for social action was the only way to have their grievances remedied.

A similar conclusion was reached about the same time by another group of Mexican immigrants in Kansas City. Faced with the threat of expatriation following the War, the Mexican "colonia" organized a *Liga Protectora Mexicana* to protect the right of residence concomitant with their legal immigrant status. The *Liga Protectora* was a grass roots organization in structure serving during the short two years of its existence a series of functions ranging from finding jobs for the unemployed to providing food and clothes for the needy. With the end of the post-war depression which had provoked the threat of expatriation, the organization lost its major reason for existence and dissolved in 1923.[8]

Although, initially there was a concern for social action and politics among many of the early examples of Mexican community organization in this country, their major concern was providing fundamental social and economic benefits for their members while offering a focal point for entertainment and social activity in the Mexican American community. Cognizance of their minor concern for politics should not lead one to underestimate the importance of such mutual aid societies as *La Alianza Hispano Americana, La Sociedad Progresista Mexicana, Comité de Beneficiencia Mexicana,* and the *Sociedad Unión Cultural Mexicana* in the history of the Mexican minority. For, as Paul Taylor points out, "these societies represent the only continuous organized life among the Mexicans in which the initiative comes wholly from the Mexicans themselves. . . ."[9] In addition, due to their size and popularity they offer a potential source of great political strength in the Mexican community.[10]

Orden Hijos de América

Although many of the "mutualistas" in their inceptions participated somewhat in social action and politics, a growing number of Mexican community leaders in the 1920's began to realize that more specialized organizations were needed if the Mexican Americans' interests were to be well defended in American society. One of the first signs of this awakening arose in San Antonio, Texas, where a small group of Mexican American community leaders in 1921 organized the *Orden Hijos de America* (Order Sons of America). Unlike the "mutualistas" which were open to United States citizens and non-citizens alike, the Orden restricted its membership exclusively to "citizens of the United States of Mexican or Spanish extraction, either native or naturalized."[11] This limitation of membership to American citizens indicated a growing realization by Mexican American leaders that political power is essential for the achievement of the minority's aims in this country, and that political power only arises with the organization of a solid voting bloc of citizens. This awakening was evident in the Orden's Declaration of Principles where the founders asserted that members should "use their influence in all fields of social, economic, and political action in order to realize the greatest enjoyment possible of all the rights and privileges and prerogatives extended by the American Constitution."[12]

The Orden's activities, however, were not limited to voter registration but also involved direct political action. One of its earliest acts in the Corpus Christi area, according to Paul Taylor, "was to seek opportunities for qualified Mexican Americans to serve on juries." Previous to this action Spanish-surnamed citizens were automatically dropped from the eligible lists without ever being summoned. As one of the Orden leaders explained, "the first thing we did was to write a request that we be admitted to the jury. I had noticed that in court cases, Mexicans were sent to jail for offenses for which Americans were given suspended sentences or let off."[13]

Due to this political awakening and their successful efforts in remedying the above such inequities, the Orden succeeded by 1928 in establishing seven councils with its most politically active branches located in Corpus Christi and San Antonio. Unfortunately, an organizational split soon developed which was to characterize many subsequent Mexican American political organizations. The division arose over the dissatisfaction of the two more activist councils with the other slower moving elements of the Orden. The result was the secession of the Corpus Christi and San Antonio Councils and their founding of what later was to become the League of United Latin American Citizens.

League of United Latin American Citizens (LULACS)

Established in 1929 as the League of United Latin American Citizens, LULACS was originally intended to incorporate the Orden Hijos de América and other interested Corpus Christi and San Antonio Mexican organizations into a single united body of concerned Mexican American citizens. Because of the reluctance of the Orden Hijos de América to subordinate itself to a younger organization, however, LULACS was forced to establish an entirely new membership composed of "native born or naturalized citizens eighteen years of age or older, of Latin extraction." While framing its first Constitution on the general model of the Orden Hijos de América, LULACS placed much more emphasis on their members' absorption into American society and on their commitment to improving the political and economic position of the Mexican American community.

The first LULACS Constitution makes explicit in its first article that a major aim of the organization is "to develop within the members of our race the best, purest and most perfect type of a true and loyal citizen of the United States of America." The Organization's founders simultaneously committed its members and their families to total assimilation into American society, believing that "in order to claim our rights and fulfill our duties it is necessary for us to assimilate all we can that is best in the new civilization amidst which we shall have to live."[14] Toward this end, the Constitution stipulated that English would be the official language of LULACS and each member must pledge himself "to learn and speak and teach same to our children."

This talk of assimilation was facilitated by the fundamentally middle class nature of the membership, which at that time was the only element of the Mexican community that tended to be American citizens anyway. LULACS decision not to become a grass-roots based organization, however, was a conscious one in the belief that the entire Mexican American community would be better served if LULACS "remained a small concentrated group unified in purpose and better fitted to fight the battles of the less fortunate."[15] This argument was also predicated on the belief that by remaining middle class and elitest LULACS could do more to reduce the stereotype that many Anglo-Americans held of Mexican Americans as "foreigners" and "unpatriotic."

In spite of this elitest approach to the organization's membership, LULACS from its inception displayed a sincere concern for the well-being of the less fortunate Mexican Americans. This concern led the various LULACS Councils to take an interest in political issues affecting the Mexican American commnuity even though its first Constitution expressly stated that "this Organization is not a political club." The succeeding paragraph in Article II of the LULACS Constitution, however, defends the membership's involvement in politics by advocating that "with our vote and influence we shall endeavor to place in public office men who show by their deeds, respect and consideration for our people."

The apparent contradiction in the above two proclamations of the LULACS Constitution is explicable if one takes into consideration the negative connotation which the term "politics" held and to a certain degree still holds for many Mexican Americans. One explanation for the Mexican American's reticence to refer to their organization's activities as political may be the legacy of disillusionment with politics stemming from the Mexican immigrant's political experiences prior to leaving Mexico. The memory of political corruption and instability in Mexico which provoked many to leave their homeland was so deeply ingrained in their psyches that it was only natural these early immigrants carry this abhorrence for politics with them and transmit it on to their offspring. It is no wonder then that one of the early leaders of LULACS, Alonso Perales, defined a political organization in the following terms:

If a political organization is understood to be an association of unscrupulous individuals whose sole intention is to elevate to and maintain in public power some leader for the sole purpose of dividing with him the crumbs or scraps of the spoils of office, then our organization is not political.[16]

Although local LULACS Councils are to be found in 21 states of the Union, the organization's strength lies primarily in Texas, the state of its origin. Here efforts have been made to involve the entire family in LULACS activities by means of Ladies' Auxiliaries along with special programs and benefits for the young. The most celebrated of these LULACS Youth Service Programs was their summer school for Texas preschool children which many view as the precursor of the War on Poverty's Head Start program in the Southwest.

Although intended to be a national Organization, LULACS has been less successful in instituting comprehensive community action programs in other states where Councils have been established. Due in part to a lack of sufficient supportive funds and the competition with other Mexican American organizations, California LULACS, organized since 1947, has been slower than some other groups to implement community action programs. Its lack of tight organizational unity, however, has also served to discourage the rise of dictatorial leadership cults by any individual or group of individuals so characteristic of many other Mexican American organizations. The nature of LULACS, nevertheless, is rapidly changing with its co-sponsorship of Operation Service, the federally funded War on Poverty program in the Southwest. For new demands have been placed on LULACS recently both to coordinate its local councils' activities more effectively and to take a more active role in promoting community action programs. One only hopes that these new pressures for change will not unleash in LULACS the same forces of disunity which were seen in the Orden Hijos de América and in such subsequent organizations as the Mexican Congress.

Mexican Congress

Organized in 1938 as a federation of Mexican American organizations in the Southwestern states, the purpose of the Mexican Congress was to work for "the economic and social and cultural betterment of the Mexican people, to have an understanding between the Anglo-Americans and Mexicans, to promote organizations of working people by aiding trade unions and to fight discrimination actively."[17] While its efforts in the Southern California area were directed primarily at reducing discrimination, it also took an active interest in politics. The Mexican Congress was instrumental in the Los Angeles Mexican community's unsuccessful attempt to get one of their own, Ed Quevedo, elected to the Los Angeles City Council before the war.

Although at its peak of activity, the Mexican Congress boasted a membership of 6,000, its popularity soon waned until its total disappearance during the Second World War. One reason given for its short existence was disagreement over the major functions of the Congress with the older membership criticizing the organization's activities for being too politically radical.[18] The more basic cause for its demise, however, lay in the fundamentally Mexico-oriented perspective retained by much of the Mexican minority in the Southwest up until World War II. As recent immigrants to the United States, many of them expected ultimately to return to Mexico and had little interest in establishing permanent affiliations with groups in this country. John Burma notes, that even many of those who had lived in the United States for twenty years continued to think of themselves as "Mexicans temporarily in the United States."[19]

Some reasons for the persistence of the Mexican community's identification with Mexico and reluctance to establish permanent organizational ties in this country were the geographic proximity of the Mexican "colonias" to the old country and the ease with which the Mexican pattern of life could be preserved in the Southwestern States up until the War. A third reason was the growing atmosphere of hostility in the Southwest against Mexicans fostered by the apprehensions of many Americans about the growing numbers of Mexican immigrants inhabiting the area. This hostility ultimately reached its peak in the 1930's with the repatriation of 500,000 Mexican residents of the Southwest, many of whom were born in the United States and eligible for citizenship.

1940–1970

During the warm days of June, 1943, a sequence of events occurred which exposed the poor condition of community organization and the lack of effective leadership in the Mexican American community of Los Angeles. The events were the Zoot Suit Riots in which Mexican American youth and servicemen clashed in the streets of East Los Angeles climaxing in a full fledged riot and the threat of massive reprisals against the Mexican American minority. In the months following the riots great attention was focused on the problems of the Mexican American minority in an effort to determine and remedy the causes of the disturbances. Organizations both public and private undertook programs to aid the long-neglected Mexican American youth.

When efforts were made to contact the leading spokesmen and community groups of the Mexican American minority, these outside organizations found they had no viable counterparts in the Mexican community. Their surprise was only equalled by the embarrassment of many Mexican Americans who realized the urgent need to organize the "barrio" more effectively for social action and political representation. These men were aware that East Los Angeles was full of small neighborhood groupings and social clubs, but saw with a few exceptions none of them able to offer the political leadership so vital to the Mexican community's improvement.

One of these exceptions was the *Coordinating Council for Latin American Youth,* organized in 1942 for the purpose of directing the attention of public authorities and American society in general to the plight of the Mexican American youth. Representing a multitude of smaller organizations, the Coordinating Council as early as November, 1942, presented to the Los Angeles County Board of Supervisors a petition urging enactment of a list of remedial actions to increase opportunities for Mexican American youth. If this petition had been promptly acted upon by the County officials, it is the opinion of Ruth Tuck that these reforms "might have obviated the events (Zoot Suit Riots) seven months later."[20]

Unity Leagues

In response to the growing need for community organizations particularly suited to achieve political objectives, Mexican Americans of the Pomona Valley (California) founded the first in a series of Unity Leagues. Although aided and encouraged by such educated professionals as Ignacio Lopez (editor, *El Espectador*) and Fred Ross (organizer from the Industrial Areas Foundation), the Unity League's membership primarily consisted of economically lower class Mexican Americans. In this way, it differs sharply from the traditionally middle-class membership of most of the earlier Mexican American political organizations discussed, and served as the model for many subsequent efforts at grass roots political organization in the Mexican American community.

The Unity League's first political success occurred in Chino, California, with the election of the first Mexican American to a city, council seat in years. The campaign organized by the Unity League to get Andrew Morales elected to the city council of Chino is significant for it reveals the degree to which Mexican Americans were learning effective techniques of political organization. Twenty deputy registrars were enlisted from the Mexican community to assure 100 percent Mexican voter turnout with the aid of a block captain system organized throughout the "colonia." A fund raising drive was also inaugurated with even non-citizens contributing to the ultimate collection of $450 in donations.

The result of these efforts was the registration of almost the entire eligible Mexican American community and their near perfect turnout at the polls resulting in the election of Morales by over 100 votes.[21] Crucial to the Unity League's success in Chino was its ability to manipulate into a crisis the issue of no representation on the City Council for the 38 percent of Chino's population who were Mexican American thereby capturing the attention of the entire Mexican community. This same organizing tactic was also employed by Fred Ross in his subsequent efforts to establish Unity Leagues in San Bernardino and Riverside, California. In both cases Fred Ross found a potentially explosive issue upon which to rally the Mexican American community into supporting the efforts of the Unity League to eliminate school discrimination.

Community Service Organization (CSO)

The end of the War saw the return of a very different Mexican American than had left for War four years previous. Having risked his life for the United States, the returning Mexican American G.I. came back with a desire to participate actively in American society. These American-oriented war veterans were to transform the traditionally Mexico-oriented mentality of much of the Mexican American community into a growing identification with American society and the Mexican Americans' contribution to it. Upon their return from overseas, many Mexican American veterans were also quick to notice the inferior position their minority occupied in relation to the rest of American society. Their desires to improve the conditions of life in the "barrio," however, at first were thwarted by the lack of opportunities for Mexican Americans to assume leadership in the existing assistance programs, since most of the responsible positions in these organizations were already occupied by Anglo-Americans. Cognizance of this fact led a number of these dedicated young Mexican Americans to consider forming their own community organizations.

77

One of the first of these organizations to be established in California was the *Community Service Organization*. Founded in Los Angeles during September, 1947, by a small group of Mexican American veterans and factory workers, the CSO began attacking a series of problems plaguing the East Los Angeles area from educational reform in the local schools to cases of police mistreatment of Mexican American youth. Starting with a membership of only fifteen, the group's activities soon attracted a grass roots membership of over 250 meeting in open forum in a local elementary school to discuss the issues of concern to the Mexican American community.

As the CSO wrestled with an unresponsive municipal government, the membership soon became aware of the need for Mexican American political representation in City Hall. After the failure to elect a Mexican American by the name of Edward Roybal to the Los Angeles City Council, the leadership of CSO resolved to undertake a massive voter registration drive in the Mexican American community in order to assure Roybal's victory in the next election. Assisted by Fred Ross, who brought with him the experience of the early Unity Leagues, the CSO swore sixty-three of its members in as Deputy Registrars and succeeded in registering 12,000 Mexican American citizens by the end of the year. The struggle to get the first Mexican American elected to the City Council since 1881 had just begun. Using the technique of "House Meetings" in which neighbors invited other neighbors into their homes to listen to a representative of CSO, the organization was able to bring the voter registration in East Los Angeles up to 40,000 and expand its own membership to 3,000 strong.[22] The result of these efforts was the election in 1949 of the first Mexican American to the Los Angeles City Council in 68 years. In addition, a heightened sense of their own political potential was injected into the Mexican American community which was to serve as the basis for the future political mobilization of Spanish-speaking citizens.

In spite of these successes, the CSO soon forsook overt participation in the political arena for a growing concern with providing the Mexican American minority community services of a mutual aid type. This is not to say that the CSO did not continue to work for increased Mexican American voter registration or push for legislation beneficial to the Spanish-speaking community. This change in approach, however, did mean that the CSO would never again publicly support a candidate for political office even though unofficial fund raising functions continued to be held for those candidates responsive to the problems of the Mexican American minority.

The adoption of a mutual aid approach to community organization represented the CSO leadership's response to the question of how does the organization solidify its membership in order to pursue a program of long-term pressure on public authorities to improve the conditions of the Mexican American community? Their motives for reviving this traditional philosophy of mutual aid, so characteristic of the earliest efforts at Mexican American community organization, were best expressed in the following passage from the CSO's Twentieth Anniversary Commemorative publication:

> During the first seventeen-year period CSO, like many crusading groups, was subjected to strong opposition and this was compounded with an unsolidified membership. The L.A. CSO leadership, realizing that these factors could be the seed of its own destruction adopted in 1964 the mutual aid philosophy as the best insurance to solidify its membership and to develop into a strong contending pressure group.[23]

The Los Angeles CSO in recent years has developed a number of mutual benefit programs ranging from the traditional death benefit insurance and credit union to the more innovative Buyers' Club and Consumer Complaint Center. As for the other approximately thirty CSO chapters throughout the State of California, little progress toward coordinating the organization's efforts on a statewide basis has been made due to what Joan Moore calls "the extreme localism of Mexican American leadership and action."[24] The one major exception to the above observation is the CSO's eight year crusade to have the State Legislature pass a bill granting old age pensions to non-citizens. Although their efforts were successful with the bill's passage in 1962, criticism has been directed toward the CSO for its single-minded concern in the political sphere with the problems of the elderly at the expense of other equally crucial problems. The Los Angeles CSO of late has responded to this pressure for a multi-issue orientation with an attack on zoning regulations in East Los Angeles and its advocacy of subdividing City Government into Neighborhood Community Councils for greater citizen participation in government.

American G.I. Forum

The same year that the Community Service Organization was being organized, an increasing number of returning Mexican

American veterans in Texas and elsewhere were experiencing discrimination in education, employment, medical attention, and housing. In a manner typical of many Mexican American community political organizations, the American G.I. Forum grew out of one specific incident of discrimination against a war veteran who was refused burial by a funeral home in Three Rivers, Texas. Angered by this and other earlier acts of prejudice against Mexican American G.I.'s, a respected Mexican American physician, Dr. Hector Garcia, and a group of other concerned Mexican American veterans from Corpus Christi, Texas, decided to organize themselves into a veterans organization dedicated to combating such acts of discrimination and improving the status of Mexican Americans in Texas. Calling themselves the American G.I. Forum, they succeeded their first year not only in having the Mexican American G.I. in question buried in Arlington Cemetery with the assistance of then Congressman Lyndon Johnson, but also eliminated discriminatory practices in the Corpus Christi Veterans Hospital. Urged on by their initial achievements in reducing discrimination the G.I. Forum succeeded in establishing over 100 Forums in Texas by the end of 1949. Today the G.I. Forum is organized in 23 states with a membership of over 20,000.

Although officially non-partisan, the organization's members are encouraged to participate actively in politics. Recognizing the dearth of Mexican American representation in government, the G.I. Forum urges its members to run for political office, and actively recommends Mexican Americans for appointive positions in government. Typical of the G.I. Forum's activist role in promoting Mexican Americans for public office was the organization's chastizing of Kansas Governor William Avery for failing to reappoint a Mexican American to the State's Civil Rights Commission at their 1965 Convention in Kansas City.

The G.I. Forum's period of greatest success in promoting political reform and social action benefiting the Mexican American community was during the 1950's, at a time when other groups timidly shrank from adopting an activist posture for fear of being called Communist. This unique role of the G.I. Forum during the 1950's was made possible by its leaders' skillful manipulation of patriotic symbols and their veteran status to combat accusations that the organization was advocating leftist programs. Although the organization is now criticized by some for being too status quo oriented, the G.I. Forum's effective use of American symbols to cloak such political action as their opposition to the importation of agricultural laborers from Mexico assured the existence of at least one organization committed to protecting the rights of Mexican American citizens during those tense years.

The G.I. Forum has also been active in providing community services to the Mexican American minority. Some examples of its benefit programs are its "back to school" drives, scholarship programs, and more recently low-cost housing through their co-sponsorship of Operation Ser. Of special interest is the G.I. Forum's deliberate attempt to involve the entire family in its activities. Recognizing that members' competing obligations to both the organization and their families has spelled the downfall of many Mexican American organizations, the Forum established both a Ladies' Auxiliary and Junior G.I. Forums for the youth. In addition, the local chapters of the Forum have attempted to meet the social needs of their members' families by sponsoring dances, picnics, and annual Queen contests. By attempting to fulfill a series of varied functions for its members, the G.I. Forum has succeeded in solidifying its membership and remaining a "strong contending pressure group" for Mexican American rights.

Mexican American Political Association (MAPA)

Although all of the Mexican American community organizations discussed at one time or another have taken an active interest in politics, most have hesitated to openly admit the political nature of many of their activities for some of the reasons discussed earlier. One of the first organizations in the Mexican American community, however, to formally declare its primary function as political is the *Mexican American Political Association.* Organized on a statewide basis throughout California in 1958, MAPA grew out of the realization by many concerned Mexican American leaders that their community no longer could depend upon the Democratic Party structure to champion the political cause of the Mexican American in California. Shocked by the defeat of Edward Roybal for Lieutenant Governor in 1954 and Henry Lopez for Secretary of State in 1958 during a year of otherwise Democratic landslide, these leaders came to recognize the need for an organization solely dedicated to advancing the political interests of the Mexican American in California.

Constitutionally committed to a bi-partisan stance, MAPA is concerned primarily with electing Mexican Americans to public office and supporting candidates for both parties who are dedicated to bettering the status of the Mexican American minority.

Due in part to MAPA's efforts to increase Mexican American political representation in California, two state assemblymen, one Congressman, three Superior Court Judges and three Municipal Court Judges of Mexican American descent were subsequently elected. In the political arena, MAPA has also pressed for legislation beneficial to the Mexican American and has undertaken voter registration drives and programs of political education such as "floating seminars" throughout the state.

In the sphere of social action, individual MAPA chapters have also taken the initiative in promoting the interests of the Mexican American community. Numerous examples exist of MAPA chapters coming to the defense of Mexican Americans over all sorts of issues ranging from police malpractices to school discrimination. A case in point was the Compton, California Chapter's successful efforts to improve the educational conditions at a local public school where 90 percent of the students are Mexican American.[25] In its efforts to meet the various needs of the minority, MAPA also encourages family involvement in many of its activities. This is stimulated through a system of dual membership for wives of members at no extra cost, and by the organization's recruitment of women for positions of responsibility in MAPA.

The efforts of MAPA to promote political organization and social action among the economically lower class Mexican Americans have been hindered in the past by the predominantly middle class membership of the organization. As Ralph Guzman noted, this class consciousness among the Mexican American community has prevented many of the organizational achievements of the Mexican American middle class from serving to increase community participation among lower class Mexican Americans.[26] One reason for this has been up until recently the Mexico-oriented perspective of the poorer Mexican American compared with the assimilative orientation of the middle class Mexican American. Each group, in turn, has been aroused by differing symbols with middle class organizations such as LULACS emphasizing American symbols of patriotism while such "grass roots" organizations as the early "mutualistas" employed Mexican names and emblems to satisfy the greater ethnic consciousness of the Mexican American poor.

Recognizing the need to bridge this gap between their middle class members and the poorer Mexican American if MAPA is to achieve its stated objectives, the organization's leadership recently has attempted to increase lower class participation in MAPA by intensifying the organization's ethnic identification and by facilitating the poor's access to MAPA functions. The former tactic involves the implementation of ethnically-charged symbols in public statements and closer collaboration with such highly ethnic-conscious young Mexican American groups as the United Mexican American Students (UMAS). The lower class Mexican American's access to MAPA functions has been facilitated by recent attempts to locate MAPA Conventions and other events in close proximity to poorer Mexican neighborhoods. As explained by the current President of MAPA, "this . . . was done in order that we might attract more of our barrio poor who in the past have been excluded from our conventions." He goes on to say that "we must eliminate this is in our organization if we ever hope to gain the respect and understanding from those who do not participate due to their economic status."[27]

A second difficulty plaguing previous Mexican American organizations which MAPA's founders strove to avoid was the danger of dictatorial leaders ("Liderismo") assuming control of the organization and perpetuating their rule by encouraging a personality cult of loyal followers ("cultismo"). Recognizing the Mexican Americans' susceptibility to personalistic leadership in which the individual's loyalty is first to his chosen leader and second to the organization, the framers of MAPA's Bylaws sought to decentralize the organization's structure enough to assure the autonomy of each chapter within its respective Assembly District. As the major author of the Bylaws explains, "the State Executive Board (of MAPA) is provided with no powers to initiate or make local endorsements, which field is reserved to the locally chartered assembly, congressional and county district organizations."[28]

The fact that the State Executive Board of MAPA does insist that all state-wide political endorsements for such offices as Governor be reserved to the annual state-wide MAPA Conventions in which all chapters are represented does not obliterate the fact expressed by Manuel Ruiz that "the basic elements in MAPA are the practical realities of local political autonomy."[29] The original MAPA leadership recognized that only by conscientiously respecting the autonomy of its local chapters could they assure organizational vitality and the participation of all its members. Under no circumstances was the decentralization of its structure intended to discourage strong leadership in MAPA. Rather they hoped through local autonomy to assure the blessings of dynamic leadership without the curse of either "liderismo" or "cultismo."

Efforts to Coordinate Mexican American Organizations

After discussing the benefits of a decentralized organizational structure, the question now arises whether efforts to unite all Mexican American community organizations under one permanent coordinating body have been successful. One attempt to establish such a united front in California dates back to 1953 when the *Council of Mexican American Affairs* was founded in Los Angeles. As a "non-partisan, non-sectarian, and non-profit citizens organization dedicated to the development of leadership among Americans of Mexican descent and to coordinating the efforts of all the various organizations and groups concerned with the betterment of the Mexican American in the Los Angeles region," CMAA began with 44 member organizations.[30]

With the above goal of coordinating all other existing Mexican American organizations in mind, CMAA maintained an office and full-time executive director who organized conferences on issues of concern to the community and provided member organizations with assistance in the form of information and new channels of communication. Unfortunately, CMAA's laudatory efforts to unite the multitude of organizations in the Mexican American community met with failure due to the member organizations' refusal to pay their dues and their lack of sufficient financial resources to accomplish such a task.

After a period of dormancy, the CMAA in 1963 was revitalized under new leadership and with a completely new approach to serving the Mexican American community. Instead of attempting to coordinate the grass-roots organizations in the community for a more unified Mexican American voice in civic affairs, CMAA has accepted the role of a small elitest organization of successful Mexican American professional and businessmen functioning as a high-level pressure group for the Mexican American minority. By organizing political banquets and community forums in which public officials are invited to address the Mexican American community, the CMAA serves to support Mexican Americans in public office and pressure other public officials to take a greater concern for the minority.

The failure of CMAA to coordinate the various organizations in the Mexican American community during its earlier years is due in part to the significance of class homogeneity for the success of a Mexican American community organization. As mentioned earlier, organizations with a middle class membership seldom hold much attraction for lower class Mexican Americans. Since most of the efforts to unite community organizations stem from the middle class segments of the Mexican American minority, it naturally follows that these attempts would hold little interest for the poorer members of grass-roots Mexican American organizations. Dr. Ernesto Galarza refers to this problem in discussing the possibility of organizing the minority into a national organization:

> The higher one goes toward national organization the greater the preference of Mexican Americans to express themselves in English and to use symbols that mean something only to English-speaking people. Reverse the direction and one finds the more intense symbolism and greater use of Spanish at the grass-roots. This weakens both the organizational strength and the emotional strands upon which organization depends.[31]

A more recent attempt to organize the Mexican American minority into a unified national body was undertaken by the *Political Association of Spanish Speaking Organizations* (PASSO). Founded in the early 1960's in Texas as an outgrowth of the Viva Kennedy Movement, PASSO was dedicated to organizing the Mexican Americans of the Southwest into a united national political organization capable of exerting political pressure at all levels of government. After experiencing great success in organizing chapters among the Mexican Americans of Texas, PASSO's leadership then attempted to organize chapters in Arizona as part of the larger goal of a national organization. The Arizona Mexican American community, however, was unresponsive to the overtures of PASSO preferring what Juan Martinez describes as "an organization more suited to the needs of the Arizona Spanish-speaking." In response to this demand for an Arizona-based organization, the *American Coordinating Council on Political Education* (ACCPE) was established with a paid membership of 2500 Mexican Americans and chapters in ten of Arizona's fourteen counties.[32]

The failure of PASSO to expand successfully into Arizona reflects a second major obstacle confronting efforts to coordinate the organizational activities of Mexican Americans. This is the intense "localism" or emotional identification with a local region so prevalent among Mexican Americans throughout the Southwest. This localism, however, is not simply emotional but also reflects marked differences in the political attitudes of Mexican Americans living in different areas of the Southwest. As Joan Moore notes, "tactics defined as rather cautious in one setting may be viewed as 'trouble making' in another, with the attendant withdrawal of support by other Mexican Americans in either situation." She goes on to say that "these 'local' variations may occur even within the same metropolitan area."[33]

One recent organizing effort which is displaying an awareness of these above obstacles in its attempts to coordinate the activities of Mexican American organizations is the *Southwest Council of La Raza*. Established in 1968 as a non-profit corporation of Mexican Americans, dedicated to "assisting local Mexican American community efforts to organize themselves more effectively," the Council respects the autonomy and integrity of the local community organizations it is working to assist. As its First Annual Report reiterates, "it is not a mass-membership organization nor was it created for the purpose of giving any one organization a 'base.'" Rather all of the Council's efforts "are aimed at the development of the barrio through the organization and encouragement of local cooperative community groups in the barrio," with its own activities "being supportive in the broadest sense."[34]

In order to avoid the divisions arising from middle class control over grass-roots operations and intense "localist" sensitivities, the Southwest Council has encouraged the formation of "action-oriented local councils," composed of representatives from the "barrio." It is the function of these local councils to advise and assist the Southwest Council in its efforts to appreciate and meet the needs of community organizations. Unlike the earlier efforts of the Council of Mexican American Affairs, the Southwest Council has not had to depend upon its participant members for financial support due to a $630,000 grant from the Ford Foundation. The future success of the Southwest Council as a self-sufficient body will, therefore, depend upon its leadership's willingness to reject what Ernesto Galarza calls "ready-made patterns" of national organization for methods more suited to the personality of the Mexican American community.[35]

Historical Lessons

One of the results of the preceding historical analysis is a refutation of the assumption that the Mexican American minority has been politically apathetic and slow to develop community action organizations. Rather, the above historical study leads to the conclusion that major elements of the Mexican American community have consistently expressed an interest in politics and have organized themselves over the years into community action groups for the purpose of improving the minority's relative status in American society. The Mexican American minority, however, has expressed this concern for politics and desire for social action in a very different way than other segments of American society. As Arthur Rubel observes, "Chicanos seem no less interested in political issues than do Anglos."[36] By overlooking this fact, many observers erroneously have concluded that the Mexican American was politically unconcerned since they were unable to detect in the Mexican American community any political organizations comparable to the ones used in the Anglo American community for political expression.

Unlike the Anglo American, the Mexican American traditionally has not developed highly specialized organizations for the sole purpose of political action. Rather he has preferred to establish undifferentiated multi-purpose organizations which will serve not only his political needs but also his economic, social, and cultural ones as well. Considering the previously discussed Mexican reticence to describe one's activities as "political" due to the negative connotations the term holds for the Mexican American community, it has also been customary for such all-purpose organizations to avoid using the term "political" either in their title or statement of purpose. The fact that these Mexican American community organizations do not refer to themselves or their activities as political in nature does not in any way, however, negate their willingness to undertake political action in the form of pressure on public officials or support of legislation when the need arises. Julian Samora and Richard Lamanna confirm this in the following quote from their study of Mexican Americans in East Chicago, Indiana:

> With the exception of the associations ancillary to the religious institutions and the strictly recreational groups . . . all associations have a *political overtone,* and urgent need for unity, a sense of contributing to the adjustment of its members to the community, a feeling that through the effort of the association the community is made aware of the presence and the needs of the Mexican American.[37]

In addition to exposing the unfamiliarity of many non-Mexican American observers with the actual nature of organizations in our community, the previous historical analysis has also revealed the Mexican American's ignorance about the nature of his own organizations and what makes them prosper. For the one major indictment to be thrown at Mexican American efforts at political organization on the "grass-roots" community level is their generally short-lived nature. Originally organized in response to a crisis or specific case of discrimination, these community action groups often fade away as the crisis passes, leaving the community just as unprepared when the next crisis develops. Some formula to assure the continued vitality of Mexican American community political organizations, therefore, is needed if the Mexican American community is to develop and maintain what was referred to earlier as "strong contending pressure groups" in the struggle for social, political, and economic quality.

From our analysis of those Mexican American organizations which have endured longest while maintaining much of their original vitality, five clues emerge to how a Mexican American community political organization can best retain both its membership and vigor for years of political combat and social action.

1. Multi-Functional

As mentioned above, most Mexican American community political organizations in the past have been characterized by their willingness to serve many different functions for their membership. Most successful Mexican American political organizations, for example, also seem to offer mutual aid benefits of some sort to help their members in time of financial need. They attempt to meet the social needs of their community by sponsoring dances, picnics, banquets, etc. Mexican American political organizations that ignored these various other needs of their members have often found it difficult to retain the interest and support of their membership after a political issue or crisis has ceased to be current.

In their multi-purpose orientation these Mexican American community organizations resemble the political organizations of the early European immigrants to this country who, experiencing the same poverty as the Mexican American today, were forced to rely on their own organizations for services they otherwise could not afford. In this sense, the multi-functional attribute of successful Mexican American political organizations may be more characteristic of any organization of poor people rather than a uniquely Mexican phenomenon.

2. Family Involvement

Related to the quality of multi-functionalism is the second attribute of those Mexican American community political organizations demonstrating greater longevity and vitality. This is their provision for the involvement of members' families in the activities of the organization, either through the establishment of women's and young persons' auxiliaries or through regular group social activities in which the members' families can participate. In the case of MAPA, dual membership for both husband and wife was found to be an effective technique for incorporating the family in MAPA's activities. No matter how achieved there is little doubt that family involvement is crucial to the success of a Mexican American organization. Emanating from a culture that places great emphasis on loyalty to family, a Mexican American political organization member will experience a conflict in his obligations to family and to the organization he belongs to with the former usually winning out unless provision is made by the latter to reduce this tension. The best way to reconcile these demands on the individual member is to encourage the family's equal identification with the organization.

3. Single Issue Area Crisis Approach

Most voluntary political organizations in the Mexican American community develop initially around a crisis issue or series of related issues of crucial importance to the community. As the crisis passes or the issue fades in importance, the organization is confronted with a decline in membership and support unless its leadership has learned to either provoke or capitalize upon another series of crises. As the previous study of successful Mexican American political organizations reveals, the crisis orientation and its perpetuation is essential until the "grass roots" membership has developed enough political sophistication to actively support the organization even during periods of relative calm.

One of the dangers in this "crisis issue" approach, however, is the strain that it places upon the organization's limited resources of manpower and money. For as the organization's reputation for success grows, so also does the community's demand for it to undertake newer and larger tasks. One possible solution to this dilemma may be an attempt to limit the organization's scope of responsibility to a specific "issue area" such as discrimination in education or housing where the organization's limited resources can effectively cope with the crises that develop. The success of such a "single issue area approach" depends, however, upon the degree to which other "single issue" oriented community organizations emerge to attack the other areas of concern to the community. If these other bodies do not appear, the organization will be forced by community pressure to undertake tasks unrelated to its original scope of responsibility thereby running the risk of overextending its resources and failing. To avoid this, many of the successful Mexican American political organizations discussed have satisfied the pressure upon them to expand their activities by taking on one issue area at a time in a sequential manner, thereby concentrating enough of its resources on each crisis to assure success.

4. Personalistic Consensual Leadership/Decentralized Structure

The most often observed characteristic of Mexican American political behavior is its emphasis on personalism or the need to personally identify with a candidate or leader. Whereas many will support a candidate primarily based on their intellectual agreement with his beliefs, the Mexican American voter has been observed to support more often that candidate whose personality he can identify with and relate to. As Arthur Rubel notes, "unlike Anglo Americans, Chicanos vote for persons with whom they can establish relationships amenable to personalistic instrumental activities."[38]

This subjective criteria for political leadership also arises in the Mexican American's selection of a community organization leader. The success of a Mexican American political organization, therefore, depends upon leadership by a man who not only can capture the devotion of the membership but also will respect the personalities and opinions of the other members. In short, the type of leader best suited for promoting organizational longevity and vitality is one with a magnetic personality who recognizes the need for developing a consensus of opinion among the membership before acting.

Unfortunately, this combination of personal magnetism and respect for the sensibilities of other members is difficult to find in a leader and attempts to promote it frequently have led to dictatorial leadership and a reign of cultism. Recognizing these dangers of strong personalistic leadership, several successful Mexican American organizations already discussed have discovered a safeguard against dictatorial leadership and greater assurance of a consensual decision making approach in the form of a decentralized administrative structure. By distributing leadership responsibilities among several elected officers, or among its local chapters in the case of a larger body, an organization can protect against its domination by an autocratic leader. The tactic of decentralizing power in the organization also encourages the development of experienced younger leadership for the future.

5. Ethnic Symbolism

In our discussion of the effect of class differences on the nature of Mexican American political organizations, it was observed that differing symbols were used to attract various segments of the

Mexican American community to membership in organizations. The G.I. Forum, and LULACS, for example, effectively used the symbols of American patriotism to attract assimilative conscious middle class Mexican Americans to their ranks. In turn, one sees such newer organizations as the *Crusade for Justice* in Colorado and the *National Farm Workers Association* in California employing ethnically charged symbols such as "La Raza" to induce poor Mexican Americans to join them. The above success of "Corky" Gonzalez and Cesar Chavez in attracting supporters through the effective use of ethnic symbolism leaves little doubt that any attempt to organize successfully the Mexican American community especially at the grass roots level must involve a strong appeal to ethnic loyalty.

In conclusion, the above five ingredients for Mexican American organizational success should not be construed to be either exclusive or inclusive. Rather they should simply be viewed as some clues to why certain Mexican American political organizations in the past have prospered and why some may have failed to endure. The five hypotheses may also serve as a useful formula in evaluating the potential effectiveness and longevity of recently established Mexican American organizations. For until those currently involved in the political organization of the Mexican American community begin to study the earlier organizing efforts of equally dedicated Mexican American leaders, they are destined to perpetuate many of the same conditions which have inhibited the effective political organization of the Mexican American minority in the past.

Notes

1. William V. D'Antonio and William H. Form, *Influentials in Two Border Cities, A Study in Community Decision-Making,* 1965, p. 30.
2. Letter from Ed. Idar, Jr. to Franklin Roosevelt, Jr., published in Albert Pena, Jr., "Needed: A Marshall Plan for Mexican Americans" The Texas Observer, April 15, 1966, p. 1.
3. D'Antonio and Form, *op. cit.,* p. 246. See also Alphonso Pinckney, "Prejudice Toward Mexican and Negro Americans," *Phylon,* Winter 1963, no. 24, p. 358.
4. John Gregory Dunne, *Delano, The Story of the California Grape Strike,* 1967, p. 55.
5. Paul Taylor, *Mexican Labor in the United States,* 1928; p. 45.
6. Manuel Gamio, *Mexican Immigration to the United States,* 1930, p. 133.
7. Richard Thurston, *Urbanization and Socio-Economic Change in a Mexican American Enclave,* Ph.D. Thesis, UCLA, pp. 36–37.
8. Paul Ming Chang-lin, *Voluntary Kinship—Voluntary Association in a Mexican-American Community,* Master's Thesis, University of Kansas, pp. 93–94.
9. Paul Taylor, *op. cit.*
10. The Sociedad Progresista Mexicana organized in 1929 has 18,000 members and 65 lodges throughout the State of California alone.
11. Article III, Constitucion y Leyes de la Orden Hijos de América in O. Douglas Weeks, "Lulacs" in *Southwestern Political and Social Science Quarterly,* December 1929, pp. 260–261.
12. Section I, Declaration of Principles, *ibid.*
13. Paul Taylor, *An American Mexican Frontier, Nueces, County, Texas,* 1934, p. 247.
14. Quote of J. Luz Saenz, LULACS Founder, from *El Paladin,* Corpus Christi, Texas, May 17, 1929, in O. D. Weeks, *op. cit.,* p. 274.
15. O. D. Weeks, *ibid.,* p. 272.
16. O. D. Weeks, *ibid.,* p. 275.
17. John Burma, *Spanish Speaking Groups in the United States,* 1954, p. 103.
18. *Ibid.*
19. *Ibid.,* p. 104.
20. Ruth D. Tuck, "Behind the Zoot Suit Riots," *Survey Graphic,* August, 1943, p. 316.
21. Interview with Ignacio Lopez (editor of *El Espectador* and founder of the Unity Leagues), April 28, 1969, Los Angeles, California.
22. Fred Ross, *Get Out If You Can, the Saga of Sal Si Puedes,* California Federation for Civic Unity, 1953, pp. 12–13.
23. Community Service Organization, *20th Anniversary Commemorative Publication,* March 25, 1967, p. 18.
24. Joan Moore, *Mexican American Problems and Prospects Special Report,* University of Wisconsin, 1966, p. 54.
25. "MAPA and the Community," *The Voice* (Official MAPA publication), December 31, 1965, Vol. 1, No. 3, p. 3.
26. Lecture by Ralph Guzman, Fall Quarter 1968, California State College, Los Angeles.
27. Abe Tapia, Welcoming Address to the Ninth Annual Convention of MAPA, Pico Rivera, California, June 29, 1968.
28. Letter of Mr. Manuel Ruiz to former MAPA President Edward Quevedo, December 18, 1963.

29. Letter of Mr. Ruiz to Mr. Bert Corona (a former President of MAPA), June 13, 1967.

30. Paul M. Sheldon, "Community Participation and the Emerging Middle Class," in Julian Samora, *La Raza, Forgotten Americans*, p. 39.

31. Ernesto Galarza, "Program for Action; The Mexican American, a National Concern," *Common Ground*, Summer 1949, published as a pamphlet by the Common Council for American Unity, p. 37.

32. Juan Martinez, "Leadership and Politics," in Julian Samora, *La Raza, Forgotten Americans*, 1966, p. 54.

33. Joan Moore, *op. cit.*, p. 55.

34. Southwest Council of La Raza, *First Annual Report*, February 1968 to February 1969, pp. 2–3.

UNDECIDED LEADERSHIP AND TRADITION COMBINE TO KEEP LA RAZA IN DEMOCRATIC PARTY

By Delfino Varela

The election campaign just past was of great interest to La Raza because it marked the first time since 1948 that any section of the community made a serious attempt to break with the long tradition of an overwhelming allegiance to the Democratic Party. This overwhelming allegiance, especially in the heavily populated urban areas, has caused the Mexican-American vote throughout the United States to have little political leverage. The Democrats justifiably took it for granted as theirs, and the Republicans made only hopeless gestures at capturing it from the Democrats.

For the past two years, however, there has been a growing determination on the part of the Chicano activists throughout California and the Southwest to chart an independent political road for the community by either voting Republican when necessary, or preferably by organizing a voter bloc outside both political parties. This political ethnic bloc, if it could be organized, would certainly provide an attraction center for both major parties and both would adopt its issues in order to vie for its votes, since in many elections the difference between victory and defeat for the major parties is between a fraction of a percent and five percent. This would mean that a well-organized voter bloc could be pivotal.

As a result of the growing awareness of the very bad political situation of the community because of its overwhelming tie to the Democratic Party, and given the dreary alternative offered by the Republican Party, La Raza Unida Party was organized in Colorado and Texas. In Texas a number of local races were won where the Mexican vote is compact, cohesive, and a large majority of the total. For this campaign, however, La Raza Unida was prevented from getting on the ballot in three heavy Mexican-American counties in Texas — Dimmit, Lasalle, and Zavala — and where they did get on the ballot in Hidalgo county, the legal fight was prolonged and prevented a strong buildup.

REGENERACION, 1970, Vol. 1, No. 8, p. 3.

In Colorado, the Chicano candidate for governor in La Raza Unida Party, Albert L. Gurule, got 12,296 or 1.7 percent of the 665,000 total votes cast. Coloado is tough about allowing third parties to stay on the ballot, and La Raza Unida would have had to receive ten percent of the total to have kept its ballot status.

MAPA in California

In California, where the Mexican-American population is the largest in the United States, the Mexican American Political Association decided on a statewide basis to stay with the Democratic Party in some of the state constitutional races, but to go for the Peace and Freedom Party's Chicano candidate for Governor, Ricardo Romo, as a beginning towards the formation of an independent voter bloc.

Since MAPA does have a large number of local chapters throughout the state, it was expected that the Peace and Freedom Party candidacy of Ricardo Romo, who described himself as the Cesar Chavez of the political field, would poll large votes especially in the urban barrios around Los Angeles and in some of the strongly organized towns throughout the state. The Romo vote was a disappointing one percent however, and the Peace and Freedom candidate for Attorney General, Marge Buckley, got three times the Romo vote. This means, of course, that not only was Romo not supported by the California Chicano voter, but that he was even passed up by the supposedly progressive Peace and Freedom voters in many cases.

Not All Bleak

While no tangible gains were registered in the independent efforts, it cannot be said, of course, that the entire results were bad. Congressman Edward Roybal from California, Senator Joseph Montoya, Congressman Manuel Lujan from New Mexico were retained in the Democratic Party, as were Congressman Henry Gonzalez and Congressman Eligio de la Garza from Texas.

One more Chicano Assemblyman in California, Peter Chacon, won in the San Diego area, raising the total in the California legislature to two. These two will have their hands full, however, in the new Democratic nominated assembly to get any kind of deal   for the community in the coming reapportionment, since the Democrats naturally tend to spread our heavy Democratic vote into as many adjoining areas as possible to increase the total number of Democratic districts.

While all of the voting trends throughout the West Coast and Southwest indicate a continuing heavy loyalty to the Democratic Party, the election does mark a first effort towards independent political action. That it did not realize its full potential is probably due as much to inexperience and lack of funds as it was to the basic newness of the approach for political activists so long trained in the Democratic tradition and uncertain as to how definite and irrevocable a break to make.

The answer as to the future course of the move away from the Democrats probably depends to an extent on the Democrats themselves. If they regard the results as confirmation of their feelings that nothing can drive the Mexican vote away from the fold, the consequent disregard will lead inevitably to continued defection on the part of the young voter, and sooner or later to significant defections of the community as a whole. If the trend of more and more accommodation to the Conservative Middle that was nationally evident in the last campaign by Democrats at all levels remains a trend within the party structure, then the defections will not only be inevitable, but more and more necessary.

The Mexican-American and the Church

César E. Chávez

The following article was prepared by Mr. Chavez during his 25-day "spiritual fast" and was presented to a meeting on "Mexican-Americans and the Church" at the Second Annual Mexican-American Conference in Sacramento, California on March 8-10, 1968.

The place to begin is with our own experience with the Church in the strike which has gone on for thirty-one months in Delano. For in Delano the Church has been involved with the poor in a unique way which should stand as a symbol to other communities. Of course, when we refer to the Church we should define the word a little. We mean the whole Church, the Church as an ecumenical body spread around the world, and not just its particular form in a parish in a local community. The Church we are talking about is a tremendously powerful institution in our society, and in the world. That Church is one form of the Presence of God on Earth, and so naturally it is powerful. It is powerful by definition. It is a powerful moral and spiritual force which cannot be ignored by any movement. Furthermore, it is an organization with tremendous wealth. Since the Church is to be servant to the poor, it is *our* fault if that wealth is not channeled to help the poor in our world.

In a small way we have been able, in the Delano strike, to work together with the Church in such a way as to bring some of its moral and economic power to bear on those who want to maintain the status quo, keeping farm workers in virtual enslavement. In brief, here is what happened in Delano.

Some years ago, when some of us were working with the Community Service Organization, we began to realize the powerful effect which the Church can have on the conscience of the opposition. In scattered instances, in San Jose, Sacramento, Oakland, Los Angeles and other places, priests would speak out loudly and clearly against specific instances of oppression, and in some cases, stand with the people who were being hurt. Furthermore, a small group of priests, Frs. McDonald, McCollough, Duggan and others, began

EL GRITO, Summer 1968, pp. 9-12.

to pinpoint attention on the terrible situation of the farm workers in our state.

At about that same time, we began to run into the California Migrant Ministry in the camps and fields. They were about the only ones there, and a lot of us were very suspicious, since we were Catholics and they were Protestants. However, they had developed a very clear conception of the Church. It was called to serve, to be at the mercy of the poor, and not to try to use them. After a while this made a lot of sense to us, and we began to find ourselves working side by side with them. In fact, it forced us to raise the question why OUR Church was not doing the same. We would ask, "Why do the Protestants come out here and help the people, demand nothing, and give all their time to serving farm workers, while our own parish priests stay in their churches, where only a few people come, and usually feel uncomfortable?"

It was not until some of us moved to Delano and began working to build the National Farm Workers Association that we really saw how far removed from the people the parish Church was. In fact, we could not get any help at all from the priests of Delano. When the strike began, they told us we could not even use the Church's auditorium for the meetings. The farm workers' money helped build that auditorium! But the Protestants were there again, in the form of the California Migrant Ministry, and they began to help in little ways, here and there.

When the strike started in 1965, most of our "friends" forsook us for a while. They ran — or were just too busy to help. But the California Migrant Ministry held a meeting with its staff and decided that the strike was a matter of life or death for farm workers everywhere, and that even if it meant the end of the Migrant Ministry they would turn over their resources to the strikers. The political pressure on the Protestant Churches was tremendous and the Migrant Ministry lost a lot of money. But they stuck it out, and they began to point the way to the rest of the Church. In fact, when 30 of the strikers were arrested for shouting Huelga, 11 ministers went to jail with them. They were in Delano that day at the request of Chris Hartmire, director of the California Migrant Ministry.

Then the workers began to raise the question: "Why ministers? Why not priests? What does the Bishop say?" But the Bishop said nothing. But slowly the pressure of the people grew and grew, until finally we have in Delano a priest sent by the new Bishop, Timothy Manning, who is there to help minister to the needs of farm workers. His name is Father Mark Day and he is the Union's chaplain.

Finally, our own Catholic Church has decided to recognize that we have our own peculiar needs, just as the growers have theirs.

But outside of the local diocese, the pressure built up on growers to negotiate was tremendous. Though we were not allowed to have our own priest, the power of the ecumenical body of the Church was tremendous. The work of the Church, for example, in the Schenley, Di Giorgio, Perelli-Minetti strikes was fantastic. They applied pressure — and they mediated.

When poor people get involved in a long conflict, such as a strike, or a civil rights drive, and the pressure increases each day, there is a deep need for spiritual advice. Without it we see families crumble, leadership weaken, and hard workers grow tired. And in such a situation the spiritual advice must be given by a *friend,* not by the opposition. What sense does it make to go to Mass on Sunday and reach out for spiritual help, and instead get sermons about the wickedness of your cause? That only drives one to question and to despair. The growers in Delano have their spiritual problems . . . we do not deny that. They have every right to have priests and ministers who serve their needs. BUT WE HAVE DIFFERENT NEEDS, AND SO WE NEEDED A FRIENDLY SPIRITUAL GUIDE. And this is true in every community in this state where the poor face tremendous problems.

But the opposition raises a tremendous howl about this. They don't want us to have our spiritual advisors, friendly to our needs. Why is this? Why indeed except that THERE IS TREMENDOUS SPIRITUAL AND ECONOMIC POWER IN THE CHURCH. The rich know it, and for that reason they choose to keep it from the people.

The leadership of the Mexican-American Community must admit that we have fallen far short in our task of helping provide spiritual guidance for our people. We may say, "I don't feel any such need. I can get along." But that is a poor excuse for not helping provide such help for others. For we can also say, "I don't need any welfare help. I can take care of my own problems." But we are all willing to fight like hell for welfare aid for those who truly need it, who would starve without it. Likewise we may have gotten an education and not care about scholarship money for ourselves, or our children. But we would, we should, fight like hell to see to it that our state provides aid for any child needing it so that he can get the education he desires. LIKEWISE WE CAN SAY WE DON'T NEED THE CHURCH. THAT IS OUR BUSINESS. BUT THERE ARE HUNDREDS OF THOUSANDS OF OUR PEOPLE WHO DES-

PERATELY NEED SOME HELP FROM THAT POWERFUL INSTITUTION, THE CHURCH, AND WE ARE FOOLISH NOT TO HELP THEM GET IT.

For example, the Catholic Charities agencies of the Catholic Church has millions of dollars earmarked for the poor. But often the money is spent for food baskets for the needy instead of for effective action to eradicate the causes of poverty. The men and women who administer this money sincerely want to help their brothers. It should be our duty to help direct the attention to the basic needs of the Mexican-Americans in our society . . . needs which cannot be satisfied with baskets of food, but rather with effective organizing at the grass roots level.

Therefore, I am calling for Mexican-American groups to stop ignoring this source of power. It is not just our right to appeal to the Church to use its power effectively for the poor, it is our duty to do so. It should be as natural as appealing to government . . . and we do that often enough.

Furthermore, we should be prepared to come to the defense of that priest, rabbi, minister, or layman of the Church, who out of commitment to truth and justice gets into a tight place with his pastor or bishop. It behooves us to stand with that man and help him see his trial through. It is our duty to see to it that his rights of conscience are respected and that no bishop, pastor or other higher body takes that God-given, human right away.

Finally, in a nutshell, what do we want the Church to do? We don't ask for more cathedrals. We don't ask for bigger churches or fine gifts. We ask for its presence with us, beside us, as Christ among us. We ask the Church to *sacrifice with the people* for social change, for justice, and for love of brother. We don't ask for words. We ask for deeds. We don't ask for paternalism. We ask for servanthood.

PART IV

ACCOMMODATION POLITICS

SPEECH: "THE HATE ISSUE"

Representative Henry Gonzalez

The SPEAKER pro tempore. Under a previous order of the House the gentleman from Texas (Mr. GONZALEZ) is recognized for 15 minutes.

Mr. GONZALEZ. Mr. Speaker, we are a nation of immigrants. Every one of us, save the Indians, is either an immigrant or the descendant of immigrants. All immigrants or their ancestors are either members of some racial or religious minority or their descendants have been, at one time or another. There is not a living American who either is, or has been, or has a descendant who was a member of some minority. As it happens I am myself a member of an ethnic minority and am so classified by the census. I think that there is not a Member of this body who is unaware of the effects that minority status can have on an individual life.

Eric Hoffer has observed that no matter how protective the laws may be, no minority group is ever truly secure; a minority exists in the knowledge that its rights are protected only on the consent of the majority, or at least on the benevolent neutrality of the majority. Minority rights are protected, but only as long as the majority is willing. It does not matter whether you happen to be in a political minority or a racial minority, but that you realize deep in your soul that your position is tolerated, but never secure. Perhaps it is never said, maybe even never thought, but somehow the feeling is inescapable that there may be something wrong with you or your position, because after all it is a minority position. One feels safety, but not security. It is a fortunate thing that all of us can understand this, that most of us recognize that we are or may be in a minority, and that therefore minority rights must be—and generally are—protected.

An ethnic minority is in a peculiar position. I happen to be an American of Spanish surname and of Mexican descent. As it happens my parents were born in Mexico and came to this country seeking safety from a violent revolution. It follows that I, and many other residents of my part of Texas and other Southwestern States—happen to be what is commonly referred to as a Mexican American. That label sums up most of the elements of a vast conflict affecting perhaps most of the 5 million southwestern citizens who happen to bear it. The individual finds himself in a conflict, sometimes with himself, sometimes with his family, sometimes with his whole world. What is he to be? Mexican? American? Both? How can he choose? Should he have pride and joy in his heritage, or bear it as a shame and sorrow? Should he live in one world or another, or attempt to bridge them both?

There is comfort in remaining in the closed walls of a minority society, but this means making certain sacrifices; but it sometimes seems disloyal to abandon old ideas and old friends; you never know whether you will be accepted or rejected in the larger world, or whether your old friends will despise you for making a wrong choice. For a member of this minority, like any other, life begins with making hard choices about personal identity. These lonely conflicts are magnified in the social crises so clearly evident all over the Southwest today. There are some groups who demand

CONGRESSIONAL RECORD, April 22, 1969, Vol. 115, Part 8, pp. 9951-9954.

brown power, some who display a curious chauvinism, and some who affect the other extreme. There is furious debate about what one should be and what one should do. There is argument about what one's goals are, and how to accomplish them. I understand all this, but I am profoundly distressed by what I see happening today. I have said that I am against certain tactics, and against certain elements, and now I find yet more confusion. Mr. Speaker, the issue at hand in this minority group today is hate, and my purpose in addressing the House is to state where I stand: I am against hate and against the spreaders of hate; I am for justice, and for honest tactics in obtaining justice.

The question facing the Mexican American people today is what do we want, and how do we get it?

What I want is justice. By justice I mean decent work at decent wages for all who want work; decent support for those who cannot support themselves; full and equal opportunity in employment, in education, in schools; I mean by justice the full, fair, and impartial protection of the law for every man; I mean by justice decent homes, adequate streets and public services; and I mean by justice no man being asked to do more than his fair share, but none being expected to do less. In short, I seek a justice that amounts to full, free, and equal opportunity for all; I believe in a justice that does not tolerate evil or evil doing; and I believe in a justice that is for all the people all the time.

I do not believe that justice comes only to those who want it; I am not so foolish as to believe that good will alone achieves good works. I believe that justice requires work and vigilance, and I am willing to do that work and maintain that vigilance.

I do not believe that it is possible to obtain justice by vague and empty gestures, or by high slogans uttered by orators who are present today and gone tomorrow. I do believe that justice can be obtained by those who know exactly what they seek, and know exactly how they plan to seek it. And I believe that justice can be obtained by those whose cause is just and whose means are honest.

It may well be that I agree with the goals stated by militants; but whether I agree or disagree, I do not now, nor have I ever believed that the end justifies the means, and I condemn those who do. I cannot accept the belief that racism in reverse is the answer for racism and discrimination; I cannot accept the belief that simple, blind, and stupid hatred is an adequate response to simple, blind, and stupid hatred; I cannot accept the belief that playing at revolution produces anything beyond an excited imagination; and I cannot accept the belief that imitation leadership is a substitute for the real thing. Developments over the past few months indicate that there are those who believe that the best answer for hate is hate in reverse, and that the best leadership is that which is loudest and most arrogant; but my observation is that arrogance is no cure for emptiness.

All over the Southwest new organizations are springing up; some promote pride in heritage, which is good, but others promote chauvinism, which is not; some promote community organization, which is good, but some promote race tension and hatred, which is not good; some seek redress of just grievances, which is good, but others seek only opportunities for self aggrandizement, which is not good.

All of these elements, good and bad, exist and all of them must be taken into account. The tragic thing is that in situations where people have honest grievances, dishonest tactics can prevent their obtaining redress; and where genuine problems exist, careless or unthinking or consciously mean behavior can unloose forces that will create new problems that might require generations to solve. I want to go forward, not backward; I want the creation of trust, not fear; and I want to see Americans together, not apart.

Just a few days ago, in Denver there was a demonstration mounted by a priest and a few others. The priest and eight others pledged that they would fast for 8 days in behalf of legislation to protect migrant farmworkers. About 30 people were on hand to support them. Within 2 hours a convention of militants arrived and took over; they refused to listen to legislators who were working for the legislation they supposedly supported. After a while, someone pulled down the flag of the State of Colorado and mutilated it. The militants left and marched back to their convention, jeering at police along the way and generally behaving in imitation militant manner. The original protest was drowned, its purpose obscured, and justice moved forward not at all, The priest remarked sadly:

The group who destroyed the flag was not part of our group. We don't agree with that philosophy.

In this case I doubt that the plight of migrant farmworkers was ever called to public attention, but was lost in the antics and hoopla mounted by unthinking people who apparently got bored with their own meeting and decided to take over another one. I fear that this is an instance where the cause of justice took a back seat to the cause of publicity.

Assuredly there is cause for wrath among people who have suffered long and endured much. But the question that must be answered is whether wrath alone will bring about justice, or whether it will merely obfuscate the real remedy. It is easy to be angry, but it is hard to have that moral indignation that alone reveals the depth of injustice, and lights the corridors of truth.

It is not simply a case today where a local protest is taken over in an isolated incident; the Denver situation is not at all unique. In fact the very day after that incident, a demonstration in Del Rio, Tex., attracted militant types, who sought to turn it to their advantage. Militants attempted to provoke police and plastered their slogans all over the premises where a meeting was held. Even the local Republican organizer hung stickers around, so that he might possibly gain some converts. The organizer of this protest said:

We have nothing to do with militant leaders who infiltrated the Del Rio march.

In the midst of change and unrest there are always parties who want to use that unrest to their own advantage. It is no secret that militants want to use others for their own ends and purposes; but it should also be no secret to the perceptive that there are also people who want to use the militants for their purposes. It is no secret that a political party organizer hopes to promote militant action as a means to win votes, or possibly embarrass political opponents. But that is a game that many can play. If people should not be shocked that my minority party friends had a paid organizer running a hospitality suite in Del Rio, then neither should they be shocked that sympathizers of the Cuban regime might also hope to turn the incident to their advantage. Protests can advance the ambitions of many, and the ambitious will attempt to advance their interests if they can by taking advantage of the unwary and the naive.

Unfortunately it seems that in the face of rising hopes and expectations among Mexican Americans there are more leaders with political ambitions at heart than there are with the interests of the poor at heart; they do not care what is accomplished in fact, as long as they can create and ride the winds of protest as far as possible. Thus we have those who play at revolution, those who make speeches but do no work, and those who imitate what they have seen others do, but lack the initiative and imagination to set forth actual programs for progress.

Indeed there are even those with the best of intentions who find their efforts misguided. Foundation grants meant to achieve harmony and unity have created greater divisions and hatreds; funds meant to support the development of new leadership have only been used for the friends of grantees, who might or might not have any potential for constructive leadership and action. Like Tolstoy's Count Bezukhov, a foundation with the best of intentions may be able to produce only greater misery by entrusting its funds to ambitious but ruthless and self-seeking overseers. No one could quarrel with the good intentions of the bumbling Count or the great foundation, but one can and must examine what has happened to that benevolent intent. After all, the best of programs must be translated into action by human beings, and not all human beings interpret an idea in the same way. One man's facade is another man's empty and crumbling building; it all depends on who is looking at it.

About 3 years ago the Ford Foundation, by far the greatest of all foundations devoted to the advancement of humanity, took an interest in the Mexican-American minority group. What the foundation saw was an opportunity to help. That opportunity, coupled with the best of intentions, has produced what I could classify only as a very grave problem in the district I am privileged to represent. As deeply as I must respect the intentions of the foundation, I must at the same time say that where it aimed to produce unity it has so far created disunity; and where it aimed to coordinate it has only further unloosed the conflicting aims and desires of various groups and individuals; and where it aimed to help it has hurt. I hope that all of this will change; but before it can change the facts must be examined.

The Ford Foundation believed that the greatest need of this particular minority group was to have some kind of effective national organization that could coordinate the actions of the many that already existed, and give for once an effective and united voice to this minority group. This good desire may have rested on a false assumption; namely, that such a disparate group could, any more than our black brothers or our white "Anglo" brothers, be brought under one large tent. There are conflicting interests in any group of any race or creed, and this must be recognized. Whatever the case may be, the Ford Foundation established the Southwest Council of La Raza and gave it a treasury of $630,000.

Not long after the Southwest Council of La Raza opened for business, it gave $110,000 to the Mexican-American Unity Council of San Antonio; this group was apparently invented for the purpose of receiving the grant. Whatever the purposes of this group may be, thus far it has not given any assistance that I know of to bring anybody together; rather it has freely dispensed funds to people who promote the rather odd and I might say generally unaccepted and unpopular views of its directors. The Mexican-American Unity Council appears to specialize in creating still other organizations and equipping them with quarters, mimeograph machines and other essentials of life. Thus, the "unity council" has created a parents' association in a poor school district, a neighborhood council, a group known as the barrios unidos—or roughly, united neighborhoods—a committee on voter registration and has given funds to the militant Mexican-American Youth Organization—MAYO: it has also created a vague entity known as the "Universidad de los Barrios" which is a local gang operation. Now assuredly all these efforts may be well intended; however it is questionable to my mind that a very young and inexperienced man can prescribe the social and political organizations of a complex and troubled community; there is no reason whatever to believe that for all the money this group has spent, there is any understanding of what it is actually being spent for, except to employ friends of the director and advance his preconceived notions. The people who are to be united apparently don't get much say in what the "unity council" is up to.

As an example, the president of MAYO is not on the Unity Council payroll; but he is on the payroll of another Ford Foundation group, the Mexican-American Legal Defense Fund. He is an investigator but appears to spend his time on projects not related to his defense fund work. This handy device enables him to appear independent of Foundation activities and still make a living

from the Foundation. Of course, his MAYO speeches denigrating the "gringos" and calling for their elimination by "killing them if all else fails" do little for unity, and nothing for law, but that bothers neither him nor his associates.

As another example, the "Universidad de los Barrios" is operated by a college junior and two others. The "universidad" has no curriculum and offers no courses, and the young toughs it works with have become what some neighbors believe to be a threat to safety and even life itself. After a murder took place on the doorstep of this place in January, witnesses described the place as a "trouble spot." Neighbors told me that they were terrified of the young men who hung around there, that their children had been threatened and that they were afraid to call the police. After the murder, the "dean" of this "university" said that he could not be there all the time and was not responsible for what happened while he was away. This might be true, but the general fear of the neighbors indicates that the "university" is not under reliable guidance at any time. I note that since I have made criticisms of this operation its leader says it is ready to enter a "second phase." I hope so.

Militant groups like MAYO regularly distribute literature that I can only describe as hate sheets, designed to inflame passions and reinforce old wounds or open new ones; these sheets spew forth racism and hatred designed to do no man good. The practice is defended as one that will build race pride, but I never heard of pride being built on spleen. There is no way to adequately describe the damage that such sheets can do; and there is no way to assess how minds that distribute this tripe operate. But, Mr. Speaker, I say that those who believe the wellsprings of hate can be closed as easily as they are opened make a fearful mistake; they who lay out poison cannot be certain that it will kill no one, or make no one ill, or harm no innocent bystander.

I have no way of knowing whether foundation money goes into the publication of these hate sheets, but I cannot see why the foundation would permit its money to support groups that published these sheets either, and I cannot see how good can come from the building of passions that have throughout the history of mankind brought about only distrust, fear, hate, and violence.

I fear very much that the Ford Foundation miscalculated in choosing those who have charge over their grant money.

We see a strange thing in San Antonio today; we have those who play at revolution and those who imitate the militance of others. We have a situation in Denver where the local leader said, "This is our Selma," and not a week later a situation in Del Rio where the local leader said, "This is our Selma." But try as they might, Selma was neither in Denver nor in Del Rio. We have those who cry "brown power" only because they have heard "black power" and we have those who yell "oink" or "pig" at police, only because they have heard others use the term. We have those who wear beards and berets, not because they attach any meaning to it, but because they have seen it done elsewhere. But neither fervor nor fashion alone will bring justice. Those who cry for justice, but hold it in contempt cannot win it for themselves or for anyone else. Those who prize power for its own sake will never be able to use it for any benefit but their own; and those who can only follow the fashions of protest will never understand what true protest is.

I believe that a just and decent cause demands a just and decent program of action. I believe that a just and decent cause can be undermined by those who believe that there is no decency, and who demand for themselves what they would deny others. I have stood against racists before, and I will do it again; and I have stood against blind passion before and I will gladly do so again. I pray that the day will come when all men know justice; and I pray that that day has not been put further away by the architects of discord, the prophets of violence. I pray that these great tasks that face us in the quest for justice and progress will be taken up by all men; and I know that when all is said and done and the tumult and shouting die down those who only spoke with passion cast aside, and those who spoke with conviction and integrity will still be around. I am willing to let time be my judge.

SUBORDINATE LEADERSHIP IN A BICULTURAL COMMUNITY: AN ANALYSIS

JAMES B. WATSON and JULIAN SAMORA

Iᴛ is held in the present paper that the ability of a subordinate group to generate effective leadership in its relations with a dominant alien people is a critical aspect of dominant-subordinate group relationships. The subordinate group in question here is the Spanish of the Southwest. We wish to see Spanish leadership in its autonomous setting, to see it in relation to the intercultural system which is emerging between Spanish and Anglo-Americans, and to consider leadership and some of its accultural consequences.

REGIONAL BACKGROUND OF THE CASE

The Spanish-speaking people are one of the largest United States ethnic minorities, and are concentrated principally in the southwestern part of the nation. Those whose forefathers were in the area in 1848

AMERICAN SOCIOLOGICAL REVIEW, 1954, Vol. 19, pp. 413-421.

when the United States acquired the territory are also among the oldest ethnic groups, although many others have entered the region from Mexico over the intervening years. The Spanish-speaking are not powerful politically, a fact closely related to the perennial lack of leadership among them. They are seen by some authorities as surprisingly undifferentiated, compared to other large American ethnic groups, in schooling, in occupation, in income, and in degree of acculturation.[1] Perhaps the most outstanding fact about the Spanish, besides their lack of leadership is their low rate of acculturation. The special historical status of the Spanish may have a bearing upon the two facts, and the broad historical context suggests linkages between the leadership question and that of low assimilation.

The Southwestern Spanish[2] were a separate society when they came into contact with, and in a sense were conquered by Anglo-Americans, or "Anglos." Speaking a separate language and practicing separate customs, they were highly visible culturally. They represented nevertheless a modified branch of European civilization, unlike the Indians from whom they had received many influences, and unlike African slaves. In contrast to many Europeans who migrated to the United States, however, they had not voluntarily elected to adopt the lifeways of the dominant group. Moreover, they were more "native" and ecologically more adapted to their habitat in the Southwest than the dominant group. In these two respects they were more like Indians than immigrants. In the growing similarity of their goals with those of the dominant group, the Spanish are comparable to the present United States Negro, though their cultural similarity to Anglos is much less. In the sense of being a "conquered people" enslaved by their conquerors, the Spanish are somewhat like colonial people but more strictly comparable to the French of Canada. They differ from the French, however, in having smaller numerical strength relative to the dominant

group, and they did not occupy the beachhead and focal areas of the Anglo-American culture and society. Their relative isolation (1650–1900) from the parent culture as well as from the Anglo culture is also an important factor with respect to assimilation.

Hence, historically having less motivation toward assimilation and deeper environmental and traditional roots than most U. S. immigrants, less commitment to and a less exclusive need for identification with the dominant cultural system than U. S. Negroes, but smaller numerical strength and less strategic position than the Canadian French, the Spanish as a group might be expected, more than others, to sense ambivalences about assimilation. Again, beside the fact of an increasing struggle for status in the Anglo system, one must place the opposing fact—peculiar to the Southwestern Spanish—that they have at their backs an effective reservoir of Spanish language and national Mexican culture to help reinforce and stabilize any tendency toward cultural separatism.

All of these broad, contradictory factors probably play their part in the default of Spanish leadership, as well as the more specific factors discussed below. In the larger Southwestern setting ambivalence about nativism vs. assimilation would obscure the direction Spanish leadership should take and thus hamstring the development of effective leadership.

Turning to the present, there is singularly little controversy concerning whether Spanish leadership is weak, regardless of the point of view of different commentators. Agreement is all but unanimous among scientific investigators,[3] among social workers and

[1] Leonard Broom and Eshref Shevky, "Mexicans in the United States: A Problem in Social Differentiation," *Sociology and Social Research,* 36 (January, 1952), pp. 150–158.

[2] The term "Spanish," used throughout the paper refers to "the Spanish-speaking people."

[3] Cf. Robert C. Jones, "Mexican Youth in the United States," *The American Teacher,* 28 (March, 1944), pp. 11–15; Olen Leonard and C. P. Loomis, *Culture of a Contemporary Rural Community, El Cerrito, New Mexico,* Washington: USDA, BAE, 1940; R. W. Roskelley and C. R. Clark, *When Different Cultures Meet,* Denver: Rocky Mountain Council on Inter-American Affairs, 1949; George I. Sanchez, "The Default of Leadership," in *Summarized Proceedings IV,* Southwest Council on the Education of the Spanish-Speaking People, Fourth Regional Conference, Albuquerque, New Mexico, January 23–25, 1950; Ozzie G. Simmons, *Anglo Americans and Mexican Americans in South Texas, A Study in Dominant-Subordinate Group Relations*

public and private agencies interested in the Spanish-speaking people, among Anglo politicians, and among the people themselves. The Spanish of "Mountain Town," the subject of the present paper, are no exception.

THE COMMUNITY STUDIED

In the summers of 1949 and 1950, students from the Department of Sociology and Anthropology of Washington University, under James B. Watson's direction, carried out part of an intended long-range study of a small Anglo-Spanish community. Samora further pursued field work in the community, relating particularly to the question of Spanish-speaking leadership and organization, in the spring and summer of 1952.[4] It is largely with the findings from this bi-ethnic community that we propose to explore the question of weak leadership, but with the general background of the region always in mind.

Mountain Town, as we have called the community, is located in a high mountain valley of southern Colorado. It is at about 7000 feet above sea level, in an area of mixed truck farming and cattle and sheep ranching. Its 1950 population was close to 2500, comprising approximately 58 per cent Spanish-speaking and 42 per cent Anglos. (Hence the Spanish-speaking are not numerically a "minority" in the community itself, and will not be so called.) Founded around 1870, Mountain Town developed as a community of Anglo miners, storekeepers, and homesteaders. There were at the time but few "Old Spanish" families in the area, and they did not precede the Anglos by more than a decade or two. Mountain Town, hence, developed differently from the older established Spanish communities to the south which Anglos have come to dominate. The difference may have a bearing on the discussion which follows.

Descendents of original Spanish settlers still live in or near Mountain Town. It is probable that at least some of them could

(Ph.D. Thesis, Harvard University, 1952); Ruth D. Tuck, *Not With The Fist: Mexican-Americans in a Southwest City*, New York: Harcourt, Brace and Company, 1949.

[4] Julian Samora, *Minority Leadership in a Bi-Cultural Community* (Ph.D. Thesis, Washington University, St. Louis, 1953).

have been classed as *Patrón* families. Two or three are still landowners. However, the vast majority of Spanish-speaking families in Mountain Town came at a later date, many possibly around 1920. Much of this migration was from the Spanish villages of northern New Mexico, and kinsmen can often still be traced to or from that area. Practically none of these people are landowners, except for house plots; nor are they often proprietors in any other sense. The largest number are still seasonal wage workers, unskilled or semiskilled "stoop labor." Some of the women work as domestics, but many more work in the fields or produce-packing sheds. As a group, the Spanish-speaking depend for employment on the prosperity of local agriculture.

While the foregoing generalizations stand, some Spanish are now making their way slowly up the socioeconomic ladder as store clerks, garage or filling station employees, a few as operators of small groceries or oil stations, and several as salaried clerical personnel. There has been a gradual increase over the last 25 years in the number of Spanish-speaking who have eighth grade schooling, and gradually more go on or complete high school.[5] The war industries of the Pacific Coast attracted a number from Mountain Town and materially raised their economic level, and service in the armed forces broadened the ethnic outlook of not only Spanish but also of some Mountain Town Anglos. There is no question of palpable Spanish acculturation. Bilingualism, to mention an important facet, now prevails among a majority of the Spanish and increasingly one finds older people the only strict monolinguals.

Many older Anglo residents of Mountain Town feel that they have seen a definite change in the social and economic status of the Spanish-speaking, but there is no denying that traditional attitudes and traditional ethnic relationships still generally prevail. The Anglo and Spanish-speaking groups are sharply distinguishable as to religion, economic status, occupational status, language, surnames, residence, and usually physical

[5] James B. Watson, *Preliminary Observations Based On the Community of Mountain Town* (Unpublished manuscript, Washington University, St. Louis, n.d.).

appearance. Ethnic distinctions along these lines are made by nearly all members of both groups. The Spanish are nearly all nominally Catholic and the Anglos are nearly all nominally Protestant. Political and economic control of the community is in the hands of the Anglos. There is not the slightest question of their superordinate position in relation to the Spanish as a whole, though certain individuals of Spanish background clearly receive personal respect and prestige well above that of many Anglos.

The Anglo-Spanish relationship has some of the properties of a caste system. Spanish and Anglo are practically endogamous. Religious participation is mostly along ethnic lines, and many Anglo Protestants would not want the conversion of non-Protestants at the expense of any sizeable Spanish attendance in their churches. Although somewhat ill defined, there is residential distinctness in Mountain Town, and distress is felt by some Anglos at having close "Mexican" neighbors. The Spanish are excluded almost completely from Anglo social and civic organizations (e.g., lodges, Volunteer Firemen, Chamber of Commerce, Junior C of C, Rotary), except, to some extent, the P.T.A. and a veterans' group. In the cases of many of these organizations, the vast majority do not qualify for membership (e.g., in Rotary), but the lack of qualifications appears to be largely incidental. Parties, dancing, picnics, and visiting are uniformly intra-ethnic, as are bridge, sewing circles, teas, and bazaars. As in a true caste system, obviously the sharp differentiation of interaction is not simply the will and doing of one group by itself. The Anglos, for example, find out, when they decide to broaden the membership of the Parent-Teachers Association, that it is not easy to enlist Spanish parents or to have them assume office.

SPANISH DISUNITY

The disunity among the Spanish group is quite evident in Mountain Town. Disunity does not mean the existence of factionalism, it refers, rather, to the lack of common action and to limited group cohesion. When an issue of import to the members of the group comes up, few people will do anything about it. This has been proved many times in such things as politics, school segregation, employment, arrests, welfare aid, and in general discrimination.

Considering the distinctness of sociocultural boundaries, the disunity of the Spanish group is striking, for the rigid exclusiveness of the Anglos might theoretically be a strong factor in their cohesion. Nor can Spanish disunity find its explanation in any wide socioeconomic disparity within the group. Nevertheless, Spanish cohesion seldom transcends such verbalizations as *nosotros* ("we") or *la raza* ("our people"), a generalized resentment of Anglo dominance and discrimination, and a readiness to perceive injustice in Spanish-Anglo dealings.

Disunity is a large factor in the lack of political power of the Spanish. In Mountain Town numbers do not explain the failure of the subordinate group—a majority—to put people they trust into critical offices. The Spanish are not wholly indifferent about certain elective offices, the sheriff, for example, who, if prejudiced, may enforce the laws quite one-sidedly. The school board offices are also thought to be ethnically critical or sensitive because of constant fear of segregation. But the election of an avowedly pro-Spanish candidate is rare indeed. Perhaps few Anglo politicians have understood the basic disunity of the Spanish, but a good many have at least recognized it. Occasionally, however, a direct appeal is made to the Spanish as Spanish. The results in Mountain Town bear out the cynical who feel it is better to ignore the ethnic issue. "They will not even vote for their own people" is commonly asserted, and this is bitterly conceded by most Spanish.

The failure of unity and leadership in politics is not the only type of weakness of the Spanish group. There is, of course, a more informal type of leadership in interethnic relations. The spokesman, as he is often called, is a leader to whom politicians or others may turn for advice and commitments on matters seen as affecting the interests of the ethnic group. There are two or three Spanish individuals in Mountain Town —one in particular—whom most Anglos consider to be spokesmen. The same individuals were cited by the majority of the Spanish when asked by Samora who were the leaders of their group. Yet these individuals usually make commitments for their group only at great risk. Actually, they generally refuse to do more than express an opinion or give very general advice. Investigation failed to show that any individual among the Spanish, including those most mentioned as leaders by Spanish and by Anglos, was willing to assume the responsibilities of a real spokesman for the group. There was no reason to believe that any of the persons mentioned could actually keep significant commitments if he made them.

But if a distinction is made between the inter-ethnic leadership described above and intra-ethnic leadership,[6] is the picture of the latter more favorable? Investigation was made by the junior author and his wife of 16 *sociedades* and *mutualistas*, lodges and mutual benefit organizations, which exist in Mountain Town with exclusively Spanish membership and objectives, as well as of lay societies ancillary to the Roman Catholic Church. The findings, reported in detail elsewhere, were rather uniform.[7] On the whole, the non-church associations were characterized by ineffectual leadership, very poor attendance, irregularity of procedure and schedule, lack of decisive action—even in inducting new members, and often a precarious existence. Careful comparison of the church-sponsored sodalities (*e.g.*, Altar Society, Family Society) revealed the priest as central to their direction and probably instrumental in their better showing compared to the secular groups. Even when the priest tried to play a less prominent role, circumstances, if not his own inclinations, tended to thrust him into a position more beside than behind the figure in the chair. Lay leadership, by the priest's admission, from observation of the members, and by their testimony, was not considered adequate.

The facts about the Mountain Town Spanish suggest deficiency, then, both as to leadership in inter-ethnic relations and as to leadership of purely ethnic organizations, except those ancillary to the Church. Yet strong factors for cohesion unmistakably exist—Anglo exclusiveness, a relatively undifferentiated Spanish group, a common ethnic tongue, Spanish group concepts, recognition of group-wide grievances, their majority voting position, and even some Anglo political attempts to unify the Spanish vote. In the light of such factors, we may ask why leadership is so ineffectual among the Spanish.

THE HYPOTHESIS OF LEADERSHIP DEFICIENCY

It is the contention of this paper that four principal conditions account for the inadequacy of Spanish leadership in Mountain Town and probably to some extent among the Spanish of the larger Southwest.

(1) Traditional forms (patterns) of leadership, which functioned well enough in pre-Anglo-Spanish culture, have been unadaptable and possibly a handicap to the development of adequate patterns of group leadership in the contact situation.

(2) Increasingly, the status goals of the Spanish group as a whole lie in the direction of Anglo culture; for the achievement of such goals, hence, leaders relatively well adapted to the Anglo system are increasingly indicated.

(3) General ambivalence and suspicion are accorded individuals of Spanish background who are "successful" since the terms of success are now largely Anglo terms (viz. (2) above), and it is widely assumed that success is bought by cooperation with the outgroup and betrayal of one's own.

(4) Although caste-like enough to give sharp definition to the two groups, Anglo structure is relatively open to competent Spanish and thus permits the siphoning off of potential Spanish leadership, individuals relatively well adapted to the Anglo system.

The net result of these conditions is that, in the lack of adaptable traditional types, the only potential leaders who might be qualified to provide the kind of leadership indicated today are by virtue of their very qualifications absorbed into the larger body politic and are disqualified in the minds of their own fellows.

DISCUSSION

(1) The conclusion is widespread that what can be said about traditions of authority in Mexico, and even Latin America, applies on the whole to the Spanish of the Southwest. If so, the pre-Anglo-Spanish picture was one of strong authoritarian roles, the padre, the *patrón*, and the *jefe de*

[6] Julian Samora, *op. cit.*, p. 52.
[7] *Ibid.*, pp. 13–51.

familia.[8] The *caudillo* is of course a classic Latin American type. In fact, a suggestive interpretation can be made of these roles in Spanish culture as variations on the same fundamental theme, strong and decisive authority, and F. R. Kluckhohn has commented that the Spanish-American is quite systematically trained for dependence upon such authority.[9] Such a pattern would scarcely appear by itself to be an impediment to the existence of effective Spanish leadership in inter-ethnic relations.

But the traditional pattern of local, secular authority among the Spanish is of the wrong kind. First, in many places, the *patrón* pattern was simply unable to survive the innovations of Anglo contact. In Mountain Town the *patrón-peón* relationship has no strong personal relevance for the majority of Spanish. They probably still possess some cultural adjustments to the pattern, but many lack deep roots in the community and hence lack any long-standing familial connection with local *patrón* lineages. Moreover, there is relatively little tenant or even employee relationship nowadays except with Anglo landlords or employers. Crew bosses and labor middlemen exist, to be sure, but these intercultural agents are usually themselves committed to Anglo employers.

Yet there are two *patrón*-like figures in Mountain Town, and these were the ones most often mentioned as leaders by the Spanish Samora interviewed. There was some ambivalence about them, however. Many who named these "leaders," apparently in default of anyone else, declared that they could not be counted on in a pinch or that they would not do all that they could for the Spanish people.[10] Investigation showed that these pseudo-*patrones*, when called upon, usually served their fellow Spanish in limited and personal ways. They might give an individual help in the form of advice or instructions. They sometimes helped him fill in an official form or make out an application. They might, though

rarely, intercede, using their personal influence with some governmental (*i.e.*, Anglo) agency, typically the County Welfare bureau. Intercession in these cases would almost never be insistent; in fact, it is ordinarily reluctant. The pseudo-*patrones* were not reported by anyone as ever attempting to organize their people for some lasting and broadly based social action.

Interestingly enough, leadership in approximately these limited terms matches fairly well the authors' understanding of the older *patrón* pattern. The *patrón* did not form committees, found organizations, or often refer formally to his followers for common assent to social decisions. He bound them to him on a personalistic basis, with advice and counsel and by providing assistance to those lacking other resources. Such paternalistic leadership could function in the status system of colonial Mexican culture; it cannot function very extensively where the *patrón* cannot assure his followers of security in reward for their loyalty—they work for Anglos—and where even the status of the *patrón* himself is guaranteed by no *latifundium* manned with loyal retainers. Too often his status depends—even more than that of successful Anglos, he feels—upon the sufferance and approval of those in dominant positions. In such a situation erstwhile leader and follower can do little for each other in the traditional terms which were the very core of the *patrón-peón* relationship.

It may be relevant to add that the *patrón* himself was usually identified with the same general social class as those who held most of the important formal offices in the government. Ties of kinship were traditionally common between *patrón* and official. It is probably not going too far to suggest that the *patrón* himself tended in many instances to act informally as an agent of government in relation to the *peones*—"His word was law." To the extent that *patrón* status was adjusted to fit such an identification with and informal extension of governmental authority, it would likely not be an adaptable form of leadership when kinship and status identification with the dominant group were made ambivalent or impossible through their replacement by aliens.

It will be recalled that the church-spon-

[8] Cf. R. L. Beals, *op. cit.*, pp. 8–10; and O. Leonard and C. P. Loomis, *op. cit.*, p. 15.

[9] F. R. Kluckhohn, "Dominant and Variant Value Orientations," in C. Kluckhohn and H. A. Murray, *Personality in Nature, Society, and Culture*, 2nd ed. rev., New York: Knopf, 1953.

[10] Julian Samora, *op. cit.*, pp. 74–76.

sored societies in Mountain Town are generally the most effective ones among the Spanish. The lack of inter-ethnic leadership by the church certainly cannot be blamed, like that of the *patrón*, on any local restriction of the church's ability to function, nor probably on any intrinsic maladaptation of church leadership. Rather, the reason is probably that the Roman Church in the United States is only indirectly political and that not all its communicants are Spanish. In any event the church does not attempt to provide local leadership for the Spanish as a group in their common struggle for status. A special factor in Mountain Town is the national origin of the priests, who come from Spain. This factor may be of no consequence, however, as Southwestern Spanish parishes with American-born priests may have no greater church leadership than Mountain Town in inter-ethnic relations.

(2) No attempt will be made to argue that traditional Spanish culture everywhere in the Southwest approximates that of Anglos in all its basic values. The case to the contrary has been effectively presented elsewhere, *e.g.*, concerning time orientation and the value attached to formal schooling.[11] Even with only superficial observation it is clear that "go-getter" tendencies are much less typical of Spanish than of Anglos, and there may be some basis in fact for other traits ascribed to the Spanish in the Anglo stereotype, as well as *vice-versa*.

Nevertheless, it is possible to carry the emphasis of Spanish-Anglo cultural differences to the point where certain obvious and growing similarities of goal and value are overlooked or omitted. Generalizing, necessarily, the Spanish in Mountain Town are interested in better jobs, better pay, and more material things, such as automobiles, housing, and appliances. There is increasingly a concern for having children complete at least grammar schooling and learn at least moderately fluent English. Measures taken by the school system, which either are, or are interpreted by the Spanish to be, attempts at segregation (such as a special first grade

for English-deficient children), are strongly resented, as is discrimination in hiring and firing in employment, and alleged inequality in the administration of Old Age Pensions. The Spanish in Mountain Town, however, as we are emphasizing, are not very effective in changing conditions as they would.

It may be that the Mountain Town Spanish differ somewhat as to goals from those in some other parts of the Southwest. They are almost entirely landless, and are predominantly low-paid agricultural labor, a kind of rural proletariat. Yet they are resident, not essentially a migratory group. However, we are not convinced that Mountain Town is markedly unrepresentative of Spanish elsewhere in the Southwest.

The Spanish goals sketched lie in the direction of Anglo goals and for their realization a mastery of Anglo techniques and behavior patterns is necessary. Insofar as advancement toward such goals involves group-wide status, Spanish leader qualifications must necessarily include such skills as literacy, relatively high control of the English language, and knowledge of social, political, and legal usages primarily based on the dominant culture. Few Spanish in Mountain Town possess such thorough adjustment to and broad familiarity with Anglo culture, dependent as it largely is upon extensive schooling.

(3) Only a handful of eight Spanish individuals in Mountain Town possess the necessary qualifications in markedly higher degree than their fellows. As a matter of fact, it is essentially individuals with proven ability in Anglo culture who are singled out for mention as "leaders" in the survey conducted by Samora. What, then, if anything, keeps these persons from exercising the leadership functions so generally desired by the Spanish? As was mentioned, a good deal of ambivalence exists concerning these people (almost all men) in the minds of most Spanish questioned. It is often stated that these "leaders" will not really accept an active part in directing a struggle for Spanish equality; they will only do such things for their fellow Spanish as they think will not antagonize the Anglos. They are even frequently accused of working for the Anglos and not for *la raza*. And not a few feel that such leaders could only have achieved their

---

11 Cf. F. R. Kluckhohn, *op. cit.*, pp. 352–4; R. L. Beals, *op. cit.*, pp. 5–13. Arthur Campa, "Mañana is Today," in T. M. Pearce and A. P. Thomason, *Southwesterners Write*, Albuquerque: University of Mexico Press, 1947.

—usually modest—socioeconomic position at the expense of "selling out to the Anglo" or "by climbing over their own people." They are referred to as "proud" (*orgullosos*). Another adjective has been coined in Spanish especially to describe such relatively successful members of the Spanish community. Samora found that they are called *"agringados"*—"gringoized."

Here, then, is the dilemma: that the very traits which would qualify an individual to provide the sort of leadership called for are such as to cast suspicion upon his loyalty in the eyes of many he would lead. Is it that the qualified "leaders" make little effort to lead effectively because they feel—perhaps correctly—that they would have difficulty in getting an effective followership? Or is it that they get no effective following largely because of their own reluctance to exert leadership? No simple answer to the question will do, of course, particularly as leadership and followership are reciprocal roles and the lack of either precludes the other. It may be hard to say if there is a causal priority in Mountain Town between the two factors, but something more like a vicious circle is suggested by the frequent testimony of Mountain Town Spanish: many agree, on the one hand, that the relatively assimilated "leaders" are "proud" (*orgullosos*) but admit, on the other, that the people are "envious" (*envidiosos*) and are themselves unable to "follow" (*seguir*) anyone. It appears to be the case both that the hypothetical leaders are unwilling to lead and that the hypothetical followers are unable to accept followership.

(4) The factors so far suggested for the default of Spanish leadership clearly have their inter-cultural aspects, though they appear in some respects intrinsic to the Spanish culture. The fourth factor is more completely extrinsic to the Spanish side of the picture. It is that the ranks of the Anglo social structure are not completely closed to the exceptional Spanish individual who achieves appreciable mastery of Anglo culture. There is obviously no question about discrimination against individuals of Spanish background for equally competent Spanish and Anglos do not have an equal probability of success. But Anglo discrimination is paradoxically not rigid enough, in a sense, for the "good"

of the Spanish as a group. That is, those able to deal with Anglos on their own terms frequently have a chance to do so—as individuals. Hence, they are not completely frustrated, embittered, or thrust back into their own group where they must either quit the struggle altogether or turn their energies and skills to leading their people in competition with the Anglos. Instead, although against greater obstacles than an Anglo, the unusual person frequently achieves a degree of success to some extent commensurate with his abilities relative to those of his fellows.

From the standpoint of leadership the Spanish situation is not helped by Anglo mythology. The Anglo social myth recognizes two racial types among the Spanish-speaking. One is the "Real Spanish," with higher intelligence, industry, and dependability, while the other is the "Mexican," a term frequently preceded by opprobrious adjectives according to the context. The latter type, according to the Anglo, lack ambition, and generally possess just the qualities which lodge them where they are found in the social order.

The Spanish themselves make no distinction between "Real Spanish" and "Mexicans." When referring to themselves in Spanish they use the term *"mejicanos"*; when referring to themselves in English they use the term "Spanish." When the Anglos refer to them, the Spanish prefer that they use the term "Spanish" rather than "Mexican," because of the derogatory connotation of the latter term.

There is greater social acceptance of the "Real Spanish" by Anglos, particularly when they show mastery of Anglo culture—which tends to corroborate the myth. This divisive effect of Anglo mythology on the Spanish group, although difficult to assess, is nonetheless real.

The net result of these characteristics of the Anglo system is to lower the motivation of qualified persons to lead, and perhaps to contaminate the successful individual in the view of his group. His partial acceptance by the Anglo gives seeming verification to Spanish suspicions of disloyalty. The intercultural source of this effect on subordinate leadership is dramatically underscored by the Mountain Town evidence.

The three most overtly successful Spanish

individuals in Mountain Town confirm in every major respect mentioned what has been said above. They are much more competent and successful in the Anglo system than most Anglos; they are given a social acceptance by the Anglo group which, although far from unqualified, sets them markedly apart from the great majority of the Spanish; they are predominantly regarded by Anglos as "spokesmen" for the Spanish group, although by no means are they themselves willing to play the role intensively; they are mentioned with the highest frequency by the Spanish interviewed as "leaders" and the only people of their own to whom one could turn for certain kinds of assistance; but they are complained against as *orgullosos*, as being unwilling to do as much for the *raza* as they easily might, and as being subservient to the Anglo and unwilling to risk offending him. These individuals are, then, leaders largely by default and would not otherwise be mentioned as leaders. Although almost uniquely qualified in some respects to lead, they do not. In a situation where adequate inter-ethnic leadership would call for the exercise of organizing skill and close indentification of the destinies of leader and follower, these individuals largely limit themselves to personalistic functions roughly comparable to those of the *patrón* of yore, and a social distance tends to be kept which is in some respects as great as between *patrón* and *peón*. Though the comparison with traditional patterns is suggestive, we need not, as has been discussed, hark back to the *patrón* system to explain everything in the situation found today. Inter-cultural factors in the Spanish relationship with Anglos are of strategic importance in explaining leadership deficiency.

Nosotros Venceremos: Chicano Consciousness and Change Strategies

GEORGE RIVERA, JR.

It is better to die standing
Than to continue living on one's knees

—EMILIANO ZAPATA

INTRODUCTION   Chicanos first became visible to the nation in the Sixties, through the Delano (California) Grape Strike. Mexican Americans were never invisible; they were simply ignored in a decade when the glamour of the civil rights struggle focused upon Black America. Mexican Americans became, to use George Sanchez' (1967) term, the "forgotten people." Even Martin Luther King forgot Mexican Americans until late in his life, and Stokely Carmichael began to understand the "Latino" problem only when he visited Cuba. Most of the Sixties was a time when Black Panthers rarely shook hands with Chicano activists. To blacks, Chicanos were white—though the Mexican American experience proved otherwise to Chicanos living in the Southwest. Thus, the civil rights movement in the Sixties was primarily a black movement. If Chicanos desired social change, they would have to turn toward creating their own independent movement.

The Chicano Movement emerged, to the surprise of many social scientists, in direct contradiction to the "passive, apathetic" image of the Mexican commonly held in sociological and anthropological circles. Today, many of these Anglo "experts" on

JOURNAL OF APPLIED BEHAVIORAL SCIENCE, 1972, Vol. 8, No. 1, pp. 56-71.

Mexican American life are being replaced by young Chicano scholars who possess relevant perspectives on the problem. Things are as they should be: Chicanos are speaking for themselves.

Though *barrio* voices have always existed, as omnipresent as the "Echo of a Scream" in the Siqueiros painting, a Chicano intellectual presence has only recently begun to be felt. Educational opportunities have always been poor for the Mexican American. One major difference between the Chicano Movement and the Black Movement is that blacks, though they had segregated, inferior colleges, nevertheless did have access to higher education. In such institutions, intellectual critics could ponder diverse ideologies and positions in order to articulate their own position on society. Why is there no Mexican American W. E. B. Du Bois, Ralph Ellison, or James Baldwin? Because Chicanos had been systematically deprived of higher education. However, limited but increasing opportunities in education are now giving rise to a Chicano consciousness that is being felt throughout the Southwest.

This paper proceeds with a brief discussion of change strategies producing Chicano consciousness and of the conditions which best seem to suit particular strategies. One condition in particular, the presence of a Chicano majority in a rural *pueblo* (town), has recently led to breakthroughs in Chicano participation. What took place in Crystal City, Texas, is included as a case description to exemplify what can happen when Chicanos organize themselves into a political party "to play the gringo's game." I believe the Chicano Party, La Raza Unida, will become a force to be dealt with in American politics, and I follow the Crystal City case with some comments to further the cause. Help in organization and support in numbers are both needed, and will be taken from well-intentioned experts as well as from those who feel the forces of American oppression. Opportunities for such coalitions are discussed.

CHANGE STRATEGIES TO DATE

Chicano consciousness made success possible in the Cesar Chavez-led Delano Grape Strike. The families in the fields were supported by Mexican Americans as well as by sympathetic Anglos in generating an economic boycott of undreamed-of proportions. The philosophy of nonviolent protest gained widespread support for the movement. At the other end of the continuum of change strategies evolved by the Chicano Movement is Reies Lopez Tijerina's armed courthouse raid in Tierra Amarilla, New Mexico: a militant attempt to regain thousands of acres of stolen land.

The struggle continues. At least one effective urban leader has emerged: Rodolfo "Corky" Gonzales, head of the Crusade for Justice in Denver, Colorado. Gonzales has been instrumental in creating the Chicano Youth Liberation Conference held every year in Colorado, and has been actively involved in Chicano politics and Chicano draft resistance. Gonzales has recently helped in setting up an all-Chicano school—Tlatelolco. Opened in October 1970, it offers day care, preschool, elementary, secondary, undergraduate, and adult basic education, as well as vocational training. This past year Tlatelolco graduated three Chicanos and educated over 150 students, many of whom were victims of Anglo schools—the so-called "push-outs."

Where Chicanos comprise a substantial percentage of the populace, it should be possible to express Chicano consciousness through the established democratic political system. However, throughout the Southwest there are areas where Chicano cultural and/or ethnic majorities are governed by a white numerical minority who are nevertheless an economic majority. Until recently democratic processes were impervious to Chicano participation and/or influence under these conditions.

The efficacy of any change strategy is ultimately dependent on sociological conditions. At least four conditions occur to me, each implying a different strategy for the expression of Chicano consciousness. These conditions are named in Table 1 and described below.

Type I.
Pueblo Milieu
A rural area with a Chicano numerical majority best exemplifies Type I. Many of these areas are highly agricultural and can be found in *pueblos* in most of south Texas, north central New Mexico, two locations at the southern border of Arizona (Nogales in Santa Cruz County and Douglas—a mining area—in Cochise County), and two counties in southern Colorado (Conejos and Costilla). The potential for political change in these

TABLE 1. A Typology of Areas for Potential Chicano Political Activity

| | Numerical Ethnic Composition | |
Area	Chicano Majority	Chicano Minority
Rural	Type I Pueblo Milieu	Type II Calle Milieu
Urban	Type IV Ciudad Milieu	Type III Barrio Milieu

areas is very high, since a Chicano numerical majority could possibly win control of school board, city, and county offices.

The change strategy which holds the most potential for the *pueblo* milieu is seizure of the democratic process. (The Crystal City case to be discussed in detail below exemplifies the effectiveness of this strategy.) Though Chicanos in *pueblos* are in a numerical majority, change by ballot or other legitimate channels (courts) sometimes does not occur. In such locales, violence has been known to erupt (e.g., the Tierra Amarilla Courthouse Raid in New Mexico).

Type II.
Calle Milieu
An area which is rural and contains a Chicano numerical minority has perhaps the least potential for political change. In such areas, Chicanos are usually found residing on segregated *calles* (streets); and since there are usually not many *calles*, one cannot categorically call the area a *barrio*. Many Chicanos in these areas can also be found scattered on small farms outside the town. Since Chicanos are generally highly urbanized, the proportion of Chicanos in these areas is relatively small. However, countless areas throughout the Southwest exemplify this type.

Since Chicanos are not in a numerical majority in the *calle* milieu, farm worker concentrations provide the germinating seeds for change. Cesar Chavez' strike in Delano is an impressive example of the Type II potential for nonviolent change. However, there are innumerable areas of rural minority where Chicanos do not have union potential. For example, in Glidden and Columbus, Texas, most Mexican Americans work in diffused locations such as gravel pits or in service stations. These areas are not likely to produce collectives striking for change, and thus it probably will be a while before the mores of small-town America are modified, at least as they relate to Mexican Americans.

Type III.
Barrio Milieu

An urban area where Chicanos are in a numerical minority is the most characteristic sociological condition in the Southwest. Since these areas contain highly concentrated Mexican American subcommunities (*barrios*), the potential for political activity is very high, in terms of gaining some representation. The biggest threat to organizational efforts in the *barrio* milieu is the problem of gerrymandering and redistricting. The two most politically explosive areas of this type are Los Angeles, California and San Antonio, Texas. Other areas which characterize Type III are Corpus Christi. Texas; Albuquerque, New Mexico; Denver, Colorado; Fresno, California; Tucson, Arizona; Houston, Texas; and numerous other areas throughout the Southwest (Grebler, Moore & Guzman, 1970).

Change strategies in the *barrio* milieu have manifested themselves in the form of urban confrontations. The threat of violence is high in these areas; violence has in fact already occurred in the form of police overreactions to peaceful Chicano demonstrations (e.g., the Chicano Moratorium police riot in Los Angeles and the police raid on the Crusade for Justice headquarters in Denver). The trick will be to turn this threat around so that it is the Chicano community which threatens those who would deprive us of fair representation. Present outbreaks of violence hurt the wrong community.

Type IV.
Ciudad Milieu

Type IV is rare in the Southwest since there are relatively few cities with Chicano majorities. This type, known as a *ciudad* (city) can be found only in southern Texas along the border: in Laredo, Brownsville, and El Paso. The potential for Chicano political power in these areas is undoubtedly quite high since Chicanos can elect local officials and also state representatives.

Since Chicanos are in a numerical majority in these areas, strategies for change have taken the route of the democratic process. However, many "establishment" Mexican Americans control the political offices, which could ultimately mean intraminority conflict. If the people's needs are not heard and if *their* representatives are not elected, new change strategies will have to emerge to make the *ciudad* representative of *all* of the people, and not just another stronghold of the Mexican American middle class.

There are many opportunities for political activity to develop in the Chicano Movement. Texas probably represents the state with the greatest potential, since it has many cities and towns with Chicano majorities (Types I and IV). Since the Chicano constituencies in Texas are poor and uneducated, it is probable that poverty and substandard education will become the rallying points for Chicano action.

To date, political change in the *barrio* has taken the direction of building an independent Chicano political party. In Colorado, Chicanos ran candidates as high as the gubernatorial level on a La Raza Unida Party ticket in 1970. None of their candidates was elected. However, the campaign was primarily *educational*, using the "equal time" ruling of the FCC to convey Chicano perspectives and alternatives to present *barrio* life. Similarly, Chicanos in California and Arizona have taken steps to place La Raza Unida Party on the ballot for 1972. And there is one area where La Raza Unida sponsored successful candidates and accomplished major change through the democratic political process. This took place in Crystal City, Texas, under conditions I consider a *pueblo* milieu. Chicanos in Crystal City expected to win; the spirit had been with them since 1963.

CRYSTAL CITY: A CASE OF POLITICAL CHANGE ACCOMPLISHED BY THE CHICANO MOVEMENT

Crystal City is located in Zavala County, south Texas. Like most of south Texas, it is an agricultural community. The warm climate is conducive to growing vegetables in the late winter and early spring, and the entire locale is popularly known as the "winter garden area." Crystal City is considered "the Spinach Capital of the World," and its economy is controlled almost exclusively by the Del Monte Company, which processes the spinach grown there. Its work force consists almost entirely of Mexican Americans employed either as farm workers or as laborers in the processing plant. In 1960, the median years of education among Mexican Americans was 2.3, and the median income was $1,732.

Though the 1960 Census showed Mexican Americans comprising 74.4 per cent of the population of Zavala County and 85 per cent of the population of Crystal City (Browning & McLemore, 1964; Martinez, 1969), control of political power

121

had always been in the hands of Anglos. Moreover, all agricultural land and 95 per cent of the city's businesses were owned by Anglos (Comejo, 1970). In brief, an Anglo numerical minority controlled the destiny of *la raza*.

Political participation has always been theoretically possible. Traditionally, however, Mexican Americans had either been discouraged from voting or had only been encouraged to vote in a *patron* system dominated by political bosses. More recently, participation within existing parties was seriously limited by (a) a poll tax (until 1966), (b) primary election dates, (c) the cost of primary run-offs, (d) mobility of migrant workers, (e) cultural differences, and (f) the low level of education among Mexican Americans.

Strains have always existed between Anglos and Chicanos. Skin color and cultural differences often provided the rationale for differential treatment of Chicanos by Anglos. Police harassment has been the most blatant form of discrimination. The Texas Rangers, as well as local police officials were widely known for their brutality;[1] only within recent years has *one* Mexican American been added to the Texas Ranger force as a token appeasement by *los rinches*.

The PASO "Pilot Project" In 1963 Crystal City made history. Through the organizational efforts of the Political Association of Spanish-Speaking Organizations (PASO), in coalition with the Teamsters Union, Crystal City witnessed a revolution by ballot. PASO's "pilot project" in Crystal City had worked: An Anglo-dominated political structure was toppled by Mexican American candidates elected by a Chicano numerical majority. An Anglo mayor of some 38 years was thrown out, and an all-Chicano city council was set up. The event was historic for the Chicano: it not only represented the first time that an all-Anglo political structure had been substantially overthrown, but more importantly, it represented the political potential of the Mexican American. However, PASO's hopes that there would be "more Crystal Cities" went unfulfilled. All Chicanos in Crystal City political offices,

1. For an excellent discussion of discrimination against Mexican Americans by law enforcement agencies, *see* U. S. Commission on Civil Rights (1970). *See* Procter (1970) for a discussion of Mexican American encounters with the Texas Rangers.

incumbents as well as new candidates, were defeated within four years.

Reasons for failure. Why did an event that was so politically equitable eventually fail? In an article on "Leadership and Politics," Martinez (1969) suggests two major reasons: (a) fighting among members of the all-Chicano Council over municipal affairs, and (b) unsolved city problems which caused even Chicanos to doubt the ability of their leaders. Mexican Americans subsequently turned against one another. Some were seen as opposing the interests of *la raza* and came to be known as *vendidos* (sell-outs). In addition to these factors, it is my belief that the Chicano Movement had not developed its own organization adequately to sustain this victory.

PASO originated the idea of a "pilot project" to illustrate the political potential of the "sleeping giant," but what eventually resulted was a Teamster-manned campaign fronted by PASO.[2] After PASO had demonstrated to the Democratic Party that it could successfully mobilize Chicanos, it abandoned the candidates to survive on their own. PASO's showing had gained for it a stronger coalition status in the Democratic Party, which appeared to be PASO's major concern.

The Chicano Movement lacked the organization necessary to replace PASO in Crystal City. What would have happened if the SNCC (Student Nonviolent Coordinating Committee) had abandoned the first southern community that they politically organized?

In another sense, the 1963 Crystal City revolt was premature. As Bill Richey, La Raza Unida's first City Manager of Crystal City, stated in an interview: "First, no programs were introduced to financially aid those candidates who might lose their jobs for political participation; and second, the campaign only focused on the city's elections." If precautions are not taken to protect a movement's victories, ground gained will soon be lost. Those who have lost, as the Anglos did in Crystal City, will reorganize and retaliate with new resources.

Economic reprisals should have been expected. Many Mexi-

2. *See* Conde (1963) and *Look* Magazine (1963).

123

can Americans who gained city council positions were fired from their jobs. Until an economic base could be built to absorb such victimized candidates, economic pressures posed serious threats to political and organization participation.

The failure in Crystal City demoralized the Movement. The conditions were not right. Trained leadership and Chicano consciousness among the masses needed to be developed. Six years passed before political change strategies were attempted again in the struggle for Chicano representation.

The MAYO
"Winter Garden"
Project

The Mexican American Youth Organization (MAYO) took the first steps to try out the newly formed La Raza Unida political party in Texas. This represented a major step toward Chicano political consciousness. The Chicano vote would no longer be taken for granted.

Formed in San Antonio, this student organization was originally financed by the Southwest Council of La Raza, a Ford Foundation project. Beginning with involvement in Chicano school walkouts in south Texas during 1968, MAYO has participated in almost every innovative change in the Texas Chicano Movement. In 1969 Mario Compean, José Angel Gutierrez, and several other MAYO members designed a two-year project to create a model for Chicano political activity. As a result, Crystal City and the "winter garden area" were chosen for a concentration of efforts; and the development of a national political party, La Raza Unida, began.

Precipitating factors. A school walkout at the local high school rekindled the political flame in Crystal City. On December 9, 1969, 1,700 students walked out of school and organized the Youth Association (YA) to negotiate their demands. Chicano students were protesting several issues, among which were the lack of bilingual-bicultural education and the discriminatory selection of cheerleaders. In order for a girl to qualify for cheerleader candidacy, Crystal City High School required that she have parents who had been graduated from high school in Crystal City—a modern-day version of the "grandfather clause."

Though school board officials still had not met their demands, students returned to school in January. YA continued to struggle, and later was subsumed by a broader community organization formed by MAYO's representative, Gutierrez. This new organization, called Ciudadanos Unidos, registered with the county clerk in January 1970. Its specified purpose was mobilization of local Chicanos as a political force. Ciudadanos Unidos, prompted by the school boycott and supported by Gutierrez' organizing abilities, filed for all school board positions on a La Raza Unida Party slate. A massive voter registration campaign followed.

Mobilization for action. La Raza Unida Party took advantage of three ensuing elections to mobilize Chicanos for political action: (1) city and school board elections in April 1970; (2) the Zavala County elections in November 1970; and (3) city and school board elections in April 1971. Three school board seats contested in the April 1970 elections were won by La Raza Unida candidates; defeated were two so-called *vendidos* and an Anglo who claimed to be half Mexican. Though this was not an elected majority, control became a reality when an already elected school board member switched his support to La Raza Unida, giving the latter four seats out of seven. In the city council elections, Pablo Puente and Ventura Gonzales, two La Raza Unida candidates, were elected to a five-member board. Again, an already-elected Mexican American switched his support to La Raza Unida, giving them another majority.

Immediately following this victory, Puente and Gonzales lost their jobs at local Anglo-owned business establishments. However, because La Raza Unida Party had control of the school board, both men were hired as teacher aides.

Changes effected. During the interim between April and November, La Raza Unida Party majorities were able to accomplish several major changes. Some of the changes made in the school system included bilingual education from kindergarten to third grade, bicultural education (Chicano Studies) in the secondary schools, and free breakfast and lunch programs. In addition, a moratorium was declared on the use of IQ and English proficiency tests, because such tests traditionally had been used to keep Chicanos out of college. Student records were declared confidential and therefore unavailable to selective ser-

125

vice boards. There were important changes in municipal government also. The city council passed a resolution revoking the jurisdiction of the state police and Texas Rangers from any road other than a state highway. Minor municipal offenses that were formerly tried by a judge were now to be heard by a Chicano jury—*barrio* peers. Finally, the local Del Monte processing plant, which had heretofore avoided paying city taxes, was annexed to the city in order to bring in added revenue.

Counter-Tactics. The April elections stimulated an intensive Anglo counter-movement. To get on the ballot for the November county elections, La Raza Unida held its county convention and selected six candidates. But in Zavala County the party was denied ballot status due to a typographical error stating 1969 instead of 1970 (McKnight, 1970). As a consequence of three state rulings and a federal court ruling, La Raza Unida was forced to run a write-in campaign.

When voters misspelled the name of one or more of the write-in candidates, election officials counted these votes for someone other than La Raza candidates. In addition, Mexican Americans were intimidated by Texas Rangers, county sheriffs, and Texas highway patrolmen; were given illegal literacy tests; were told that they had already voted; and were not given aid when illiterates desired it. Furthermore, Chicano poll watchers were not allowed to carry out their duties. One poll watcher was told by a county sheriff: "I ain't here to argue the law. That's a lawyer's job. I'm just saying I'm goin' to arrest you if you don't move on." With no federal authorities to monitor the elections, La Raza was helpless at the hands of county and state officials (McKnight, 1970).

The implementation of visible changes via representation locally and on the school board brought increased numbers of voters to the polls in the November 1970 county elections. La Raza Unida ran six candidates for county positions: a county judge, a county treasurer, a county clerk, a justice of the peace, and two county commissioners. Though La Raza Unida Party did not win any of the contested positions, it made a strong showing, obtaining between 34 and 45 per cent of the total votes for each position, on a *write-in* basis (McKnight, 1970, p. 6).

Nor did the county defeat demoralize La Raza Unida. In April 1971, three positions on the Crystal City council and two positions on the local school board were up for election. La Raza Unida Party candidates won all three city council positions (a mayor and two city councilmen) and both school board positions. La Raza Unida now had a solid majority on the board of education (5 seats out of 7) and all five positions on the city council.

These elections were also characterized by Anglo retaliations. The Texas Education Commission issued a series of complaints against the Crystal City school system the week before elections. Though the harassment was well timed, La Raza was able to counter criticisms and win the elections.

LA RAZA UNIDA
PARTY AND
ITS FUTURE
Experiences in Zavala County, south Texas, demonstrate how the development of La Raza Unida Party constitutes a major step in Chicano political consciousness. The Chicano vote can no longer be taken for granted. A report (Comejo, 1971) on a study by the League of United Latin American Citizens (LU-LAC) and the Mexican American Bar Association suggests that an all-out campaign to get Chicanos in the states of Texas, California, Illinois, and New Mexico to register and block vote could result in determining the outcome of the 1972 Presidential election. If the total Chicano vote in the Southwest and Midwest is to have such political potency, and if La Raza Unida Party is going to mobilize this potency, party organizers must begin now to cope with philosophical issues and problems in organization.

Political Machismo
The Chicano Youth Conference of Aztlan held in Denver, Colorado, in March 1969 issued a political position in *El Plan Espiritual de Aztlan* which read:

Political liberation can only come through an independent action on our part. . . . Where we are in a majority we will control; where we are in a minority we will represent a pressure group; nationally, we will represent one party: La Familia de La Raza.

In June 1971, the Chicano Youth Conference Political Workshop passed a resolution stating that "La Raza Unida will support only La Raza Unida candidates, and under no circumstances will it support either the Democratic or Republican parties."

The disillusionment of Chicanos with existing political parties cannot be overstated. But organizational efforts, especially in the *barrio* milieu, will probably meet resistance from Mexican Americans who are Democrats. To abandon the Democratic Party completely is difficult for some Mexican Americans (e.g., the case of the Mexican American Political Association (Comejo, 1971). Though leading Chicano politicians, such as Albert Peña of San Antonio, have announced that they will probably run as La Raza Unida candidates in future elections, it is doubtful whether other Mexican American politicians can make the transition from the Democratic Party to La Raza Unida Party. Certainly, Representative Henry B. Gonzales (D-Texas) will not make the transition. Thus, the question remains: How will La Raza Unida mobilize already-elected Mexican American Democrats who are cautious about abandoning the Democratic Party?

Coalitions. La Raza Unida Party organizers have been primarily interested in mobilizing Chicanos to political action. Many white liberals will interpret this to mean that whites, or *gabachos*, are not wanted in the Chicano Movement. This is simply not true. What is true is that racist *gringos* are not wanted in the Chicano Movement. For example, in Crystal City, a *bolillo*, Bill Richey, played an instrumental role in helping to develop La Raza Unida Party in south Texas. In fact, he was recruited by José Angel Gutierrez and was later successfully recommended by Gutierrez for the position of City Manager when Chicanos gained control of the city council. Support from white liberals, when genuine, is invited.

Coalition with blacks represents a different problem to be dealt with, especially in the *barrio* milieu. Though some Mexican Americans are reluctant to take steps toward coalition, most Chicanos accept its inevitability, if both groups coalescing have equal power. Whatever cautions exist stem from the competitiveness between minority groups created by the dominant society, and by the fact that in the past coalition with blacks has meant playing a secondary role to blacks. Furthermore, in a coalition where all three groups are involved (blacks, Chicanos, and whites), white liberals tend to support blacks over Chicanos. Such bias probably stems from white guilt, but will have to change considerably if Chicanos are to participate effectively in a coalition.

Candidates and staff for the Movement. The need for educated leaders and trained organizers could prove a limiting factor to Chicanos in organizing counties and communities. In Crystal City (*pueblo* milieu), most of the Mexican American-elected officials' educational attainment was low. Although one should not assume that education is a necessary prerequisite for holding public office, it nevertheless is helpful in the administration of public affairs.

What will happen when Gutierrez, the one leader with organizing skills, decides to leave? Moreover, what will happen in other counties and communities if La Raza Unida Party gains control but lacks skilled organizers? For the present, this problem is not acute, but may prove so when future Chicano candidates take power.

Finances and legal fees. How will the organizational activities of La Raza Unida Party be financed? It cannot continue to grow and still be solely financed from small contributions and honoraria from Chicano leaders' speaking engagements. Such funding may have been sufficient for activities in Crystal City, but will it be sufficient when political activity spreads to other areas?

Though white liberals are eager to support black organizations financially, they rarely recognize that other minority organizations are struggling to stay solvent. This might change, but it will not happen until whites become cognizant of the needs of other minorities. Another possible source of funding could be foundations, like those which actively support black voter registration efforts in the South. Outside funding, though, always poses the question: Will strings be attached?

Since court procedures are often used as social control measures, volunteer legal counsel is also needed. Though the Mexican American Legal Defense and Educational Fund (MALDEF) exists, it cannot handle all of the Movement cases. Though white liberal lawyers sometimes volunteer their time, on occasion they handle critical cases too lightly. If white lawyers do become involved, they must realize that losing a case for Chicanos means losing a means to survival. One case comes to mind: It was a liberal white legal firm in Texas that handled La Raza Unida's case in the courts when La Raza Unida Party was attempting to get on the ballot for the county elections in Crystal City. That defeat in the courts cost Chicanos two more years of waiting to get *representation* at the county level, when two more years could have meant *control* of the county.

CONCLUSIONS The potential for the development of Chicano political power is quite high in many rural areas of the Southwest, as well as in the urban *barrios* of the West. It is highest in areas which we have labeled *pueblo, ciudad,* and *barrio* milieux. The rise in Chicano consciousness is creating new opportunities for political change.

Though we discussed a situation where nonviolent change occurred, the threat of violence is always present. If Chicanos are not able to realize social change through legitimate means within the system, violence will inevitably erupt as the last resort for changing intolerable conditions. La Raza Unida Party cannot solve all of the Chicano's problems, but it can begin to implement tangible changes for the poor. It can begin to give hope where there once was none. Even before the exploits of Cortez, an Aztec chieftain, upon his election, spoke hopefully in prayer:

> Grant me, Lord, a little light,
> Be it no more than a glowworm giveth
> Which goeth about by night,
> To guide me through this life,
> This dream which lasteth but a day,
> Wherein are many things on which to stumble,
> And many things at which to laugh,
> And others like unto a stony path
> Along which one goeth leaping.[3]

La Raza Unida Party members, like the Aztec Chieftain, believe in "a little light"; otherwise they would not have sup-

3. From Simpson, Lesley Byrd. *Many Mexicos.* Berkeley and Los Angeles, Calif.: Univer. of California Press, 1969. P. xi.

ported attempts by the Chicano community to penetrate the
political abyss of American politics.

REFERENCES   Browning, H. L., & McLemore, S. D. A. statistical profile of the
Spanish-surname population of Texas. Austin: Bureau of Busi-
ness Research, Univer. of Texas, 1964.
Comejo, A. A report from Aztlan: Texas Chicanos forge own political
power. Speeches by Mario Compean and José Angel Gutierrez.
La raza unida party in Texas. New York: Pathfinder Press
(Merit Pamphlet), 1970.
Comejo, A. MAPA weighs political action for la raza. *The Militant,*
August 6, 1971, pp. 11 and 30.
Conde, C. Crystal City gave PASO the pilot project it needed. *The
Dallas Morning News,* May 7, 1963, pp. 17-18.
Grebler, L., Moore, J. W., & Guzman, R. *The Mexican American
people.* New York: Free Press, 1970.
Look Magazine. Other Texans: The last angry Americans. October
8, 1963, 68-70.
McKnight, P. How they stole la raza unida party's vote. *The Mili-
tant,* November 20, 1970, p. 6.
Martinez, J. R. Leadership and politics. In J. Samora (Ed.), *La raza:
Forgotten Americans.* New York: Harper and Row, 1969. Pp.
47-62.
Procter, B. H. The modern Texas Rangers: A law enforcement dilem-
ma in the Rio Grande Valley. In M. P. Servin (Ed.), *The Mexi-
can American: An awakening minority.* Beverly Hills, Calif.:
Glencoe Press, 1970. Pp. 212-227.
Sanchez, G. I. *Forgotten people—A study of New Mexicans.* Al-
buquerque, N. M.: Calvin Horn, Publisher, 1967.
U. S. Commission on Civil Rights. *Mexican Americans and the ad-
ministration of justice in the Southwest.* Washington, D. C.:
G.P.O., March 1970.

EL PARTIDO LA RAZA UNIDA:
CHICANOS IN POLITICS

Richard A. Santillan

In the last two years has appeared a new phenomena in the Chicano barrios of the Southwest.
There appears to be a significant move to establish
an independent Chicano political party. In fact, the
partido has already developed in Texas and Colorado. In Texas, for example, four counties are under
the control of El Partido La Raza Unida (the Party
of the United Race). There is also a possibility that
26 counties in Texas will be under the control of the
new partido in the future including San Antonio and
Corpus Christi. In Colorado in 1970, an entire slate
of Chicanos ran for almost every political office in
the state. The partido received 2-5 percent of the
vote. This was the largest total ever given to a third
party in the history of Colorado.[1] The vote total was
significant for two other reasons: (1) the campaign
was conducted without any real financing and (2)
the Chicano slate appeared late in the campaign.

In New Mexico a few years ago, Reis Tijerina ran
for Governor but was ruled off the ballot. Tijerina
was one of the leaders of the incident known as "the
Courthouse Raid" in New Mexico in 1967. Tijerina's
successor in 1970 was a Pueblo Indian Jose Alfredo
Masestias, the first Indian to run for Governor of
New Mexico since 1837. Currently, in New Mexico
there is talk of establishing a new Chicano political
partido (party). In California, groups of Chicanos
are now developing such a partido. The Chicanos
are trying to encourage Chicano voters to switch
from the Democratic party to the new partido. Many
Chicanos are optimistic that the party will become
official before the 1972 elections. This year Arizona
will host a Partido La Raza Unida conference. Its

THE BLACK POLITICIAN, July 1971, pp. 45-52.

main objective will be to develop the partido in Arizona.

This Chicano movement towards the establishment of an independent political party is new, but the fact that Chicanos are involved in politics is not. The Mexican-American has been involved in politics for many years. Before one can discuss the new partido, it is important that we look at those earlier political organizations which laid down the foundation and gave direction towards the development of a new partido.

We often hear the argument that most minorities who came from Europe to the United States were able to achieve middle-class status by becoming involved in American politics, "So why can't the Mexican-American do the same thing?" There is one important difference between groups that came from Europe and the Chicano: the European groups came here voluntarily whereas the Chicano was conquered by war. As history has shown, the victor of war does not give political equality to those they have conquered. In fact, it has been a policy of conquerers to deny the people they have conquered any political voice or representation. One has only to look at the American Indian. Where there was resistance by Mexican-Americans, it was crushed. Politically, the Mexican-American was crushed in two ways after the Mexican-American War: through the use of the "anglo" political machinery and through violence. A good example would be what occurred in California. In 1891, English as a requirement to vote was introduced by A. J. Bledsoe, a one-time member of the vigilante Committee of Fifteen, which had expelled every person of Chinese ancestry from Humboldt County. Bledsoe, quoted from a political platform of the day, warned of the necessity to "protect the purity of the ballot box from corrupting influences of the disturbing element...[2] The requirement of English was ratified in the form of a constitutional amendment in 1894 by popular vote. It was not until March 25, 1970 that the California Supreme Court declared that literate Spanish-speaking voters could vote in elections even though they cannot read English. The decision was unanimous. Justice Raymond L. Sullivan stated:

> ...It is hardly so compelling that it justifies denying the vote to a group of United States citizens who already face similar problems of discrimination and exclusion in other areas and

need a *political voice* if they are to have any realistic hope of ameliorating the conditions in which they live . . .[3]

But, besides the "legal" obstacles set up by the political powers, there were bloody confrontations between Anglos and Chicanos. Because the Chicano many times was without arms, he usually was the one who lost. In Texas from 1908-1925 there were hundreds of bloody battles. Cary McWilliams states:

> Like Texas and California, Arizona has a long record of Mexican lynchings. One Mariano Tisnado was lynched in Phoenix on July 3, 1873; Leonardo Cordoba, Clement Lopez, and Jesus Saguaripa were lynched in Tucson on August fourth of the same year, with a coroner's jury defending the lynchings. Still another Mexican was lynched in Bisbee, a stronghold of anti-Mexican sentiment, on August 11, 1882. So firmly were the Anglo-Americans entrenched in power that, in the 1890's, one reads of the enactment of ordinances outlawing Mexican fiestas in Arizona. There is also a record of a number of Mexican lynchings in Colorado.[4]

It was estimated that after the period of the Mexican-American War, thousands of Mexicans were killed because of anti-Mexican feelings. In an editorial of November 18, 1922 in the New York Times it was stated that "the killings of Mexicans without provocation is so common as to pass almost unnoticed."[5] This editorial was written almost 80 years after the Mexican-American War.

There were some groups of Mexican-Americans who were able to defeat the Anglo. These "outlaws," as they were referred to by Anglos, were found throughout the Southwest. These men have become heroes to many in the Chicano movement. In Texas, there was Juan Cortina and Juan Flores; in California, there was Tiburcio Vasquez and Joaquin Murrieta, among others.

It was not until the 1920's that several Mexican-American organizations were established. There are many reasons why the Mexican-American began to organize in the 1920's. First, many realized that the Southwest would never become part of Mexico again. Therefore, they knew that they now had to try and work within the American system. A second factor was the arrival of many Mexicans into the United States because of the revolution in Mexico.

The Mexican was now in the majority in many
areas, thus he did not fear the Anglo as much as
before. He could now try to organize without the
fear of being killed or sent to jail. The third factor
was that many Mexican-American servicemen came
home from World War I with a broader experience
of the political system of the United States. Their
conversations with other Mexican-Americans from
other parts of the nation made them realize that the
Chicano was discriminated as a group and not only
in one area. The fourth factor is described by
Miquel David Tirado:

> Some of the earliest organizations formed by
> the Mexican community in the United States
> were mutual benefit and protective associa-
> tions whose functions were similar to those
> served by the mutual aid societies set up by
> earlier immigrant groups to this country. By
> pooling their meager resources the Mexican
> immigrants learned they could provide each
> other with low cost funeral and insurance bene-
> fits, low interest loans and other forms of eco-
> nomic assistance.[6]

Some of these organizations formed in the 1920's
were: Liga Protectoria Mexicana which was established around 1923 to protect residents from expor-
tation from Kansas City; the Orden Hijos de
American established in 1921; and the League of
United Latin American Citizens (LULAC), formed in
1929. LULAC councils are found in 21 states and
this organization has a reported membership of
100,000. In 1938, a federation of Mexican-American
organizations in the Southwest organized into the
Mexican Congress. The Mexican Congress was to
work for the "economic, social and cultural betterment of the Mexican people, for a better understanding between Anglos and Mexicans, to promote organizations of working people by aiding
trade unions and to fight discrimination actively."[7]
In 1942, the Coordinating Council for Latin American Youth was organized for the purpose of exposing the plight of the Mexican youth. Most of the
organizations so far discussed were social in nature,
yet I agree with Tirado who states: ". . . that many
Mexican-American community organizations, although not manifesting the traditional attributes of
a politically-oriented body, have served a vital
function in advancing the political interests of the
Mexican-American minority, and may therefore be

referred to as community political organizations."[8]

It was not until after World War II that many Mexican-American organizations became political both in philosophy and action. There are two groups that organized in 1947 (the Community Service Organization (CSO) and the G.I. Forum). Both of these organizations were established by Mexican-American servicemen who returned from the war. Tirado described the Mexican-American serviceman who returned:

> The end of the War saw the return of a very different Mexican-American than had left for war four years previous. Having risked his life for the United States, the returning Mexican-American G.I. came back with a desire to participate actively in American society. These American-oriented war veterans were to transform the traditionally Mexico-oriented mentality of much of the Mexican-American community into a growing identification with American society and the Mexican-Americans' contribution to it.[9]

One of the first projects that CSO was involved in was the election of Edward Roybal to the Los Angeles City Council. Roybal had lost the previous election, and thus, CSO made it a point to try to get him elected in the next one. CSO succeeded in registering 12,000 Mexican-Americans by the end of the year. Before the election, CSO had registered 40,000 people in East Los Angeles. The result was that Roybal became the first Mexican-American (1949) to be a member of the Los Angeles City Council in 68 years. CSO later realized that its priorities should be in attacking the social problems of the barrio and that in so doing it would be impossible to work hard for a candidate for political office. The CSO has continued to work for voter registration but only to a limited extent. "This change in approach, however, did mean that CSO would never again publicly support a candidate for political office even though unofficial fundraising functions are held for those candidates responsive to the problem of the Mexican-American minority."[10]

The American G.I. Forum was established in Texas. A Mexican-American war veteran was refused burial by a funeral home in Three Rivers. A group of Mexican-American servicemen decided to organize and fight so that this kind of treatment would never occur again. The G.I. Forum is now organized in 23 states and believed to have a membership of 20,000. It was during the 1950's that the Forum had its greatest success in political elections. Once considered by many to be conservative, one now only has to read its newsletter to realize that the Forum is beginning to support many of the issues raised by the current Chicano movement.

Even with Mexican-American organizations working in politics, the Mexican-American still did not have a political voice at the end of the 1950's. The next step would have to be the formation of political organizations whose entire philosophies and actions would only be political in nature. We note that although the CSO and the G.I. Forum were political, both were non-partisan and both were involved in other issues besides politics. Therefore, the development of MAPA, PASSO, and ACCPE came about because the Mexican-American realized that what was needed now were organizations which were strictly political.

MAPA (Mexican-American Political Association) was established in California in 1958. It was established because Mexican-Americans believed that only through group pressure could they gain political representation. (MAPA will be discussed more in detail in the second article.) PASSO (Political Association of Spanish-Speaking Organizations) was established in Texas. It was the result of the "Viva Kennedy" movement in the 1960's. Many Mexican-American leaders and groups believe that the Mexican-American vote won the state of Texas for President Kennedy in the 1960 election. Therefore, many of them realized that the Mexican-American did have potential political power and thus decided to form PASSO. PASSO was very instrumental in the elections of Chicanos to the City Council of Crystal City, Texas in 1963. They have also been involved in voter registration and active in other elections. ACCPE (American Coordinating Council on Political Education) is located in Arizona. PASSO tried to organize in Arizona but was refuted. Instead, ACCPE was formed. It has a paid membership of 2,500 and chapters in 10 of Arizona's 14 counties.

Two-Party System Failed

After 1968, the Mexican-American again looked

at the American political system and found that the Mexican-American after almost 120 years of being an American citizen did not have any real political voice. The Mexican-American tried to work in the two-party system, but the system failed him. In 1968, the California Legislature did not have one Mexican-American in the Assembly nor the Senate, although there are nearly 3 million Spanish-speaking people in California. The Los Angeles City Council and the L.A. County Board of Supervisors did not and still do not have a Mexican-American member, although there are nearly 1 million Spanish-speaking people who reside in Los Angeles County. The United States Sénate has only one Spanish-surname member, Joseph Montoya of New Mexico. The United States House of Representatives has only five Congressmen with Spanish-surnames: Edward Roybal from California; Herman Badillo from New York; Manuel Luzan from New Mexico; Henry Gonzalez and Eligio de la Garza, both of Texas.[11] There is not one Mexican-American governor or mayor of any large city in the United States. This was the predicament in which the Chicano found himself in the late 1960's. Thus, the Chicano now realized that he could no longer work within the two-party system; especially the Democratic party. In the campaigns of 1956, 1958, 1960, 1962, and 1964, the Chicano population voted 95 percent or higher for the Democratic party.[12] Yet the Democratic party has given the Chicano "nada" (nothing). It is at this point that I would like to discuss the development of El Partido La Raza Unida in Texas and Colorado.

The Partido La Raza Unida was first established in Texas. One of the leaders of the partido in Texas is Jose Angel Gutierrez. In a speech in San Antonio on May 4, 1970, Gutierrez explained why and how the partido came into existence in South Texas. He stated that the partido was necessary because of the critical need for people to experience justice. Also, he said that Chicanos are tired of being represented by politicians who did not care about the people. Gutierrez believes that the most important reason for the establishment of the partido is that Chicanos need to be in control of their destiny. "We need to make the decisions that are going to affect our brothers and maybe our children. We have been complacent for too long."[13]

The conditions were ripe for a new political party in South Texas. The education level in Zavala county is 2.3 years. In La Salle county, it is 1.5 years. In Crystal City, the drop-out rate for Chicanos is 71 percent. The median family income in La Salle is $1,574 per year while in Zavala it is about $1,754.[14] There are other inadequacies such as police brutality, exploitation of Mexican-Americans by Anglo businessmen, and the ban against speaking Spanish in schools. Thus, Gutierrez and other members of MAYO (Mexican-American Youth Organization) realized that South Texas would be the first area where the partido might be successful. It is important to note that Gutierrez is from South Texas and so were most of the other members. The cry "outside agitators" used by Anglos to try and discredit Chicano movements did not work in this case.

Mario Compean, MAYO member, remarked that it was very important that Chicanos succeed in starting a new party. If successful, other areas in the Southwest would try and promote the new partido. "Chicanos took over the city government and inspired people elsewhere to become active. As a result of all this awakening, we have had—especially in Texas—a concentrated effort to make the Mexicano visible in every aspect of society, economically, politically and otherwise."[15] Members of MAYO believe true Chicano power should consist of controlling those institutions that will be relevant to the needs of the Chicano people.

When members of MAYO were trying to organize in Crystal City and other counties of Texas they realized that there had to be some kind of plan of action. Therefore, they set out to accomplish certain goals. The first was to establish a core of workers who would devote most of their lives to the partido. This nucleus is important because at all times there are people working to establish the party. The second was to bring real democracy to the counties of South Texas. In other words put the power in the hands of the majority. The Chicanos outnumber the Anglo about 70 percent to 30 percent and higher. Members of MAYO realized that there were 26 counties that had a Chicano majority yet not one was controlled by Chicanos. The third goal was direct confrontation with the Anglo. Members of MAYO realized that it was a necessity to polarize

Chicanos against Anglos. Chicanos wanted to expose the Anglo as he really existed: as an exploiter of the Chicano. The fourth goal was to transfer the businesses and economic establishments into the hands of Chicanos.

Before City elections were held in Crystal City, Texas in 1970, there was a massive boycott of the high school. Other schools in the area also participated. The students directed many grievances towards the school board. During the walk-outs two significant events occurred. Many Mexican parents realized how "racist" the school board members were when they refused even to hear the complaints of the Mexican community. The second event was that many Anglo businesses along with police tried to put down the Mexican community. Some businesses refused to serve Chicanos who participated in the walk-outs. One business fired two Chicanos on the spot. The owner believed that the two Chicanos were sympathetic toward the boycotts. Chicanos then boycotted Anglo establishments. Some of these businesses were forced to close and others were badly hurt. The Chicano makes up 85 percent of the consumers in Crystal City.

The school board finally gave in to the demands of Chicano students. Gutierrez explains: "Not long after capitulation by the school board did the gringos in the area learn what was next. The entire state of Texas also learned. For in this decade Aztlan would have its own political party. The new political party would be named La Raza Unida."[16] The Chicano party was legally filed in the Texas Winter Garden area and in Hidalgo County deep in the Texas Rio Grande Valley. The filing deadline was early in February, 1970. All county offices were being contested by La Raza Unida candidates in four Texas counties. A grand total of 16 Raza Unida candidates were running for political offices. After they met some technicalities thrown at them by the "establishment," the party was able to place its candidates on the ballot. The results were:

> Cotulla, Texas set the pace—two candidates for school board won and of the four city council seats contested, all now belonged to La Raza. The city government was now under new Chicano leadership.
>
> In Carriza Springs, the county seat of Dimmit, two school board seats were won by Raza

140

Unida sponsored candidates. La Raza Unida candidates in Crystal City won the school board election.

The score at the end of the day read: Raza 11; gringos 1. On April 7, 1970, a repeat performance occurred. All Chicano candidates for the city council of Carriza Springs and Crystal City won by even larger margin. The score now read: Raza 15; gringos 1.

Included in the 15 were two new mayors; two school board majorities; and two city council majorities.[17]

Since the elections, the Chicano candidates have made relevant reforms for the Chicano people of South Texas. Some of their activities include:

The school system in Crystal City quickly approved a bi-lingual and bi-cultural education from kindergarten to the third grade. Mexican counselors were sought and hired. Chicano principals, teachers, administrators, and a school attorney were hired. A free breakfast program for all elementary students was in operation by the last six weeks of school. A teacher housing package is being developed and so is the contract agreement for community control of school facilities.

An additional summer educational program for departing farmworkers' children was implemented. Mexican Independence Day (September 16) is now being considered as a school holiday. In nearby Cotulla, the new Mayor has begun preparations for a million dollar housing project, a feasibility study of street improvements; a summer recreation program; and the creation of a city manager's position.

Although the Cotulla school board does not have a Chicano majority, it has eliminated a discriminatory English proficiency examination which was used to classify Mexicans as mentally retarded. The board also dropped the prohibition of speaking Spanish on school grounds.[18]

To some outsiders these accomplishments may not seem like much, but for the Chicano people it is the first time that they have felt that someone really cared about their lives. Also, it is the first time that Chicanos are able to control their community. It is only the beginning, yet it already has done much for the people. For those who are skeptical, I can only say that the partido is spreading not only in the Southwest but also in areas such as the Midwest,

Kansas, Illinois and Wisconsin.

There are two other important changes that have come about because of the success of the partido. The first is that the partido now neutralizes two elements in the Chicano community: the "tio taco" (Mexican-American Uncle Tom) who can no longer take advantage of "his" people, and the second element it neutralizes is the Texas Rangers and other police departments. Gutierrez explained that the Texas Rangers would beat one or two Mexicans, but now that they face thousands of angry Mexicans, they are "scared shitless. The Texas Rangers have recently removed their headquarters from Carriza Springs to San Antonio, and their director, Captain Alee, has retired. The Texas Rangers finally forced him to. It takes a great load off of us here, not having a company of Texas Rangers eight miles away."[12]

The partido has made Aztlan a reality. Aztlan refers to the legendary homeland of the Aztec Indians in far northern Mexico (now the Southwest United States). It is the name young Chicanos in 1969 chose for the separate Chicano nation they declared to exist in the Southwest. It appears to many Chicanos that La Raza Unida is the latest step on the road to Aztlan. "Aztlan had to start somewhere," Gutierrez often tells Chicano audiences. "We think we've done that in Crystal City."

After the victories, Chicanos began to work to organize other Texas counties for the November, 1970 elections. In the November elections, Chicanos ran for county offices in Zavala, Dimmit, La Salle, and Hidalgo counties. In the first three counties because of "technicalities" they were barred from the ballot. The partido then decided to have a write-in campaign, but as most partido members realized, write-in campaigns have never been too successful. Yet despite the odds, they elected one write-in candidate, Raul Rodriguez, in La Salle County. Another write-in candidate lost by only 40 votes; another lost by 46 votes. But these write-ins were running in a county where the median grade level among Chicanos is 2.3 years. Gutierrez explains some of the difficulties they faced.

> "This is just unbelievable! It's like a miracle. I personally was able to teach three people how to write. They couldn't even write their own names. They just wrote the names of the candi-

142

dates. It was the first thing they ever wrote in their lives."[20]

Gutierrez believes that the November elections were also important because: (1) the popularity of the party, as opposed to half a year ago when it had its first victories; (2) it was a test of voter attitudes toward the accomplishments of the party and not just the party's name; (3) to see how the voters would stick behind the leadership of the party in spite of all the obstacles. Gutierrez believes that on all three points, the results were excellent. There were over 1,000 Chicanos at a partido rally before the election. Never have Chicano people responded in large numbers to political rallies in South Texas. As mentioned, the partido is now working to get the party on the ballot statewide for the 1972 elections.

"We are already working in three other counties, in three other communities, on the same kind of agenda we used here: a school walkout, then voter registration, and then the school board and city council elections. These are the communities of Pearsall, Frio County, Lockhard in Caldwell County and another town south of San Antonio. In January of 1971, we began organizing the party statewide."[21]

Thus, Gutierrez and other members of MAYO believe that the Chicano people are now on their way to controlling their own lives and communities through the partido.

Colorado was the second state in which the partido was established. The partido appears to be gaining momentum in Colorado. The philosophy of a new partido was first outlined in Denver in 1970. "Corky" Gonzales, who is the head of the Crusade for Justice, announced that day that a new partido would be established in Colorado and throughout the Southwest. Although the partido in Texas already existed, it was in Denver that Chicano delegates from the entire United States declared a National Chicano Party. Gonzales believes that there is "no real concrete movement until you have a political philosophy and ideology to align yourself behind."[22] The platform and philosophy of a National Chicano Party was developed. It consisted of different areas of political development. The first was that the partido would begin in the nation of Aztlan. The second was that the philosophy of the partido would be "El Plan de Espiritual de Aztlan." The third was the formation of a Chicano Congress.

143

This congress would consist of representatives from all the barrios of the United States. The fourth was that the party would not be concerned merely with elections but would work daily with and for the Chicano people. The fifth was that the Chicano Congress would be the governing body for all the party and would handle all political questions concerning the nation of Aztlan.

Although the National Chicano Party philosophy and platform was created, no national platform in reality exists. At this moment, all the state partidos are trying first to get themselves established. Once the state partidos are successful, then a National Chicano Party will be established. Gonzales discussed this situation: "I think it was a little premature to try to form the Congress of Aztlan last March (1970) at the youth conference. That wasn't really solid; it wasn't concrete. There were a lot of differences of opinion and there were no established Raza Unida candidates or representatives. I see it starting to develop now and out of this will come the Congress of Aztlan."[23]

The development of the partido in Colorado began in the town of Pueblo on May 16, 1970, at the Belmont campus of SCSC. There were over 800 Chicanos from the state who attended. Some of the candidates announced were:

Albert Gurule, for Governor. "I have the interest of the Chicano and the poor at heart. I'm perhaps more qualified than any of the other candidates running within the two party system, because I'm untarnished. I don't owe anybody anything and I don't have to worry about losing votes if I take a stand on an issue. I will be addressing myself to the needs of the people."[24]

George Garcia, for Lt. Governor. Garcia was fired from his job when it was learned that he would be running for the Chicano party.

Patricia Gomez, for the House of Representatives District 35.

The first La Raza Unida regional Conference was held in June, 1970, in Denver. More than 300 Chicanos attended. Committees gave reports on how the partido was doing and announced more candidates for office: Leo Valdez for State Treasurer and Marcus Saiz for Colorado State Board of Regents. There were other regional conferences held at Alamosa, Adams State College on June 20, 1970; Ft.

144

Collins, Colorado, June 27; and at Boulder, Colorado on July 11, in which over 1,300 Chicanos attended. At every one of these conventions candidates were chosen to run for different political offices. Over 30 Chicanos were chosen to represent the partido. It is important to note that the candidates were from almost every walk of life. The spectrum ranged from housewife to student. These candidates ran in the November, 1970, elections.

Basically the platform represented the needs of the Chicano people. The following is the official Colorado platform of the La Raza Unida party.

HOUSING: To implement and-or utilize those resources now available and to strive for those resources necessary to accomplish adequate housing for La Raza. We want our living areas to fit the needs of the family and cultural protections, and not the needs of the city pork barrel, the building corporations or architects.

EDUCATION: We resolve that schools be warm and inviting facilities, and not similar to jails in any way. We also resolve a completely free education from kindergarten to college with no fees, no lunch charges, no tuition, no dues. Spanish be the first language and English the second language and the text books be rewritten to emphasize the heritage and contributions of the Mexican-American or Indio-Hispano in the building of the Southwest.

ECONOMIC OPPORTUNITIES: We resolve that the businesses serving our community be owned by that community. Instead of our people working in big factories across the city, we want training and low interest loans to set up small industries in our communities. These industries would be co-ops with the profits staying in the community.

JOB DEVELOPMENT: We resolve training and placement programs which would develop the vast human resources available in the Southwest. In job placement, we demand that first of all racist placement tests be dropped and in their place, tests be used which relate only to the qualifications necessary for that job and we further demand non-discrimination by all probate and public agencies.

LAW ENFORCEMENT: We resolve an immediate investigation of the records of all prisoners to correct the legal errors or detect the prejudice which operated those court proceedings, causing their convictions or extra heavy sentencing. We resolve immediate suspension of officers suspected of police brutality until a full hearing is held in the neighborhood of the event.

REDISTRIBUTION OF THE WEALTH: That all citizens of this country share in the wealth of this nation by institution of economic reforms that would provide for all people and that welfare in the form of subsidies in taxes and payoffs to corporate owners be reverted to the people who in reality are the foundation of the economy and tax base for this society.

WAR IN VIETNAM: We resolve that the draft board be representative of the population and that members of the draft boards be 35 years or younger and that these draft boards be appointed every four years concurrent with the election for Governor. That this war is unjust and only a form of genocide that has been used against La Raza to eliminate our national resource—our youth! (20 percent of the killed in Vietnam.[25])

This is only a partial part of the complete platform. But it does give us the general areas which the partido sees as representing the needs of the Chicano people. With this platform, the partido campaigned in the entire state of Colorado. At the end of the election, the party received the most votes ever given to a third party in the history of Colorado. This was significant because the partido did not have any real financial backing.

After the election, Gonzales stated, "People who voted for La Raza Unida were those who were committed to our platform. And remember, 55 to 60 percent of our people are under the age of 21. As you know, in this state the 18-year-old vote was killed. We feel that if that had changed, this would have strengthened La Raza Unida by about fourfold."[26] Also, the election had indirect results for the partido. Both the Democratic and Republican parties came out with Chicano candidates to try and split the Mexican vote. What resulted was that two Chicanos running in the Democratic party were elected to the Colorado's House of Representatives. This is the most Chicanos in the House in the history of Colorado. Gonzales believes that this was not a weakness of the partido but the fear that the two-party system has of the potential partido political power.

Now that the 1970 November elections are over, the partido in Colorado is looking ahead to the '71 municipal elections. There are candidates at this time who are running for different political offices at local levels of government. In fact, a partido candidate is running for mayor in Denver and has a good chance of winning. The partido is also organizing for the 1972 elections.

Both the partidos of Texas and Colorado have so far been successful in most of their goals. This despite the obstacles that the two-party system structure has set up. Thus, Gonzales agrees with Gutierrez that "We intend to nationalize every service that's available, every institution that's in our area. Wherever we are the majority we say we are going to control, that's a democratic principle."[37]

FOOTNOTES

1. News item in *El Gallo,* December, 1970, p. 6.
2. News item in *Los Angeles Times,* March 25, 1970.
3. *Ibid.*
4. Carey McWilliams, *North from Mexico* (New York: Greenwood Press, Publishers, 1968), p. 127.
5. *Ibid,* p. 113.
6. Miquel D. Tirado, "Mexican American Community Political Organization," *Aztlan—Chicano Journal of the Social Sciences and the Arts,* Vol. I, No. I (Spring, 1970), p. 55.
7. *Ibid,* p. 59.
8. *Ibid,* p. 54.
9. *Ibid,* p. 62.
10. *Ibid,* p. 63.
11. Delfina Varela, "Undecided Leadership and Tradition Combine to Keep La Raza in Democratic Party," *Regeneracion,* Vol. I, No. 8, p. 3.
12. Stan Stener, *La Raza—The Mexican-Americans* (New York: Harper and Row, Publishers, 1969), p. 200.
13. News item in *La Raza,* Vol. I, No. 2, p. 28.
14. *Ibid,* p. 28.
15. *Ibid,* p. 25.
16. Jose Angel Guteirrez, "Aztlan: Chicano Revolt in The Winter Garden," La Raza, No. 4 (no page numbers)
17. *Ibid,* no page number.
18. *Ibid,* no page number.
19. News item in the *Militant,* December 25, 1970, p. 13.
20. *Ibid,* p. 11.
21. *Ibid,* p. 11.
22. News item in *El Gallo,* December, 1970, Vol. II, No. 10, p. 7.
23. *Ibid,* p. 7.
24. News item in *El Gallo,* Vol. II, No. 8, p. 8.
25. *Ibid.*
26. News item in *El Gallo,* Vol. II, No. 10.
27. *Ibid.*

THIRD PARTY POLITICS
OLD STORY
NEW FACES

Richard A. Santillan

As mentioned in the first article, a split is developing
between the Mexican-American community and the Democratic party in the Southwest. I've discussed the division
in Texas and Colorado. In this article I will discuss the
development of the Partido La Raza Unida in California.
This article will contain three major areas: (1) the development and philosophy of MAPA (Mexican-American
Political Association) and how it relates to the partido;
(2) some factors, political and non-political, that have
made the Chicano realize that he can no longer work
within the two-party structure and (3) the development,
philosophy, goals and accomplishments of the partido
in California.

As in the first article, it is important to understand why
the partido came into existence. Mexican-Americans in
California have been involved in politics for a long time.
But in the late 1950's, Mexican-Americans realized that
what was needed was a Mexican-American political
group. Earlier organizations were involved in politics but
they were also involved in many other areas. Therefore,
they could not concentrate their total effort in developing
political power in the Chicano community. Thus in the
late 1950's MAPA was established. Chicanos realized that
an organization such as MAPA had to come into existence
for several reasons: (1) there was no real Mexican-
American political representative in the local, state, and
federal level; (2) in 1958 Henry Lopez was defeated
for Secretary of State of California. In both 1954 and 1958
it was a Democratic landslide and Mexican-Americans
voted 95 percent or higher for the Democrats, yet not one
Mexican-American was elected; (3) There was a need for
a Mexican-American political pressure to elect Mexican-
Americans and other people sensitive to the needs of
the Spanish-speaking communities. One of MAPA's strategies was to establish a MAPA chapter in every assembly
district that had a Chicano population.

THE BLACK POLITICIAN, October 1971, pp. 10-18.

MAPA's Philosophy

After MAPA was established, it announced certain goals. Some of the goals were "the social, economic, cultural, and civic betterment of Mexican-Americans and all Spanish-speaking Americans through political action; the election and appointment to public office of Mexican-Americans and other persons sympathetic to our aims; to take stands on political issues, to present and endorse candidates for public office, to launch a voter registration drive throughout the state of California and to carry on a program for political education"[2] MAPA's philosophy was to get involved in the community not only politically but also in issues involving education, welfare, and economics. MAPA has been one of the leading forces against the Immigration Department and its harassment of Chicanos. MAPA understood that if it involved itself in the community, the community would realize the importance of MAPA.

After two years of existence, MAPA believed that it was ready to endorse and run candidates for political office. In 1960, the year John F. Kennedy became President, not one Mexican-American was elected despite a Democratic landslide and Mexican-Americans voting 95 percent Democratic. But MAPA did not fold under. They realized their successes as well as their mistakes. They believed with the experience of 1960, they could win in 1962. In 1962, MAPA endorsed three successful Mexican-American candidates: Edward Roybal was elected to the United States House of Representatives. He was the first Mexican-American ever elected to the federal legislature from California. Phillip Soto and John Moreno, both of Los Angeles were elected to the California assembly. Roybal is presently still a congressman. Soto was re-elected only once in 1964 and Moreno lost his bid for re-election in the same year. Thus in 1967, there was not one Chicano in the California legislature out of a total of 120 members, despite the fact that there were close to three million Spanish-speaking people in California. In 1968, Alex P. Garcia was elected and re-elected in 1970 from the 40th assembly district. In 1970, Peter Chacon, a Mexican-American, was elected from San Diego. He represents the 79th assembly district. It should be pointed out that Chacon's district comprises only about 9 percent Chicano population. On June 22, 1971, a special election was held in California for the State Senate seat in the 27th district. Assemblyman Garcia ran for the position. The race was a critical one for the Mexican-American community. There is not one Mexican-American in the Senate and there has not been one in over 120 years. MAPA's chapters 40th and 48th endorsed assemblyman Garcia. However, Garcia lost to assemblyman Roberti. Garcia did receive the second highest vote cast in the race.

149

In 12 years MAPA has not only endorsed some successful candidates but also has been instrumental in appointments of Mexican-Americans to positions of Superior Judges. But MAPA has not reached the success it had hoped for in the 1950's. There has been a confrontation within MAPA about philosophy and action. One of the major reasons why MAPA has failed is because it is basically a middle-class organization. It has not been able to relate to the masses of poor Chicanos who are the vast majority in the barrios. As explained by Ralph Guzman, "This class consciousness among the Mexican-American community has prevented many of the organizational achievements of the Mexican-American middle-class from serving to increase community participation among lower-class Mexican-Americans."[2] MAPA has also been criticized because it has been a "vote-getter" for the Democratic party. Although MAPA was to have been bi-partisan, it has almost worked entirely within the Democratic party. It has perpetuated the Mexican-American 'hip-pocket vote' for the Democrats, and, thus has lost its political leverage by putting 'all its eggs in one basket.' Another criticism is that many members have used the organization as a stepping stone to their own political careers and have not related to the Chicano community once they are elected or appointed. Their loyalty was to the Democratic party and not the community. These have been some of the obstacles which have prevented MAPA from gaining the political power that it once envisioned.

Political Evolution

The preceding has been a short summary of the development of MAPA. I have discussed its history, successes, and its failures. I believe that an organization such as MAPA had to exist before the partido. The reason is that Chicanos are now convinced that they can no longer work within the two-party system. The partido is the result of the political evolution in the Chicano community. MAPA was a necessary step in this evolutionary process. Chicanos should understand that the establishment of MAPA in its time in history was a militant move. The partido can learn much from MAPA and thus be stronger prepared in helping the Chicano community develop real Chicano political power in the barrios of California.

As pointed out earlier, it was the Democratic controlled legislature which in 1960 gerrymandered the barrios in such a way that it is almost impossible for a Chicano to win. For example, East Los Angeles, which has close to 800,000 Mexican-Americans and Mexicans, is divided into nine assembly districts, seven Senate districts and six congressional districts. The result is that not one of these districts has more than 30 percent Mexican-American registered voters.[3] This gerrymanding was accomplished under a Democratic Governor, Edmund 'Pat' Brown. This year the legislature is once again controlled by the Democrats. Chicanos feel that the Democratic party will give them nothing as they did in 1960. Assemblyman Walter Karabian, Assembly majority leader whose district encompasses a large Chicano population stated,

> When you start talking about reapportionment you're talking about a man's political career. As Assembly majority leader, I have duties to members of my party. I can't envision legislation which would sacrifice the present incumbents.[4]

Karabian reflects the opinion of most of the Democrats especially those with large Mexican-American populations. However, I will discuss more about reapportionment and gerrymandering in the next article. My purpose here was to show how the Democrats prevented Chicanos in 1960 from gaining political power and most likely will do the same in 1971.

In the 1970 elections, Mexican-American candidates planned a new strategy within the barrios of California. Their plan was two-fold: (1) to run an anti-Democratic party campaign and (2) to run on Chicano issues and unite the Chicano people into block votes. Both these plans were successful. In an article entitled "Chicanos Long Love Affair With The Democratic Party Ends," the late Ruben Salazar discussed some of the local campaigns within the barrio. Salazar observed that the Chicano candidates were not so concerned about winning as they were in trying to make the Mexican-American community more independent of the Democratic party. The Chicanos ran on barrio issues and blamed, not the Republicans, but the Democrats for the conditions in the barrio. As one worker said "We discovered that it wasn't a love affair at all, but really a kept woman situation. The party took us for granted and gave little in return."[5] Salazar concluded that "the trend in the barrios right now is Chicanos first, party second. And the emphasis is on organization more than election."[6] One of the candidates was Abe Tapia, MAPA state-wide president. He ran against the incumbent Walter Karabian of the 45th Assembly district. Tapia ran on barrio issues, he had no Anglo advisors, and promised not to compromise. He followed the advice given to him and other Chicanos by Cesar Chavez. Chavez told them not to worry about immediate results, but to work toward organizing the barrios of California. Tapia stated "I got 29 percent of the vote and the district is almost 30 percent Chicano. I went for the Chicano vote and that is what I got. Why should I complain?" Another Chicano who had an impressive loss was Oscar Z. Acosta, who ran for the office of County Sheriff. Acosta is a Chicano lawyer who has defended Chicanos in cases known as the "E.L.A. 13", "The Biltmore 5", "Catolicos por La Raza", "Corky" Gonzales, and others. He was also the first attorney to test the exclusion of Spanish surname persons from the Grand Jury and other juries as well. One of the main issues Acosta ran on was community control of the Sheriff's Department. Although many people believed that this was a radical move, Acosta received over 110,000 votes or about 10 percent of the votes cast. He didn't come close to Pitchess, but he received more votes than Everett Holladay, Monterey Park Chief of Police. It should also be pointed out that in this election the 18-20 year old votes were not cast. In many cases of police brutality it is the young Chicanos who receive the blunt force of the Sheriff's Department, yet, they were not allowed to vote. If they had, the race could have been even more interesting and much closer.

"Down With Gringos"

The last candidate to be discussed is Ricardo Romo, a Chicano who ran for Governor of California under the Peace and Freedom Party. His campaign was important for two main reasons: (1) he was running to become the first Chicano Governor in over 100 years and (2) he received endorsements from Mexican-American organizations and some labor unions which in the past endorsed the Democratic Party. A good example of this would be the State Wide MAPA convention held last year in Fresno. Both Romo and Democratic candidate Jesse Unruh appeared before the MAPA convention to ask members for their support and endorsement. When Unruh appeared before the group, there were loud boos and shouts of "down with the gringos". But more important was that the shouts were aimed at what Unruh stood for—the Democratic party. When Romo appeared, he received massive approval and shouts of "Chicano Power". After both gave reasons why he should be endorsed, the delegates cast their votes. MAPA realized that if it supported Romo, the Democratic party would act hostile toward MAPA in the future. Yet, MAPA realized that some protest had to be made clear to the Democratic party. When the votes were counted, Romo beat Unruh 79-46 and received MAPA's endorsement. Unruh was disappointed and would later suffer another set-back. The Congress of Mexican-American Unity, which was basically a "rubber stamp" for the Democratic party, also endorsed Romo over Unruh. The Congress is made up of about 250 Mexican-American organizations. Also, some Chicano unions endorsed Romo over Unruh. Labor, traditionally, in the Chicano community has been Democratic yet they, too, are becoming dissatisfied with the Democratic party. In reality Romo did not have a chance to win. But defeat can also accomplish positive effects. His campaign was a warning to the Democratic party that the Chicano community was tired and dissatisfied with it. Over 67,000 people voted for Romo. The majority of them were Chicanos. Thus, we can note that the Democratic party cannot afford to lose Chicanos in such numbers. Again this vote did not reflect the 18 30 year old vote. It should be pointed out that the Chicano community is the youngest minority in the United States. It is reported that 50 percent of its population is under 25 years of age. After MAPA endorsed Romo, one worker stated, "Chicanos have usually voted Democratic. This has served to placate the Mexican-American community. With us in their pocket, they didn't have to do anything for us. By splitting off into a third party if we're organized, we could swing the election either way and determine what candidate is going to be elected. This puts a hell of a lot of pressure on the major party candidates to give us attention."[8] After being endorsed, Romo immediately called for unification of all Chicano organizations. Romo told the delegates to turn their backs on "self-serving" politicians and to begin thinking about forming a third party. Many Chicanos believe that 1970 was a milestone for Chicanos in politics. It was the beginning of a new decade that would bring political power to the barrios of California.

Dormant Congressman

Some Chicanos went so far as not endorsing Congressman Edward Roybal. In February 1970, the Congress of Mexican-American Unity did not endorse Roybal for political office. Although Roybal is the only Mexican-American from California in the federal legislature, many Chicanos believe that he is not meeting the needs of the Mexican-American community. One Chicano law student stated, "he's been more or less a dormant congressman and has been in office for 8 years."[9] The vote was 217-134 to hold back the endorsement. Again, it must be emphasized that the vote was not only against Roybal's record, but because he is a Democrat. Chicanos are demanding more than just token representation.

Campaigning by Democrats in East Los Angeles was not only tough but a little "dangerous" as well. One example was what occurred in October, 1970 with former Congressman John V. Tunny. Tunny went into East Los Angeles to try and convince the people to vote for him for United States Senator. Within a few minutes, he was forced to flee by car from the barrio. A large group of Angry Chicanos began to complain about how the Democratic party was insensitive to the needs of the community. Tunney later stated that he left because he felt his life was endangered. Some newspaper reports indicated that Chicanos jumped on his car and kicked it before it left. Before the incident, Tunny had tried to give a speech but was cut short by shouts of 'Chicano power'. One of the leaders of the demonstration explained why the incident occurred, "These politicians are supposed to represent us and whenever we have problems, they never represent us."[10] He said Tunny, whose districts include Riverside and Imperial counties, "has never done anything for us—he has always represented the power structure—the farmers." This statement refers to attempts to organize farmworkers in these counties by the Farmworkers Union headed by Cesar Chavez.

But, although, most Chicano frustrations are aimed at the Democratic party, Chicanos are also dissatisfied with the Republican party. The Republican party noting the split between the Democratic party and Chicanos have tried to take advantage of this situation. But their conduct and behavior has been the same as Democrats—false promises, false hopes, and token representation. I will give some examples on how the Republican party has tried to win Chicano votes and how, they too, have exploited the Chicano community.

'More Rhetoric'

On May 29, 1969, Martin G. Castillo was sworn in as Chairman of the United States Inter-Agency Committee on Mexican-American Affairs. Also Henry Quevedo would be the committee's executive Director. Quevedo is the son of the late Eduardo Queveda, long-time President of MAPA. Castillo stated that although he was a Democrat, he felt the Democratic party had given the Mexican-American 'more rhetoric' than help and charged that under the Democratic Administrations,

> "When the time came for my people to be helped, we were overlooked or dumped together with other minorities. I am convinced that President Nixon will provide a substantial thrust at the problems of the Mexican-American. His attention and concern are more than ceremonial efforts of regination."[11]

Later President Nixon appointed Hilary Sandoval Administrator of the Small Business Administration. It was the highest appointed position ever held by a Mexican-American in this country's history. Because of Sandoval's appointment, a letter to President Nixon appeared in the Los Angeles Times. It was sent by a group of Mexican-American businessmen. The letter thanked the President for his appointment and ended with these words, "America, our country, is a great Nation, not because what government does for the people, but because

what people do for themselves and their neighbors . . .
the Bridge you design to bring us together is becoming
a human reality."[12] Within eight months after this letter
was printed, Castillo, Quevedo, Sandoval, and other
Mexican-Americans in the Republican Administration
'resigned'. Better words would be "were fired." There is
much speculation why these 'resignations' occurred. But
the Chicano community knows that there were two main
reasons: (1) In the 1970 elections, Chicanos continued to
vote Democratic and in many races, their votes defeated
Republicans and (2) the 'police riots' of East Los Angeles
embarrassed the Administration because of talks at that
time between President Nixon and Former President
Diaz-Ordaz of Mexico. At these talks, President Nixon
explained to President Diaz-Ordaz how the Mexican-
American was becoming an equal member of the American society. When the 'police riots' occurred, Nixon found
himself in a very uncomfortable position. Nixon blamed
Mexican-Americans in his Administration for not keeping him informed of the tense situation within the barrios
of the United States. Thus it became clear not only to
Chicanos but conservative Mexican-Americans that
Nixon appointments were nothing more than just token
representations. Nixon had hoped that these appointments would sway the Chicano community to vote Republican, but when it didn't he got rid of his token
Mexican-Americans. Chicanos realize that Nixon was
thinking more about 'vote getting' rather than how to
solve the cruel conditions that exist in the barrios. Chicanos can now point out that there is not really a difference between the Democrats and Republicans.

Closer To Home

My last example will be closer to home. It is regarding
Republican Governor Ronald Reagan's position on the
Chicano community. Reagan told a group of about 400
people at the Mexican Chamber of Commerce of Los
Angeles that the Mexican community was entitled to a
voice in Sacramento and Washington. He discussed reapportionment and indicated that Chicanos should get
their share of representation. Yet it was this same man
who vetoed a bill that would have allowed a Spanish-
speaking person in each polling place to aid those who
can communicate better in Spanish rather than in English. This bill would have done several things: (1) it would
have given a large segment of the Chicano community the
opportunity to vote in their native language; (2) it would
have offered more jobs for Mexican Americans; (3) it
would have given the Chicano an opportunity to participate more in the political system of California. It is also
this same man who cuts welfare, medical, education, and
the Educational Opportunity Program, each one affecting

the Mexican American community. Governor Reagan, on one hand, says that Chicanos need representation yet he is one of the main obstacles that prevent Chicanos from gaining political power.

But besides the political factors that have alienated the Chicano community from the two-party system there have also been non-political factors. Although these factors were not political in nature, I will show that politics played an important role. Many times we note incidents affecting Chicanos without realizing that politics plays a hidden part. I am going to discuss four cases in which different segments of the community were involved. The first case involves the killing of two Mexican nationals by Los Angeles and San Leandro police.

On July 16, 1970, Guillermo Beltran Sanchez and his cousin Guillardo Alcazar Sanchez were killed when police raided their apartment and opened fire. The police believed that a murder suspect was in the apartment. The police were incorrect. City officials and the police both called the incident 'a tragic mistake.' In the Los Angeles Grand Jury investigation it was reported that the police used many incorrect procedures. Also there was a conflict of testimony between police and Mexican nationals who were in the apartment and survived. It should be pointed out that the murder suspect was later found but released because of lack of evidence. Although there are many aspects to this case, I would like to discuss the political ramification as the result of these killings.

Attempt To Win Votes

It should be pointed out that the Los Angeles Grand Jury did indict the police officers but the charges against them were dropped in a Los Angeles court. On October 30, 1970, Judge David N. Fitts dismissed the criminal charges against the four officers and apparently the case was closed. But in March, 1971, a Federal Grand Jury indicted the four police officers for violating the civil rights of the two Mexican nationals who they had killed. Indicted in the case were police officers Hector R. Zepeda, Sgt. Marshall F. Gaines, William Kinsella, and Jeffrey J. Fedrizzi. The reaction to the indictments was sharp and critical of the Nixon Administration by Los Angeles city officials. Police Chief of Los Angeles, Edward M. Davis charged that the indictments were 'politically motivated' and represented an attempt by the Nixon Administration to win minority (Chicano) votes. Mayor Sam Yorty stated that the charges were a challenge 'to the integrity of the Los Angeles Department.' Yorty did state that the shootings were a 'terrible tragedy' but he said that it did not justify the action taken by the United States Attorney (Meyer). Yorty said that Meyer was a 'political apointee' who did not have much experience in these type of matters. Meyer was appointed to his office by President Nixon with the approval of the former United States Senator George Murphy. Thus it became apparent to tho Chicano community that both political parties, especially the Republicans were using the killings for their own political gain.

But the most surprising political move was yet to come. Both Yorty and Davis asked the Los Angeles City Council to provide taxpayers money to pay legal expenses for the police officers. It should be noted that the city council (15 members) does not have one Mexican-American. The Chicano community protested against this request because they did not want their money being used to defend police officers who killed Mexicans. But the City Council voted 8-5 to defend the police. Some Chicanos felt that it was now legal to murder Chicanos. Those who voted against the defense were Councilmen Mills, Bradley, Lindsay, Edelman and Councilwoman Russell. Mills, Bradley, and Lindsay are Black. Those who voted for the defense were Potter, Lorezen, Farrarro, Bernardi, Wilkinson, Stevenson, Snyder and Gibson. The following were some of the council members reaction to the vote: Wilkinson, declared that the city had no choice but to defend police in a case "where they acted in behalf of the city." John Ferrarro, "we have to defend them if we expect them to defend the city." Richard Cruz, State Chairman of the Chicano Law Students, expressed the feeling of the community when he told the Council, "you are suggesting that Chicanos have to pay for the legal defense of the murders of our own people."[13]

On August 8, 1971, the four officers were found innocent on all charges. The Judge, United States District Judge A. Andrew Houk 'cinched' the outcome, according to one juror Robert J. Bombach. Judge Houk told the jurors that "I couldn't agree more. I think you made the right decision" and added that if any of the jurors were harassed by any Chicanos, "I'll land on that person with a heavy hand that he or she will never come out of jail. They better not come around monkeying with me or they'll be sorry."[14] After the verdict, the police officers talked with the members of the jury, shook their hands and expressed their thanks. Judge Houk told the jurors before they left, "You've all done your duty and worked long and hard without prejudice, in my view. You can go back to your regular pursuits and sleep like babies."[15] But it is difficult for the Chicano community to sleep not only because of the injustices by the political system but also by the judicial system as well.

Remove Judge Chargin

Yet U.S. District Judge Houk was not the only judge to do injustice to the Chicano community. In San Jose on September 2, 1969, Judge Gerald S. Chargin presided over a case which involved an allegation that a Mexican-American youth had sexual relations with his younger sister. Within minutes after the court proceedings opened, Chargin told the youth,

> "I don't know why your parents haven't been able to teach you anything or train you. Mexican people after 13 years of age believe its perfectly all right to go out and act like an animal . . . we ought to send you out of this country—send you back to Mexico. You are lower than animals and haven't the right to live in organized society—just miserable lousy, rotten people . . . maybe Hitler was right, the animals of our society probably ought to be destroyed because they have no right to live among human beings."
>
> Mr. Lucerno, the youth's attorney, stated, "The court is indicting the whole Mexican group . . . what appalls me is that the court is saying that Hitler was right in genocide."
>
> Chargin: "What are we going to do with the mad dogs of our society? Either we have to kill them or send them to an institution or place them out of the hands of good people because that is the theory—one of the theories of punishment is if they want to act like mad dogs, then, we have to separate them from our society."[16]

The late Ruben Salazar presented this transcript in the Los Angeles Times. It caused great anger within the Chicano community. The Chicano community in San Jose demanded that Judge Chargin be removed from the Bench. The city of San Jose has the largest Chicano population of any city in Northern California, 450,000. A presiding Judge, Joseph Kelly, told a group of 30 Chicano leaders that he could do nothing in removing Chargin. Paul Sanchez one of the leaders, stated later, "He rightfully informed us that he had no jurisdiction in getting Judge Chargin off the bench. However, what shocked us is that Judge Kelly was not sufficiently morally shocked by Judge Chargin's behavior to support us even philosophically."[17] The Chicano youth was innocent and only pleaded guilty because of his lawyer's advice. Judge Chargin later told newsmen, "I am pleased to say that my entire adult life, both in law and on the Superior Court bench, has been an effort for justice for all. The most recent example of this was my nomination of the only Mexican-American presently serving on the County's Grand Jury."[18]

The political aspect of this case involves the fact that Assemblyman Alex P. Garcia and several co-authors introduced a bill in February, 1970 to impeach Judge Chargin and to remove him from the bench. The resolution needed a simple majority of 41 votes in the Assembly. A two-thirds State Senate vote is required for impeachment. Although the Assembly has majority Democrats, many with large Chicano populations, Garcia's resolution could not get enough votes. We see then that Democrats did not respond to the outcries of the Chicano community demanding Chargin's removal. Thus, Chicanos saw Garcia's resolution die in the legislature and Judge Chargin still sits on the bench in San Jose. The Chicano community became more alienated with the Democrats and Republicans because their demands fell on deaf ears.

The third case involves the United Farmworkers Organizing Committee headed by Cesar Chavez. The present discussion seems to indicate that only Chicanos in urban centers are affected by political injustices. But the rural Chicanos are also affected by political exploitation by the two-party system. One of the leading organizations attempting to bring social change for rural Chicanos has been the Farmworkers Union. Yet in June, 1971, a Democrat, Assemblyman Kenneth Cory (D-Garden Grove) introduced a bill that would have prohibited strikes and boycotts, two of Chavez's strongest weapons. Cesar Chavez and over 2,000 supporters appeared in Sacramento to try and kill the bill. They were successful, but Chavez was not too happy with the Democratic party. He warned Democratic leaders in the State legislature that if they failed to discipline party members in matters vital to labor, they could expect a defection next year at the ballot box. Farmworkers, he said, could "boycott more than just grapes and lettuce."[19] Chavez stated that a political arm would be created within the Farmworkers union.

Pressure On Cory

Assembly speaker Bob Morreti (D-North Hollywood) said that Democratic leadership put enough pressure on Cory and thus he withdrew his bill. But Chavez stated that he was not in a conciliatory mood. Chavez said to thank the Democratic leadership for killing the bill would be like, "thanking the hangman for imposing an unjust sentence and then going on to commute the sentence."

Chavez and the farmworkers realized that a Democrat tried to push a bill that would have meant the destruction of the Farmworkers Union. In addition, it is significant to note that Assemblyman Alex P. Garcia voted in committee in favor of this bill. Garcia is one of only two Mexican-Americans in the state assembly. Unknowingly, the Democratic party is actually unifying the rural and urban Chicano because of its policies toward the Chicano community.

The final case involves all segments of the Chicano community. In the past year there has been much violence in the barrios in the Southwest. The worst has occurred in the barrios of East Los Angeles. There has been a series of confrontations between Chicanos and police and other institutions that perpetuate racism toward Chicanos. The following are some of the areas and dates of the confrontations: East Los Angeles August 29-31 (3 Chicanos killed and more than 1 million dollars in damage); Wilmington and San Pedro August 30-31; Barstow September 1; Delano and Redlands September 13; East Los Angeles September 16 (3 Chicanos wounded by gunfire); East Los Angeles January 9 and 31 (1 person killed and 20 Chicanos shot). Also, this year the city of Oxnard has seen the worst rioting in its history by the Chicano in that city. But the disturbances did not only appear in California. On June 5, 1971, the worst "rioting" in Albuquerque, New Mexico occured in that city. Nine Chicanos were shot, some of them were left in critical condition. The city officials in New Mexico blamed "outside agitators" for causing the trouble. But the Alianza, a Chicano organization, blamed the trouble on "123 years of racism and oppression in New Mexico of the Indo-Hispano by the Anglo." Since the confrontations in New Mexico, there has been more violence in other parts of that state such as in Santa Fe, Canjelon, Belen, and Esponola. In Denver this year, police wounded nine Chicanos at the Platte Valley Action Center. The city council refused to hear demands and complaints of the Chicano community.

One Real Change

Although the problems in the barrios are poor housing, inferior education, health, police brutality, and exploitation by businessmen, the city officials from California to New Mexico claimed that the only reason for the violence was because of "trouble-makers." The elected officials refuse to admit that there are problems in the barrio and that they are responsible for them. During confrontations last year and this year, Los Angeles Police Chief Davis said that the trouble was due to "swimming pool Communists." Mayor Sam Yorty, whose city has the most Mexican-Americans in the United States, urged Chicano parents not to let their children get involved in demonstrations because of the influence of Communism. Sheriff Peter Pitchess said that the trouble was caused by the "hoodlum element" in the Mexican-American community. He also contradicted Davis and Yorty when he stated, ". . . this violence was caused not by outsiders but by those who live in the community."[20] The Los Angeles Board of Supervisors also reacted to the violence in East

Los Angeles. Some of the reaction was: Supervisor Warren Dorn, "I think this proves that a moratorium should be called on Chicano moratoriums."; Supervisor Frank Bonelli, "The Chicano Moratorium demonstrations are doing considerable damage to the cause of the substantial majority of excellent Americans of Mexican heritage"; Supervisor Kenneth Hahn motioned that stricter limita-tions be placed on County parks for rallies. Parks have been the starting and ending points of many of the demonstrations.

This has been a very short summary of the confrontations now being staged in the Southwest by Chicanos. My point was to show that elected and appointed city officials refuse to recognize the problems of the barrios. As one Mexican-American said, "In one incident, the oppressed have become villain, while the villains who have planted the seeds of this destruction — the perpetrators of racists policies — are absolved merely by not being identified. When is local authority going to cope with the solution to the problem rather than prepare for another battle? The violence, destruction, and looting is abhorent and indefensible, yet less defensible are the ever present racist policies that fostered these acts."[1]

One year has passed since the major disturbance of August 29 in the East Los Angeles barrio. At that time many politicians promised to do something about the conditions in the barrio. Since last year unemployment in the barrio has increased, the school drop-out statistics remain about the same and, in sum, conditions in the barrio remain the same if not worse. There has been only one real visible change and this is the presence of even more police in the community. The East Los Angeles community more than ever has the appearance of being a police state.

The last section of this article will explore the development, philosophies, goals, and accomplishments of the Partido La Raza Unida in California. I will first give a brief discussion of where the partido was first established and how it expanded throughout the state.

The partido first began in Northern California in the Bay area such as Oakland, Hayward, Berkeley, and Union City. Other chapters were later developed in San Jose and Fresno. The Stockton conference held in February of this year drew over 1,300 Chicanos. At this meeting over 14 chapters of the Partido from Northern California attended. In the same month, there were conferences held in East Los Angeles, Riverside, and San Bernardino. In March, a chapter was established in Sacramento. Since then, many areas have established chapters such as San Diego, San Fernando, Long Beach, Rio Hondo, Gilroy, Santa Cruz, Alta Loma and many others. Thus we note that the developmental process moved from Northern California down to San Diego. This process took approximately six months.

The next area of discussion will deal with the philosophies of the partido. Although there are many basic issues, there are some differences on others. I will discuss both these now. What I will do is take certain philosophies from each chapter's platform which are common to the entire partido.

One of the most important points is reflected in the platform of Northern California, it states,

> "La Raza Unida will not support any candidate in the Democratic, Republican party, or any individual who supports these parties."

This also extends to Peace and Freedom and American Independence parties. Another common and important point is

> "Any person of La Raza registered in La Raza and/or works activily to support the program and activities of the party will be considered a member with the rights to participate in all decision-making process of the party on the basis of one person and one vote. By 'La Raza,' we mean those people who are descendants of or come from Mexico, Central America, South America and the Antillas."[22]

The Sacramento chapter platform states,

> "This party is being formed as an alternative to the traditional stronghold the Democratic and Republican parties have on the United States political system. The Raza people recognize that these two parties have ignored the existing problems of the brown minority and in many cases have exploited them for their own advantage. Unify the brown minorities will be the key factor for organizing 'La Raza Unida'."[23]

The East Los Angeles platform covers several important areas. But some of the critical ones are those which the two party system have ignored. The platform states,

> "Parole conditions should be changed because of the injustices the pinto (convict) inside the pintas (prisons) suffer under today. That the political representation of La Raza Unida party will be fully involved and not partially involved in penal reform.
>
> Control of land: La Raza Unida will introduce bills into the legislature to free compesinos and give them back their land with cooperative control.

Most chapters have within them labor committees. The East Los Angeles labor committee reflects basically the view of all the chapters,

> "The majority of Chicanos in this country are working class people. Therefore, we demand an end to the deplorable working conditions, low wages, discrimination, exploitation. We demand full employment

162

for our people."

Education: "We recognize that education has been used as a tool by a racist system to keep Mexicans down, the causes of unemployment, poverty, the welfare cycle, and the lack of Chicano professionals to serve the community are related in a direct way to the inferior schools of our communities. The education we receive is designed to destroy our cultural identity and pride and thus dehumanize us; as well as to channel us into the bottom rungs of our society and the economic scale."[24]

From the San Fernando Valley platform,

"La Raza Unida will be and is a mechanism and vehicle for both political control of local government bodies, such as city and county governments, school boards, and judicial districts as well as for maximum and total bargaining power of the Chicano community in the total electoral and governmental process in this county. La Raza Unida Party through its candidates and its platform getting on the November general election ballots, shall have the power to deny our votes to the lesser-of-two-evils candidates and parties of the Anglo establishment — the Democratic and Republican party — by running our own candidates on our own platform."[25]

This is only a partial list of some of the common areas of La Raza Unida Party.

There are basically only two areas where there is a difference between Northern and Southern California. Both of these are related. Northern California has a foreign policy and Southern California does not. The second difference is that Northern California believes that "raza" means South and Central Americans, Cubans, and other Spanish-speaking people. Southern California sees "raza" as meaning Chicanos or Mexican-Americans. In some chapters in Northern California, much of the work is done by non-Mexican American Spanish-speaking people. Although Chicanos in Southern California have attempted to involve other Spanish-speaking people they have been unsuccessful. But, these differences are not a hindrance to the party. In fact the partido prides itself that it is flexible enough to be able to reflect the needs of each individual community.

The next area will be a discussion of the goals of the partido. One of the important goals is to register enough people to put the party on the ballot for next year's election (1972). It is required by state law that the partido register 66,344 people under La Raza Unida Party before December 30, 1971. If successful, the partido can run candidates in next year's primary and general election. Another goal for the partido is a reunification of Mexico ending the occupation of Northern Mexico (Atzlan). There are many who believe that Mexicans on both sides can work toward a partido that will once again unite them. A

163

third goal will be cooperative community ownership of all places of employment whether they be businesses, factories, or farms. This will be the only way to end discrimination and economic exploitation. In education the goals are as follows:

1. The establishment of a Chicano school district whose members are accountable to the community.

2. Bilingual education should be initiated in community schools. Spanish should be taught by Chicanos.

3. Open admissions in the colleges should be obtained with full support (academic and financial) for all Chicanos without regard to entrance examinations.

4. There should be expansion of efforts through the party to recruit more of our youth into the professions, e.g., health, law, education, teaching, etc.

5. We should strive to develop our own schools, from the elementary level to the University level.

6. We should strive to establish community control of our local schools. Parents should form a policy-making body to hire and fire teachers, administrators, the budget matters, etc. There should be maximum participation of the parents in all aspects of their childrens' education.[26]

Another goal of La Raza Unida Party is equality for Raza women:

> Raza men and women both, will co-operate fully in this party and at home, in the very difficult task we have before us of freeing our women and encouraging them in every way we can, at all times, to become involved in every level of the struggle, and in working actively towards the elimination of all attitudes and practices that have relegated our women to the unquestionable bondaged positions they are now in.[27]

Philosophical Aspects

The underlying theme in all these goals is the complete control of all institutions that affect the Spanish-speaking people. Philosophy and goals are almost necessarily related. Therefore, the philosophical aspects of the partido describes how things are and the goals discuss what things will be in the future for Raza.

The last area will be the accomplishments of the partido. Although La Raza Unida Party is not a "legal" party, it has already done much for the people. For the partido there are thus far two types of accomplishments: political and social. I will first discuss the political accomplishments. Candidates of La Raza Unida Party made a good showing in their first election in Oakland last April 20. Tito Lucero ran for councilman at large and received 1,087 votes. Florencia Medina, a candidate for the Oakland Board of Education, won almost 27,000 votes or 33 percent of the votes cast against the Anglo in that office. Also, Trinidad Lopez, a Raza Unida candidate for the Board of Trustees, received 25,000 votes or more than 25 percent of the votes. Two other La Raza Unida Party candidates ran in Berkeley and also had a very good showing. All the above candidates ran as Independents but reflected the idealism of La Raza Unida Party. An incident ten days before the election shows the strength of Raza Unida Party as much or perhaps more than the votes. One of the La Raza Unida candidates, Antonia Rodarte, was dropped from the slate because he endorsed a regular Democratic candidate. Thus the partido made it clear that it will not be exploited by "sell-outs" and that it does not endorse any other political party.

In San Diego, at this time, there is an Independent candidate running for Mayor under the platform of the Partido La Raza Unida. His name is Gilberto Robledo and the election will be held next month (September). The reason he is running is for more Chicano representation but also "to spread the word about La Raza Unida in the political areas. Raza Unida has had successes in such places as Texas and Colorado. It is a Party that is gaining momentum in California. The building of a political base is important in bringing our needs to the gabacho (anglo) in city government and thus he will see that we will have a basis to bargain from."[28] There are nine candidates who are running for the Mayor seat. Robledo is the only "minority" running and some believe that a large minority vote may put him in a run-off.

In voter registration, La Raza Unida has been very successful. A good example would be the East Los Angeles chapter. Every Saturday, members of La Raza Unida go into the community, house to house, and register for the partido. During the week, members attend meetings and visit various service centers. What has resulted is that from April to July of this year, approximately 10,000 people have registered in the East Los Angeles area. 47 percent have registered for La Raza Unida, 33 percent registered Democrat, 2 percent registered Peace and Freedom, and the rest registered in other parties or declined to state party affiliation. Thus, in East Los Angeles, almost 1 out of every 2 people who registers to vote are registering into the partido.

Social Effects

But there has also been social effects by the partido such as unification, organization, and grass-roots participation. The partido has been one of the strongest tools ever used to unify the Chicano community not only in California but throughout the Southwest. A good example would be Southern California. The barrios of East Los Angeles, San Fernando, Long Beach, Pico Rivera, Norwalk, and others in the past have lacked communication and have been isolated from each other. But with the partido, the Chicano barrios now have something that all can identify with. Chicanos in Southern California, like their counterparts in Northern California have met in several meetings and exchange ideas and types of action to bring change in the barrio. Thus, the partido has not only brought together Chicanos in Southern California but between North and South, urban and rural. Because of the partido, there is now better understanding and communication of all the barrios as there has never been before.

Grass Roots

Another positive factor of the partido is the involvement of grass-roots people. As mentioned before, many Mexican-American organizations have been middle-class and therefore could not relate to the poor Chicanos or Latinos. But La Raza Unida has within it, welfare recipients, ex-convicts, students, 'vatos-locos, young and old, radical and conservative and other people who have never been involved in politics before in their lives. The partido is giving raza a chance to participate in something that will bring social and political justice to their barrios. Because of its goals and aims, many poor Chicanos are better able to relate to the partido more so than to any previous organization.

There are many more positive effects, but I would like to discuss just one more. As mentioned before, violence has occurred within the barrios of the Southwest. The Chicano who strikes in anger cannot be blamed. In fact, he should be given credit for confronting the racist institutions that affect him. But nothing is being accomplished. The partido believes that it can be a peaceful tool to bring social change within the community. The philosophy of La Raza Unida is not to burn down the schools but to control them; not to burn down the stores, but to control them; not to burn down the welfare departments, but to control them; not to burn down the police stations but to control them. Chicanos and Latinos believe that "Raza Power" means controlling those institutions that affect the Spanish-speaking communities. Many Chicanos and Latinos believe that La Raza Unida Party is the way to accomplish this in the future.

Series of Events

In conclusion, I have tried to summarize the reasons why the Partido was established in California. It is not easy to isolate only one reason for the establishment of the Partido. As shown in this article, it has been a series of events which has led to the partido's existence. It is reported that by 1980, one out of every five people in California will be a Mexican-American.[29] Therefore, the importance of the partido now is very vital to the future of the Chicano community.

Since my last article, there has been good news from Texas. The partido there has had more victories. In Asherton, they won some seats on the school board. In the Pharr-San Juan-Alamo school district, two La Raza Unida candidates were elected, resulting in a total of five Chicanos out of seven on the board. Elections for Mayor and two City Commissioners were held in San Juan on April 3, 1971. All three offices were won by La Raza Unida candidates giving them complete control over the city administration. Almost all their opponents were Anglos. It is significant that the turn-out for these elections was the largest ever in that Chicano community.

It's About Time

In Denver, Colorado this May, a slate of La Raza Unida candidates ran for Mayor, City Council, and School Board. There is also going to be a Southwest Conference of all La Raza Unida Parties in Denver over the Thanksgiving weekend of this year. With the popularity of the Partido in the Southwest, this conference could prove to be a historic one for all "raza" in the United States.

In closing, I believe that the following incident expresses what La Raza Unida is trying to accomplish in the barrios. A Chicano college student approached a husky Mexican-American construction worker and asked him in Spanish if he has ever heard of the Partido La Raza Unida. The man said no and thus the student explained to him what the partido is trying to do. The man registered for La Raza Unida and then reflected, "Era Tiempo" (It's about time).

FOOTNOTES

1. Kaye Briegel, "The Development of Mexican American Organizations," Manuel P. Servin. *The Mexican Americans: An Awakening Minority*, p. 174.

2. Miguel D. Tirado, "Mexican American Community Political Organization" *Atzlan*, Spring, 1970, Vol. 1, p. 67.

3. Editorial in the *Los Angeles Times*, August 23, 1971.

167

4. News items in *Los Angeles Times*, August 8, 1971.

5. Ruben Salazar, "Chicanos' Long Love Affair With Democratic Ends," *Los Angeles Times*, May 29, 1970.

6. *Ibid.*

7. Ruben Salazar, "To The Chicanos It Is How Narrowly A Candidate Lost," *Los Angeles Times*, June 5, 1970.

8. Richard Vasquez and Frank Del Olmo, "Unruh, Romo Seek Support of Chicanos," *Los Angeles Times*, August 2, 1970.

9. Bell Boyarsky, "Latin Political Group Refuses to Endorse Roybal Re-election," *Los Angeles Times*, February 16, 1970.

10. Carl Greenberg, "Chicanos Jump On Tunney Car as He Leaves L.A. Rally," *Los Angeles Times*, October 18, 1970.

11. News item in the *Los Angeles Times*, May 29, 1969.

12. News item in the *Los Angeles Times*, February 24, 1970.

13. News item in the *Los Angeles Times*, March 6, 1971.

14. News item in the *Los Angeles Times*, August 8, 1971.

16. *El Grito*, Fall, 1969, Vol. III, No. 1, p. 5.

15. *Ibid.*

17. Ruben Salazar, "Judge's Latin Slurs Bring Call for Removal," *Los Angeles Times*, October 2, 1969.

18. *Ibid.*

19. William Endicott, "Democratic Chiefs Warned by Chavez on Labor 'Harassment'," *Los Angeles Times*, June 8, 1971.

20. News item in the *Los Angeles Times*, February 3, 1971.

21. News item in the *Los Angeles Times*, February 14, 1971.

22. Northern California Platform.

23. Sacramento Platform.

24. East Los Angeles Platform.

25. San Fernando Valley Platform.

26. East Los Angeles Platform.

27. Northern California Platform.

28. News item in *La Verdad*, July-August, 1971, p. 10.

29. Mexican American Population Commission of California, "Mexican-American Population in California," April, 1971, p. 9.

PART V

THE POLITICS OF RADICALISM

El Plan Espiritual de Aztlan

In the spirit of a new people that is conscious not only of its proud historical heritage but also of the brutal "gringo" invasion of our territories, we, the Chicano inhabitants and civilizers of the northern land of Aztlán from whence came our forefathers, reclaiming the land of their birth and consecrating the determination of our people of the sun, declare that the call of our blood is our power, our responsibility, and our inevitable destiny.

We are free and sovereign to determine those tasks which are justly called for by our house, our land, the sweat of our brows, and by our hearts. Aztlán belongs to those who plant the seeds, water the fields, and gather the crops and not to the foreign Europeans. We do not recognize capricious frontiers on the bronze continent.

Brotherhood unites us, and love for our brothers makes us a people whose time has come and who struggles against the foreigner "gabacho" who exploits our riches and destroys our culture. With our heart in our hands and our hands in the soil, we declare the independence of our mestizo nation. We are a bronze people with a bronze culture. Before the world, before all of North America, before all our brothers in the bronze continent, we are a nation, we are a union of free pueblos, we are Aztlán.

Por La Raza todo. Fuera de La Raza nada.

Program

El Plan Espiritual de Aztlán sets the theme that the Chicanos (La Raza de Bronze) must use their nationalism as the key or common denominator for mass mobilization and organization. Once we are committed to the idea and philosophy of El Plan de Aztlán, we can only conclude that the social, economic, cultural, and political independence is the only road to total liberation from oppression, exploitation, and racism. Our struggle then must be for the control of our barrios, campos, pueblos, lands, our economy, our culture, and our political life. El Plan commits all levels of Chicano society -- the barrio, the campo, the ranchero, the writer, the teacher, the worker, the professional -- to La Causa.

170

Nationalism

Nationalism as the key to organization transcends all religious, political, class, and economic factions or boundaries. Nationalism is the common denominator that all members of La Raza can agree upon.

Organisational Goals

1. UNITY in the thinking of our people concerning the barrios, the pueblo, the campo, the land, the poor, the middle class, the professional -- all committed to the liberation of La Raza.

2. ECONOMY: economic control of our lives and our communities can only come about by driving the exploiter out of our communities, our pueblos, and our lands and by controlling and developing our own talents, sweat, and resources. Cultural background and values which ignore materialism and embrace humanism will contribute to the act of cooperative buying and the distribution of resources and production to sustain an economic base for healthy growth and development. Lands rightfully ours will be fought for and defended. Land and realty owner- ship will be acquired by the community for the people's welfare. Economic ties of responsibility must be secured by nationalism and the Chicano defense units.

3. EDUCATION must be relative to our people, i.e., history, culture, bilingual education, contributions, etc. Community control of our schools, our teachers, our administrators, our counselors, and our programs.

4. INSTITUTIONS shall serve our people by providing the service necessary for a full life and their welfare on the basis of restitution, not handouts or beggar's crumbs. Restitution for past economic slavery, political exploitation, ethnic and cultural psychological destruc- tion and denial of civil and human rights. Institutions in our community which do not serve the people have no place in the community. The institutions belong to the people.

5. SELF-DEFENSE of the community must rely on the combined strength of the people. The front line defense will come from the barrios, the campos, the pueblos, and the ranchitos. Their involvement as protectors of their people will be given respect and dignity. They in turn offer their responsibility and their lives for their people. Those who place themselves in the front ranks for their people do so out of love and carnalismo. Those institutions which are fattened by our brothers to provide employment and political pork barrels for the gringo will do so only as acts of liberation and for

La Causa. For the very young there will no longer be acts of juvenile delinquency, but revolutionary acts.

6. CULTURAL values of our people strengthen our identity and the moral backbone of the movement. Our culture unites and educates the family of La Raza towards liberation with one heart and one mind. We must insure that our writers, poets, musicians, and artists produce literature and art that is appealing to our people and relates to our revolutionary culture. Our cultural values of life, family, and home will serve as a powerful weapon to defeat the gringo dollar value system and encourage the process of love and brotherhood.

7. POLITICAL LIBERATION can only come through independent action on our part, since the two-party system is the same animal with two heads that feed from the same trough. Where we are a majority, we will control; where we are a minority, we will represent a pressure group; nationally, we will represent one party: La Familia de La Raza!

Action

1. Awareness and distribution of El Plan Espiritual de Aztlán. Presented at every meeting, demonstration, confrontation, court-house, institution, administration, church, school, tree, building, car, and every place of human existence.

2. September 16, on the birthdate of Mexican Independence, a national walk-out by all Chicanos of all colleges and schools to be sustained until the complete revision of the educational system: its policy makers, administration, its curriculum, and its personnel to meet the needs of our community.

3. Self-defense against the occupying forces of the oppressors at every school, every available man, woman, and child.

4. Community nationalization and organization of all Chicanos: El Plan Espiritual de Aztlán.

5. Economic program to drive the exploiter out of our community and a welding together of our people's combined resources to control their own production through cooperative effort.

6. Creation of an independent local, regional, and national political party.

A nation autonomous and free -- culturally, socially, economically, and politically -- will make its own decisions on the usage of our lands, the taxation of our goods, the utilization of our bodies for war, the determination of justice (reward and punishment), and the profit of our sweat.

El Plan de Aztlán is the plan of liberation!

[*Resolution adopted at the first National Chicano Youth Liberation Conference, Denver, Colorado, March 1969]

TILTING WITH THE SYSTEM
AN INTERVIEW WITH CESAR CHAVEZ

Bob Fitch

FITCH: The first question I'd like to ask is "Why boycott?"

CHAVEZ: You know, when you consider everything, we don't have any options. Most of the other things that would have been options depended entirely on the good will of the government and we know enough to know that they're not going to move. Especially, they're not going to move in a conflict situation like ours. Personally, the big reason was this: I thought the American public would respond affirmatively.

F: That's optimistic. Most of the predictions now about the American public are not optimistic.

C: They're not optimistic because they're clichés now — "the country's sick," and all those things. Really, we haven't tried to understand how institutions work. The common procedure is to insult your friends and to feel that they ought to drop everything they are doing and come in and help you. Theoretically that would be great. But if you're going to organize, and if you're going to be a realist, you know how much to expect and you're not going to be disappointed. You plan accordingly, along very realistic lines.

F: What's the realistic basis for optimism about a public response to the boycott?

C: Well, first of all, I contend that not only the American public but people in general throughout the world will respond to a cause that involves injustice. It's just natural to want to be with the underdog. In a boxing match, however popular the champion may be, if he begins to really get the other guy and beat him up bad, there is a natural tendency to go with the underdog. And in this struggle it's not a contest between two people or a team but a contest between a lot of people who are poor and others who are wealthy.

F: What happened to the other options? Such as legislation?

C: When you get into legislation you're playing with a borrowed bat. Once you get into legislation then it's the whole question of compromise. The only reason growers are seeking legislation now, after 35 years, is because they are under pressure. They want to use legislation to take away that new-found right the workers have found through the boycott.

F: What do you mean?

C: Legislation that's being proposed permits unions but takes the boycott right away from the workers, and doesn't permit them to strike during harvest time. Of course that's the only time we work. The proposal comes not out of a spirit of giving the workers civil rights, but as a gimmick to further restrict their rights.

F: Why can't you stop the importing of Mexican labor?

C: It's a long history of the government and the employers working together. Not the same program but different variations. In fact, it's part of the system. Even under the most liberal administrations we wouldn't get them to enforce border controls. The immigration service and the border patrol always worked on the assumption that it is not really illegal for these people to be here provided they are working, are being useful to the growers. The moment they stop being useful — either because they strike or because they don't work any more since the crops are finished — then of course it becomes very illegal and they are thrown out. It's a very corrupt system.

175

F: "Corrupt" implies collusion to break the law, which is a very heavy charge. Do you want to make that charge?

C: Sure, sure, except that I'm not saying that money crosses hands. What I'm saying is that the guy before me did it, the guy before him did it, so I can't change it. It's that kind of setup.

F: That takes any connotation of deliberate action away from the growers.

C: No, it's a deliberate attempt, it's very deliberate, most deliberate! What I'm trying to explain is that it is more sinister than if they were paying money. This way the immigration service people are as much servants as we are. They're not getting paid off. They do it because of the power that the industry represents. So it's worse than if they were actually being paid money.

F: What happened to the strike?

C: To strike in any rural setting in any state today — and I don't care what state it is, California, Texas, Florida, Arizona — you're fighting the growers in their own bailiwick. You're fighting them in their own setting, so they are able to bring the tremendous powers from the police and the courts and all the structures against you on the picket line to break it totally. For instance, with Giumarra we had a thousand people out, and we had 'em out for four days, and there wasn't a soul in the fields — 50 people at most. At the end of the fourth or fifth day we were enjoined and we were permitted to have three people on either side of each entrance. Two days later people just went on through because the workers didn't know we were striking. The people who are being imported as strike breakers don't really know what's happening and sometimes don't care. The injunction is just a manifestation of the power they have. There isn't enough money or time or energy to be appealing all those things that they keep throwing at you. The boycott gets them out of the setting. They can't reach us in the boycott. The farther away from Delano, the more diffuse their power is.

F: Has the boycott worked?

C: We figure that we are cutting back the sales

now by about 33 per cent. But all that means is that we are forcing them to cold-storage the grape. The grape hasn't been lost yet. And in order to be 33 per cent effective we would have to keep up the same kind of pressure or increase it in the coming weeks.

F: What is the main issue of the strike?

C: The central issue is the whole question of recognition. Do, or will, workers have the right to have a union and have it recognized by their employers?

F: How do the growers respond?

C: Mostly they say that workers don't want a union, that if workers wanted a union they would give them a union. Really what they're saying is that the only way they're going to recognize the workers is if the workers bring enough economic heat on. The employers are still at the point where industrial employers were 50 years ago. They say, "If you want a union come and get it." In other words, "Force me to give you a union."

F: And what evidence is there that the workers want a union?

C: Well, I think that the only kind of evidence we have that cannot be refuted is the experience we've had in eight different cases where they've given workers a right to vote on whether they want unions or not. They have overwhelmingly voted that they want a union.

F: So you're ready to put it to a vote?

C: Oh sure. See, when the employers say that we don't recognize the workers or that workers don't want a union, we say give the workers the right to make this self-determination by giving them the right to an election, with the understanding on our part that if the workers vote against the union we'll call the thing off. But if the workers vote for the union, then the employers are duty bound to bargain collectively and to sign a contract with the union.

F: Who supports you?

C: Number one, the public. They were given something to respond with. That's important. Then labor, for money and technical assistance — and from just being around them you learn a hell of a lot, you know. Not necessarily by asking but just by keeping your eyes open and seeing what's happening. When it comes from a labor guy it means something, because they certainly have their experiences. And there are a lot of good guys in the labor movement generally. I defend them as much as I defend churches and other groups. It's funny how the guy who is so sensitive about making a general crack about blacks or browns thinks nothing about making a general crack at labor or the church or other groupings. I think the church brings the other kind of power. The moral power and the kind of assurance that what you're doing is really an important task. That fortifies you in your spirit. It legitimates the movement at least against the reckless attacks from the right.

F: What has the churches' Migrant Ministry done?

C: Well, in terms of any organized group it's the best by far. They were helping us from the first moment we came to Delano — way back, before the strike. In fact, the very first thing I did when I came to Delano was to meet with the Migrant Ministry up in the Sierras; they were having a retreat, and I spent three days with them. In C.S.O. [Community Service Organization] people used to kid me because I was very close to the Migrant Ministry. First of all, I've always been kind of — well, the word is not "religious," but "church-related." I dig it. And so whenever they had any meetings, when I could I would slip away and go to their meetings and be with them. It was relaxing. Besides being good people they were very committed and very strong. It was a joy to be there.

F: What do you want from the church?

C: It is very difficult to say what we want. The church should understand one thing that escapes many people. They are concerned to have people who are poor and dispossessed organize, but churchmen don't know the process of organization. A church group appropriates hundreds of thousands of dollars and after a few years doesn't have any results. They pull back and say, "Well, it can't be done." So many times the church makes the mistake of wanting to get something done, and not understanding that it takes a lifetime to do it. They throw in a lot of money initially to get things to change overnight, and nothing happens overnight. And it's not going to happen overnight. Then there's this general moralization, "It didn't work." They have to understand more about the workings of organizations in underprivileged groups, minority groups or farm workers. Now, in our case they need more of an understanding of how it works so that they can make wiser contributions, and make more long-term commitments.

F: The church isn't the organizer?

C: It can't be the organizer. It's got to be done by the people. But they've got to have the confidence in the people that it can be done.

F: Why are you an advocate of nonviolence?

C: Well, you see, it started before the union. The first day we took a vote to strike I asked for a nonviolent vote. I have been asked this question many times and I have really had to dig back and find out. I think it goes back to my family, particularly my mother. She's a very illiterate pacifist. She never learned how to read or write, never learned English, never went to school for a day. She has this natural childishness about how to live, and how to let people live. In the old days, at least when I was a kid — it was generally true in a lot of families, much less so now in my family — there were occasions when she would gather us around her and she would call it *consejo*. "Consejo" means to council, to advise. She didn't wait until it would happen — like: "You fight now? Well here it comes: I'm going to tell you how bad it is to fight." I remember that she would talk constantly about nonviolence — constantly. She used many *dichos*. "Dichos" are sayings, parables — for instance, things like "It takes two to fight; one guy can't fight by himself," or "Flies can't come into a closed mouth; keep your mouth shut."

F: So nonviolence was your nursery.

179

C: I would think so.

F: It's part of the family — in your blood, in your home, everything?

C: Yeah. And I've done a little tracing — not only my mother but both sides — and our people were very peaceful on both sides. We didn't have any generals or warriors. Very plain peons, so I think that's where it started. My Dad never fought. We never saw my Dad fight or drink or smoke — all the things that have a bad meaning. My parents weren't too young when they married. They were in their early 30s, so once they married they gave us children all their attention. They were with us all the time; she would never think of having a babysitter taking care of us. They enjoyed being with us. We weren't pampered either. They were strict.

F: I'm wondering if you had to do some reassessing of nonviolence in terms of some of the recent benedictions that violence has received.

C: No, no! You see, what is happening is that all or at least most of it is just theoretical violence.

F: There has been a lot of rationalizing of what is happening in the ghettos in terms of the riots. Some of it has been theological.

C: I don't buy it. How in hell can you get a theologian to accept that one or two or three lives are worth giving up for some material gain? It doesn't stop there, it's just the beginning. The real paradox here is that the people who advocate peace in Vietnam advocate violence in this country. Inconceivable; I don't understand it.

F: We've seen two movies on this trip through the eastern part of the country. One was *Midnight Cowboy,* the other was *The Battle of Britain. Midnight Cowboy* involves a rather gruesome murder in which a telephone is shoved down a man's throat. This seemed to be excused as an act of personal devotion to another man. *The Battle of Britain* involved a war to preserve a nation and its values. In both there was a high rationalization of the act. It seems to me that movies project violence as acceptable, more real, present, more of an experience, whereas nonviolence seems like an impossibility, unreal.

C: No! I think nonviolence is a very natural way of doing things, and violence is highly out of the ordinary.

F: That's an easy statement to make.

C: No, it's very true.

F: You said that nonviolence is more natural.

C: Sure. Remember, the moment you and I get together we're going to have to deal. Right? Or we're going to have to deal through violence, one or the other. If you and I talk here for 20 years no one is going to say much. But if we get into a big heated discussion and we stab each other, more people are going to know what happened here. It's not natural, you know. So what I'm saying is that a lot of good things happen. Who knows about all the contracts that we signed? With the exception of the three big battles, no one knows, because they weren't fights. Something was done without a struggle. It was nonviolent.

F: Does the United Farm Workers Organizing Committee want to be more than a union, a force for social reform?

C: I think that if the union loses the social force it has now it's going to become pretty meaningless. The most important thing is to provide an instrument with which workers, by their own actions and their own desires, can work themselves out of poverty.

F: It's an instrument or tool for poor people in this nation?

C: Yeah, for poor people. This is always the first order of business. But once that's attained and once they are well on their way to attaining the first contracts, to having the union recognized — along with that comes responsibility. If the workers keep that social consciousness and use it as an instrument, not only will they help themselves, but they will also help others less fortunate, and they will be a voice in society against those ills that are part of our life.

F: The C.I.O. started out with some of these aims.

Why do you think you can succeed whereas that union wasn't able to?

C: Well, let's say we hope that it will be different; that remains to be seen.

F: What are you doing to make it happen?

C: We're making it uncomfortable on ourselves to be quiet. We're trying to build around ourselves a sort of in-group gadfly, if you please, that is going to keep us moving ahead on some of the social ills even though we have such a big job, an overwhelming job, in building the union. That job hasn't been done yet. We're just now beginning to do it.

TIJERINA, HERO OF THE MILITANTS

Dr. Clark S. Knowlton

Reies Lopez Tijerina, leader and founder of the largest Spanish-American
militant organization in New Mexico,
the Alianza Federal de Los Pueblos
Libres, (Obs., Dec. 9, 1966), was
found innocent in an Albuquerque
courtroom last December 14 of the
capital charge of kidnapping and of
the lesser charges of false imprisonment and assault on a jail. These
charges originated in the Alianza raid
on the Tierra Amarilla courthouse,
June 5, 1967. The unexpected verdict
was harshly condemned by the New
Mexican press. It also shocked
the dominant Anglo-American political and economic establishment of
northern New Mexico. The verdict
was wildly cheered, on the other
hand, by large numbers of impoverished
Spanish-Americans living on dreams of
the past and on welfare in the slums
of Albuquerque and Santa Fe, and by
numerous Spanish-American small ranchers and farmers hurt severely by
recent National Forest regulations.
The Alianza, badly battered by two
years of constant court battles, has
now suddenly become again a threat
to the political and economic groupings that control northern New Mexico.
Convoys of cars from rural Spanish-
American villages again visit the
shot-up Alianza headquarters in
Albuquerque.

THE TEXAS OBSERVER, March 28, 1969, pp. 1-4.

Tijerina, the most important Spanish-American leader in New Mexico, was born into a poor migrant family near Falls City, Texas, September 21, 1923. He lost his mother at an early age. His father, losing three wives, supported his family of ten children by sharecropping in South Texas. Tijerina states that he saw his family driven away three times from Anglo-American farms at gunpoint when the harvests were in by farmers who refused to pay the family their share of the crop. The meek but Anglo-hating father finally settled his family in San Antonio. During the spring, summer and fall, they moved through the migrant stream in the Midwest and West Texas, wintering as best they could in San Antonio.

Although his father is still living, Tijerina says very little about him. He prefers to dwell with admiration upon his paternal grandfather and great-grandfather. He explains that his great-grandfather owned a small ranch on a land grant near Laredo. Anglo-American ranchers wanting his land, according to Tijerina, drove branded cattle onto the ranch and accused his great-grandfather of cattle rustling. Six Texas Rangers hung the accused man in front of his family. The man's son, Tijerina's grandfather, became a border raider attacking Anglo-American settlements and ranches along the border.

Tijerina is thus a product of the bitter border fighting between aggressive Mexican-hating Anglo-American ranchers and Rangers and the resident Mexican-American population in the lower Rio Grande Valley.

Tijerina's early history is somewhat shadowy. He relates that he grew up as a migrant worker attend-

ing school very infrequently. Somewhere along the line he managed to
acquire a decent knowledge of the
English language. A Baptist missionary, distributing the New
Testament to Mid-Western migrant
labor camps, visited the Tijerina
family. Reies, a boy in his middle teens, read the book through.
That night he dreamed that God
had called him to lead his people
out of bondage and poverty. In-
terpreting this as a religious
call, he enrolled in the Assembly
of God Bible School at Ysleta,
Texas, now part of El Paso.
Finishing his training, he was
licensed as a minister and sent
to assist revivals in and around
Santa Fe. He soon acquired a
reputation as a fiery, unconven-
tional preacher and missionary.
Within a few years he lost his
license to preach. He asserts it
was because he argued that the
Church should provide financial
and spiritual assistance to the
poor rather than the poor donating
money to the Church.

Somewhat disoriented, he drifted
around northern New Mexico finally
settling around the age of 23 in
Tierra Amarilla. A half abandoned
Spanish-American frontier settlement,
Tierra Amarilla has always been a
center of anti-Anglo-American agita-
tion. The people of the area were
robbed of their land grant by Anglo-
American lawyers and politicians
toward the end of the 19th century.
The inhabitants refusing to abandon
their ancestral lands have periodically cut the fences, burned the
ranch buildings and slaughtered the
livestock of intruding Anglo-American ranchers.

Married and with a growing family to
support, Tijerina (date uncertain)

finally left Tierra Amarilla. For 13 years as an itinerant Pentecostal preacher he and his family moved from California to East Texas and from the Mexican border to the Midwest as migrant workers. Developing a devoted following, he finally formed a small communal settlement of around 17 families on purchased land near Casa Grande, Arizona, in the early 1950's. The settlers built their homes, a small church, and worked for the neighboring farmers and ranchers. Friction over land questions soon developed with Anglo-Americans in the vicinity. The small settlement was burnt out. Tijerina, charged with trying to help an imprisoned brother escape, fled to Mexico.

He remained there for six years. During this period, he claims that he studied the history of land grants in Mexico and in the Southwest. Some evidence exists that he became involved in the activities of militant Mexican peasant groups and was deported by the Mexican government. His Mexican contacts have helped him raise funds and secure a sympathetic audience in Mexico. No evidence exists that he was ever a Castro sympathizer or communist. Entering Mexico as an itinerant religious leader, he left it deeply motivated by the philosophy of the Mexican revolution.

Returning to Tierra Amarilla sometime in the early 1960's, he was accused of joining clandestine groups of Spanish-American night riders trying to burn out encroaching Anglo-American ranchers from Texas and Colorado. The ranchers blamed Tijerina for the recurrence of night-riding activities and threatened him. Several attempts on his life may have taken place.

At any rate, he moved to Albuquerque. Securing employment around 1962 as a janitor in a local Presbyterian church, he began to organize the Alianza Federal de Mercedes, the Federal Alliance of Land Grantees. His first wife finally left him as he was seldom able to support his family.

The Alianza at first attracted primarily the landless, impoverished, aging, rural Spanish-American immigrants living in the slums of Albuquerque and Santa Fe. Forced to migrate to the city because of land lost to Anglo-American ranchers and merchants and because of the decline of the village economic systems, they exist upon welfare and upon their dreams of recovering their lands. More profoundly isolated from Anglo-American urban society than ever, the inhabitants of negro urban ghettoes, large numbers of them are found in almost every city in New Mexico.

Around 1965 the composition of Alianza membership changed rapidly. Thousands of bitter Spanish-American small ranchers and village farmers became members. Angered by what appeared to them to be harsh, unfair, and capricious decisions by the National Forest Service that were forcing many of them to migrate, or to seek employment outside of agriculture, they appealed for redress to state and federal agencies. Unable to secure a hearing, they turned to Tijerina and the Alianza. As members, they caused the Alianza to become more militant. Forest Service personnel living in the rural villages of northern New Mexico began to move to the larger cities, as resentment against them spread. Rangers were shot at on

mountain trails. Many fires were deliberately set in the National Forests
of New Mexico.

The Forest Service may have had good
reasons for their policy decisions,
but these reasons were never communi-
cated to the Spanish-Americans.
Grazing permits for small herds of
cattle and sheep upon which so many
Spanish-Americans depend were sharply
cut. The grazing season was reduced
from nine to six months. Those holding grazing permits were required to
fence their allotments and to move
their herds and flocks from one
allotment area to another. The fen-
cing was usually beyond the ability
of poor Spanish-Americans to purchase or to install. Although Anglo-
American ranchers with their cowboys
could move their animals without
difficulty, it was very difficult
for a Spanish-American farmer or
small rancher, often with other employment, to do so. Permits for
Spanish-Americans to graze milk cows
and work horses were cancelled even
though Anglo-American ranchers were
permitted to graze their work horses.
This decision intensified malnutri-
tion and threatened to force hundreds
of Spanish-American farmers out of
agriculture. They cannot afford to
buy tractors for their small acreage
and have no range for their work
stock. The Forest Service claims
that erosion in the forests has
forced them to make these decisions.
However, they spend far more on recreational developments for the Anglo American hunter, fisher, tourist,
or camper than they do on the improvement of grazing or the control
of erosion. Spanish-Americans, dependent upon the National Forests
that once were part of their land
grants, are today convinced that the
National Forest Service would like
to eliminate the Spanish-Americans

and replace them with Anglo-American
ranchers and tourists.

The Alianza message to the rural Spanish-American village people was very
simple and convincing. Tijerina and
Alianza organizers repeated it in
dozens of villages throughout 1965
and 1966. By now very few Spanish-
Americans have not heard it: "You
have been robbed of your lands by
Anglo Americans with some Spanish-
American accomplices. No one is
willing to help you recover your
lands, protect your water rights,
or secure your grazing permits.
The federal and state governments
are not interested in you. Join
the Alianza. Together we will
get your lands back or adequate
compensation for them, and protect your grazing and water rights.
This will be done preferably
through court action. If the
courts do not respond, then we
will have to resort to other me-
thods." These words endlessly
repeated have deeply affected
the thinking of Spanish-American
people in northern New Mexico.

Alianza tactics were also simple
and rather naive. The Forest
Service, owner of so much of
northern New Mexico, was selected
as the primary target. National
Forest lands in northern New
Mexico were carved out from
Spanish-American land grants.
Spanish-American land titles
were not completely extinguished.
Forest Boundaries were carelessly
surveyed and often included entire villages. As the Forest
Service has now become the major
focus of rural Spanish-American
hostility, it was not difficult
to mobilize Spanish-Americans
for activities against the National Forest Service.

189

Selecting a former community
land grant, the San Joaquin del
Rio Chama, (now part of the Kit
Carson National Forest), Tijerina
announced in 1966 that the original village community, now
uninhabited, had been reconsti-
tuted as the Pueblo Republica de
San Joaquin del Rio Chama and
would assert its rights to the
land grant. Community members
were drawn from the inhabitants
of the surrounding Spanish-
American villages, some of whom
were descendents of the original
villagers. In an open meeting,
village officials selected a
complete set of village officials. To emphasize their
claim, a series of camp-ins were
held at the Echo Amphitheater,
a public campsite on the grant
within the Kit Carson National
Forest. Finally on October 22, 1966,
a brief altercation broke out between
two nervous forest rangers, trying
to sell camping permits to the hostile Spanish-Americans, and Alianza
members.

The following Wednesday, Tijerina,
his brother Cristobal, and two members were arrested on a federal war-
rant, charged with assault upon two
forest rangers and appropriating
government property to personal use.
On a change of venue, the case was
transferred from friendly Rio
Arriba County, where conviction
would have been impossible, to
hostile Las Cruces. After several
postponements the trial was finally
held in November, 1967. A jury,
all Anglo-American except for two
Mexican-Americans, found the defendants guilty. The federal judge
sentenced Tijerina to two years in
jail, his brother to two years with
eighteen months suspended, and two
other defendants to 60 days. All

190

were allowed bail. The verdict was
appealed.

The tempo of events accelerated during the spring of 1967. In one
meeting after another, Tijerina and
other Alianza leaders in ever stronger language demanded the return of
the land grants and harshly criticized
state and federal governments. Fires
were set on the National Forests.
Anglo-American ranchers hired more
gunmen as their fences were cut and
property destroyed. Finally a mass
meeting for June 3, 1968, was called
at Coyote, New Mexico during which
plans would be made to take over
the land. The Anglo-American press
began to demand that law enforcement
agencies repress the Alianza and
curb its activities.

In 1969, David F. Cargo, a liberal
maverick Republican, had, unsupported
by the regular Republican leaders ,
won the governor's office with considerable Spanish-American support.
While in office, he married a Spanish-American girl who had been a
member of the Alianza. He began to
visit many Spanish-American villages
listening to the bitterly expressed
problems, resentments, and needs of
the village people. He published
a number of statements expressing
his sympathy for the Spanish-
Americans, calling them an exploited, neglected minority. The
Albuquerque papers reacted coldly
to his description of northern
New Mexico. He also met several
times with Alianza leaders and
succeeded in moderating somewhat
their ferocious attacks upon
state and federal governments.
The day before the Coyote meeting, Governor Cargo flew to
Michigan to participate with
Governor Romney in a fundraising banquet.

Cargo's plane had scarcely left the ground when District Attorney Alfonso Sanchez, the Democratic DA for Rio Arriba County, former Alianza attorney and personal enemy of Tijerina, and Captain Joseph Black, commander of the state police force, announced that the Coyote meeting was illegal and therefore banned. Any person attempting to attend the meeting would be arrested. They also stated that Tijerina was a con-man, the Alianza members were dupes, and the organization was communist-inspired. Roadblocks went up on all highways leading into the area. Warrants of arrest were issued for Alianza leaders.

Angry, not understanding the division of power in the state government, and feeling that they had been betrayed by the governor, the refugee Alianza leaders, headed by Tijerina, slipped through the roadblocks and met near Canjilon to decide future policy. Learning that a hearing was to be held at Tierra Amarilla on June 5, 1967, for Alianza members arrested while trying to attend the Coyote meeting, they decided to send a raiding party of around 20 men to release their people and to make a citizens' arrest of District Attorney Sanchez. Tijerina gave orders to the group to avoid violence.

The raiding party entered the courthouse in the early afternoon of June 5, 1967. Two deputies and a janitor were wounded by tense raiders. Unable to find the arrested Alianza members, who had been bound over for

trial and released on bail at an early
morning hearing, or Sanchez, who had
not come for the hearing, the raiders
held the courthouse for several hours.
Then, seizing two hostages—a newspaper reporter and a deputy sheriff—
they fled to the mountains near Canjilon, releasing their hostages before disappearing into the hills.

Panic and confusion swept the
governorless state administration
when news of the raid arrived in
Santa Fe. Rumors that Alianza guerrilla bands led by Cuban guerrilla
experts were moving toward Santa Fe
massacuring Anglo Americans on the way
were widely believed. Other rumors
had it that Alianza arson and assass-
ination squads were infiltrating
Albuquerque and Santa Fe. National
guardsmen equipped with tanks and
artillery moved along mountain roads
but did not penetrate into the mountains. Apache tribal police from
Dulce, New Mexico, Anglo-American
sheriff posses from central and
eastern New Mexico, and state
police units manned roadblocks and
searched for Alianza members. Guardsmen and their allies swept through
Spanish-American villages around
Canjilon breaking into homes without warrants, confiscating property,
holding suspected men, women and
children for many hours without
food or water in temporary concentration camps. A large part of Rio
Arriba County was treated as though
it were enemy territory in the process of occupation. No state emergency or martial law was declared
and no warrants were issued. One of
the most massive violations of the
American civil rights in recent years
took place without protests or open
investigation by any state or federal
agency.

Governor Cargo returned to New Mexico

early on the morning of the next day,
June 6. Within 48 hours the guardsmen
were sent home along with the Apaches
and the Anglo-American posses.
Contact was established with
the refugee raiders. Given the
assurance that their lives would
be spared, the majority surren-
dered or were conveniently
arrested by state and local
police. Preliminary hearings
were held. The defendants were
bound over for trial on charges,
among others, of kidnapping,
assault on a jail, and destruction of government property.
Within 45 days all were out on
bail. The immediate crisis was
over. However, the serious un-
punished violation of civil
rights and the mistreatment of
so many rural Spanish-Americans
will have long lasting effects
upon relationships between Anglo Americans and Spanish-Americans and upon the attitudes of
the local people toward both
state and federal governments.

Before the state had recovered
from the impact of the raid,
Eulogio Salazar, one of the
deputies wounded in the raid
and a star state witness, was
found beaten to death by unknown
assailants on a road near Tierra
Amarilla on January 3, 1968.
Once again a pall of fear and
insecurity covered northern New
Mexico. Local people refused
to discuss the murder, the
Alianza or local problems with
strangers.

The state press and law enforcement agencies all automatically
assumed that Tijerina and the
Alianza were responsible for
the murder. The governor revoked
the bonds of the Alianza defen-

dants and they were immediately
jailed. Their lawyers appealed
the jailing to the state supreme
court. Under questioning from
the court bench, District Attorney Sanchez admitted that no
evidence connecting the defendants with the murder existed.
The court ordered all the defendants released on bond except
Tijerina who was charged with a
capital crime of kidnapping. In
time he also was released when
the charges against him were
reduced by Judge Joe Angel.

The murder has not yet been solved.
Rumors emanating from Tierra Amarilla
implicate militant Anglo-American
groups anxious to besmirch the
Alianza reputation. Other rumors
hint that the deputy may have been
murdered as he was about to change
his testimony. Local observers are
rather curious why he was never given
police protection as an important
state witness against the raiders.
And still others believe that a local
feud may have been responsible for the
death of the state witness. The state
trial for the courthouse raid was
assigned to state district judge Joe
Angel of Las Vegas, New Mexico. On
February 8, 1968, the judge held extensive hearings, and, as a result,
reduced the charges against Tijerina
and ten other raiders from first degree kidnapping to false imprisonment.
They were bound over for trial and
then released on bail. Charges
against nine other defendants including Tijerina's charming 19 year old
daughter were dismissed.

Sanchez, disgruntled at the reduction
in charges, hastily impaneled a grand
jury of his own choosing in Rio Arriba
County and reinstated the original
capital charges that had been reduced by Judge Angel. Amidst legal

controversy, the state supreme court
shifted jurisdiction of the case from
Judge Angel to District Judge Paul
Larrazolo. This judge was a bit
miffed when he found out that Sanchez
had sworn in 13 men for the grand
jury rather than the 12 men specified
by law and that seemingly very scanty
records had been kept of grand jury
proceedings. Nevertheless, he
allowed the charges to stand. At
the request of the prosecution, the
case was shifted from Rio Arriba
County to Albuquerque. Tijerina was
allowed to conduct his own defense
with the assistance of two court-
appointed attorneys.

The constant legal battles have been
costly to the state and federal
governments. They have effectively slowed down Alianza activities.
Many members dropped out because
of fear and pressure from law enforcement agencies. Others suspended their membership, as the
Alianza was acquiring a reputation
for violence. Alianza funds were
drained away to pay heavy bail charges and to secure expensive legal
assistance. Tijerina and many other
Alianza leaders were spending most
of their time in jail or in the
courtroom. Militant Anglo-American groups have made several
attempts upon Tijerina's life.
Alianza headquarters in Albuquerque have been bombed and shot at.
In one attempt, an Anglo-American
deputy sheriff from Bernalillo
County lost most of one arm when
a dynamite charge misfired as he
set it against the door of the
Alianza headquarters. Although
the police were faithfully noti-
fied, no charges have been pressed
and no one is in custody.

Tijerina has become the hero of
every militant Spanish-American

and Mexican-American group in the
Southwest. He and the Alianza
have decisively broken through
the apathy and hopelessness of
the Spanish-Americans. They
have driven a gulf of fear and
antagonism between Anglo Americans and Spanish Americans in
the state of New Mexico. The
old political structure of northern New Mexico has been
destroyed. Younger men are now
organizing groups far more militant and inclined to violence than
the Alianza has ever been. Unrest
is growing rapidly. Unless programs come into existence to resolve the land question, secure
water and grazing rights, ameliorate
poverty, build roads, and recognize
the existence of the Spanish language and the Spanish-American culture, violence in rural New Mexico
is almost inevitable.

THE BROWN BERETS

Rona M. Fields
Charles J. Fox

Even in its days as the Young Chicanos for Community Action, the cadre which was to become the Brown Berets were forced to interact within the organizational world.

Of course, there had always been a rich world of organizations in Los Angeles:

> There are in Los Angeles scores of organizations whose membership and/or purpose are solely or primarily Mexican-American. In 1961 the local Spanish-language newspaper *La Opinion*, recorded 85; the publishing directory of the Health and Welfare Planning Council listed 47; and the Council of Mexican-American Affairs claimed 44 member organizations. An informed observer guessed that there were "hundreds—as of this week; next week there will be hundreds, but they will have different names and a different set of officers—and they'll still be broke."
>
> There are casual social organizations that give a dance or two a year, perhaps for the benefit of an orphanage in Mexico, or sickness and burial societies that may collect dues as the need arises.[1]

One study, conducted in 1961, estimated that 13.5 percent of the population was involved in formal

THE BLACK POLITICIAN, July 1971, pp. 53-63.

organizations. Most of these turned out to be lower-middle and middle-middle class ascendant Mexican-Americans.[2] We cannot assume, however, that only middle-class Mexicans are involved in organizations. The plethora of organizations would not be classified as formal in the Anglo-American sense, and therefore are not counted in such studies. However, a very thoroughly recognized aspect of Mexican-American culture is the way barrio gangs, car clubs and social clubs have a way of generating an all encompassing identity and loyalty from their membership. This loyalty and identity extends into adult life and adult relationships. A man never "stops" nor "resigns" his membership in a gang.

To speak only of the "formal" organizations is to skew observations. Sheldon makes the point that even many of the organizations which have been classified as formal have none of the appertances usually associated with organization structure within the Anglo community (e.g., telephone numbers, executive secretaries, bank accounts, by-laws, and offices).[3] It is erroneous to assume, on the basis of comparing organizational structures that the Mexican-American community lacks organizations.

It is not uncommon for some individuals to be involved in varying positions of leadership and authority in several groups at once. This may be attributable to the dearth of followers as Sheldon concludes.[4] It may, however, be that organizations both within the Mexican-American community and the community at large tend to engage in periodic mitosis. In the Anglo community this mitosis is often regenerative as each cell contributes in its own individual way to the survival of the species. In the Mexican-American community the tendency is for each cell to resort to cannibalism. This is another way of saying that Anglo organizations are able to work together by emphasizing that in which they agree while Mexican-American organizations tend to emphasize those things on which they disagree.

In their interactions with other organizations, and in the dynamics of their own organization, the Berets serve as a microcosm of organization among the Mexican-American population.

The organizational proliferations are a macro-

199

cosm of inter-personal individual relationships in that:

1. The prevailing attitude is that the individual who has achieved material success is somehow corrupt (a vendido) and not to be trusted. Translated into the attitudes and behaviors of the Brown Berets as an organization toward and with other organizations well-known public success figures become "jive dudes" who have "sold out their people," have been "corrupted by the Anglo establishment," and are "not to be trusted nor listened to." This, of course, effectively negates any possibility of utilizing existing channels for action or organizational coalition.

2. The father, a distant authority figure, is not involved nor concerned with the internal dynamics of the family. Rather, he is deliberately protected from it. Again translated this means that the nationally known Brown Power leaders such as Reies Tijerina, Corky Gonzales and Cesar Chavez are "distant" and not likely to help, nor are their efforts likely to be of value.

3. Machismo seems to be a truncation of what Erikson would describe as the process of moving from self-esteem through identity toward intimacy.' This truncation is culturally reinforced, and is therefore likely to be part of the institutionalization of any social interactions. Translated into group behavioral norms action is on the basis of social reactions to one's performance. This prohibits the performer from appearing to seek advice and from acknowledging criticism. One must prove oneself and gain the admiration and respect of the other through one's own operations, not through carrying out another's plan nor being part of another organism. This is a truncation rather than a movement toward self-realization. It is a seeking for ego strength rather than an action derived from ego strength.

The interactions of the Berets with other organizations might be characterized by one, another or all of these categories of relationships. For the sake of clarity, however, we shall exemplify the above categories by describing archetypical behaviors observed by the research team.

Although anyone who has become middle-class is subject to the accusation of vendido (literally—sell out) by the Berets, this appellation is usually directed at the "politicians." One need not be the holder of a political office to be a "politician." It is necessary only to be oriented toward participating in the political process through the traditional democratic mechanisms. Vendido is applied to such varieties of persons as a Mexican-American educator and school board member, ministers who are active in community affairs, successful doctors and businessmen, union officials and even an unsuccessful candidate for political office. In the Beret vernacular these are "jive dudes," people who will use you for their own political advantage. One of the explanations of this concept was made by a Beret leader during the 1969 mayorality campaign. He said:

> You see that poster. It says, Por Mi Raza Mato. Well, these politicians take it and first they say, 'por mi raza mato—Vote.' Then they come along and it says 'por mi raza—vote for Bradley.' They've corrupted it, it's a beautiful thing —for my race, everything. But they add to that and qualify it. It destroys the meaning and the beauty.

The distrust of the successful compatriot extends to a distrust of those who are accredited with being "leaders." Nothing condemns one as rapidly as being named by a news media, or anyone else, as "a spokesman" or "a leader."

It is significant that, in the Beret handbook, the sections on leadership and awareness are on facing pages. Awareness is stressed as a defense against "trickery" and leadership is stressed as resulting from responsible action and having been a good follower.

There is some justification for the Berets to be leery of alliances with adult leaders in the community for there have been instances of co-option which tended to undermine the Berets' self-determination. The expressed intent of several of the adults of a more broadly based activist group had been to develop the Berets into "the storm troops of the movement." But the Berets had no intention of having "our heads bashed in for someone else's purposes." Further, there have been instances of exploitation of the Beret image by one or another "leader" through inter-group unity boards. The Berets have generalized from these experiences: "We can't trust anyone in the community who is over thirty-five because they have already become politicians in one or another bag."

Meetings with leaders who are accounted "jive dudes" are often tense and fraught with anxiety. An example of this occurred when the chairman of a community brokerage committee handed over to the Berets the check for rent on the clinic building.

The chairman, a respected leader and Protestant clergyman, was attempting to communicate to the Beret ministers the solemnity and responsibility he felt for the use of the money. At the same time, he wanted the organization to understand that there were no strings attached in the form of supervision by the committee. He was red-faced and perspiring and had some difficulty in articulating. He was evidently attempting to get some cues from the Berets in order to phrase his concerns and proffer his good wishes. But the Berets were stony-faced. When the chairman mentioned that his aide would keep in touch for accounting purposes, the Beret Prime-Minister demanded to know what kinds of accounting and made it clear that he would not consider himself nor his organization accountable to the aide. The chairman quickly explained that the accounting would be minimal and only to satisfy the requirements of the foundation funding the committee. He handed over the check and they shook hands. Once the check was in the hands of the Berets the atmosphere seemed less tense. As the group proceeded toward the chairman's office there was a perceptable loosening of postures and words.

The Berets, or at least the Prime Minister, believes that their strength lies in their "purity." It is always their assumption that the other party in any proposed coalition will gain more from their association with the Berets than vice versa. The Berets always assume that it is they who have community legitimacy and that others seeking to work with the Berets are merely attempting to share in this aura. This has become such a dominant part of the Beret myth system that they even carry it over in their relationship with white professional groups. They believe that these groups are attempting to enhance their own image by their association with the Berets.

In pursuit of funding for the clinic and funding and advice in circumstances dealing with the courts, vandalism against their establishments, and police harassment, it might have been quite useful to the Berets to request the intervention or formal approval of some of the adult leaders who are recognized by the Anglo community and establishment. For instance, in December, 1968, when several wealthy liberals expressed interest in funding the clinic and others were willing to help organize it, they variously requested the approbation of these "leaders." Even with the knowledge that obtaining the money or services of these people was entirely dependent upon the simple recognition by one or two "names" of the legitimacy of the Berets and their project, the Berets were unwilling themselves to obtain it. Although in some instances they were willing to have the authors act unofficially as a go-between, they would not themselves meet with these people in a role of supplicant. This was rationalized as:

> Well, you're more educated and middle-class and they've been so brainwashed by the Anglo value system that they can communicate better with you than with their own people.

It is common to hear tales of one or another "traitor" who had used his position to benefit his own purse; or had used his people as a stepping stone to personal aggrandizement. Whether or not there are any evidences of an individual having acted in this fashion, the suspicion of it is frequently expressed. One clergyman who served as president of the Educational Issues Coordinating Council was attacked in the first issue of La Causa as having "sold out to the Board of Education" by putting a damper on proposals for further demonstrations in March, 1969. The committee had reportedly "decided not to pressure the school . . . for fear it might hurt the chances of the school bond issue in the April election."[6]

There is only a single instance of Berets officially acting in support of and in direct alliance with another Chicano organizational leader in 1969. This was with the female chairman of a welfare rights organization.

The unwillingness of the Berets to align themselves with reputed vendidos has strengthened their position in the eyes of their members and potential recruits. There are no aspersions cast on their independence, nor are they ever spoken of as a unit of someone else's defense. The insistence on "purity" has, however, often resulted in ineffectiveness through non-utilization of the resources available to them. The "establishment" and/or other Mexican-American groups are never looked upon as something that can be used. They are only viewed as something that would corrupt the purity of the Beret symbol.

The archetypical Mexican-American father is a distant authority figure. He does not enter into the daily workings of his domestic abode, rather he is to be protected from it by the mother. His function is primarily to relate to the world outside of the family. The children are to be obedient but this is not too much trouble because he rarely commands.

The "fathers" of the "movement" toward Brown Power are Reies Tijerina, Cesar Chavez and Corky Gonzales. The Berets may be analogized as developing through childhood to adolescence and finally to parenthood. As this process occurs the child loses his feelings about the father's infalibility and omnipotence. And if it were not for the fact that the fathers are geographically distant, an overt adolescent rebellion would likely occur. The fact of geographical distance, however, allows the Berets to maintain a kind of respectful allegiance.

Perception of Leaders

The Prime Minister described his organization's perception of these three leaders during a radio interview:

> Each particular area needs its own particular kind of organization running its own situation. In New Mexico, the violence that took place there was an absolute necessity in that particular place and that particular time. Now on the other hand, Cesar Chavez with his non-violent approach is his necessity, in his particular situation, at his particular time. As the situation

would arise in each area, each different organization is necessary. . . . We all think a lot of Corky. He's a Bobby Kennedy type of Chicano leader. He's young and he has a very good approach, more directed toward the young people and the young organizations. I think Corky Gonzales is only beginning and he'll go far and if we have a leader or he should be the leader of the Mexican-American revolution he will be one of the generals.

In February, 1968, the Berets acted as bodyguards for Tijerina in his visit to California. Many news reports mis-identified the Berets as being his private army,[7] but their relationship with Tijerina was not a subservient one. As was later explained by a former Beret leader: "The Brown Berets saw it fit to take the responsibility to protect Reies. Reies in no way started the group, we had been in the area three years in one form or another. . . ."

Cesar Chavez had played a part in activating the leadership cadre who were to become the Brown Berets. However, Chavez has increasingly identified with the Kennedy Democratic party faction and is thus a less attractive independent figure for the essentially apolitical Berets. As Chavez, and La Huelga generally became more associated with unions and national political figures, the Berets identified less with the grape pickers' strike. What has resulted in an ambivalence. They verbalize support of "their brothers who are fighting the oppressive slave labor conspirators."

Generally, the Berets have found more attraction and identification with Gonzales and Tijerina who, in contrast with Chavez's non-violence, have preached a doctrine closer to the Berets' motto, "by any means necessary."

There have been allegations that Gonzales and Tijerina are close confederates and even conspirators. It would be, not only improbable, but, more likely, impossible for this to be the case due to the varying requisites of their situations. However, both have made strong statements supporting the actions and legitimacy of the Brown Berets. Both have recognized their existence as independent groups. Both have invited Berets to lead and participate in youth conferences and both have expressed pride in them as Chicano youth.

Poor People's March

Early in their organizational history the Berets often spoke of and quoted the phrases of these two leaders in tones of near adulation. For at least two of the Beret leaders participation in Tijerina's "revolution" and becoming a part of his new community was high ambition. It was not until the Poor People's March, in May and June of 1968, that the Berets actually came into close day-to-day contacts with these two leaders. They took their cues regarding "coalition with other ethnic groups, not leadership by others" from the stance taken by Corky and Reies in that march. Some of the Berets, however, did sour somewhat on the purity of their idols. They were beginning to find the "feet of clay" of these "distant fathers." As they participated with them through the ensuing year. the reactions became more disenchanted.

One example of this disenchantment occurred after Gonzales' speech at Claremont in April of 1969. The audience had been enraptured. One Beret commented:

As that's a canned speech, he always does that, there's nothing new with Gonzales. He gets five hundred dollars plus transportation for making one of these speeches, but you can't get him to do it for less anymore.

Corky's main rap lines deal with pride in identity and educational reform. He and Tijerina converge on economic reform, but Tijerina is more concerned with courts, law enforcement and governmental reforms. Identity seems to be not so much of a problem for a Texan-New Mexican, as for a Chicano in Denver or Los Angeles.

The Berets have derived some of their reform proposals from each of these leaders and put them together with those stated by Angelenos such as Sal Castro and Black Power credos advocating segregation.

Some of the Berets now criticizing Tijerina's egoism and his connections with, or tolerance of, Anglo leftists. They have not openly attacked any of the three leaders with accusations of vendido, nor attempted to engage in "macho" duels with them. However, they are gradually recognizing the authority of the "distant father" as less relevant to their own particular interests. As they grow in their own prestige, they are less likely to express awe or affiliation with these leaders and seek instead to become distant fathers to others. In essence, this format exists, in embryonic stage, in their relationships with their thirty other chapters.

In the Mexican culture loyalty to persons tends to outweigh loyalty to ideas. The *machismo* concept defined by Beals as 'a purely masculine set of values which might, somewhat misleadingly, be translated as "manliness," ' heightens the tendency toward individualism. The recurring strong man, the *caudillo*, in Latin American politics often is admired as being *muy macho*.[8]

Although macho, or, the quest for self-esteem through the reactions of others, is present in the vendido characterizations and relationships, this is most characteristic of the relationships with other young militants.

The key manifestation of this is the recurring phenomena of secondary leaders breaking with one organization and founding a rival group and thus achieving primary leadership. One such occurrence in the Beret experience led to the founding of their chief rival, La Junta (the group).

The immediate precipitating cause of this splintering seems to have been proximity. After the school walkouts the then ministers of the Brown Berets decided to rent a house together. The personality rifts that soon appeared led shortly to the disassociation of two of the most loyal Berets from the group. These two became involved in already existing groups. The five remaining ministers then engaged in a non-violent intermitant leadership struggle which lasted several months. Two remained as leaders of the Berets while the other three founded La Junta. La Junta quickly became a serious rival with the Berets for legitimacy, as representative of working class Mexican-American youth gone militant. To bolster its position, at least financially, La Junta formed various relationships with adult radicals who are reputed to be members of the Communist Party. Several of the leaders of La Junta underwent ideological conversion.

Ongoing Series

The ideological alliances in addition to the bitterness of their dismissal from the Brown Berets led to

an on-going series of gang-type harassments. These
have had temporary abeyances when, for instance,
a Brown Beret married a girl who was in La Junta.
And, there is one instance of an attempt to reconcile
differences, when the Berets staged a rally which
both Brown Berets, La Junta and other groups participated. However, that same month, the Beret
office was ransacked and firebombed and there was
considerable suspicion afoot that the culprits were
members of La Junta.

Periodically since then, the Berets and La Junta
have joined in at each other's parties, as a token of
togetherness, but they have also engaged in fights
with each other, threats to each other and "bum
rapping" one another.

This is not to say that all secondary leaders by
some inevitable macho process perform destructive
splintering functions. One Beret minister, for instance, became very involved in a leadership position with La Vida Nueva, a militant student group.
He led them in several symbolic forays and became
an editor of their newspaper. He seemed about to
move on to lead and found other organizations. But
he displayed ambivalence by wanting to belong to
both La Vida Nueva and the Brown Berets as well
as maintain close contact with the Third World
Liberation Front. When the Prime Minister was
jailed for about a month his ambivalence was resolved in favor of loyalty to the Berets.

More recently, some second level leaders have
been assigned to organizing new chapters and have
thus become involved in regenerating mitosis. Also
in the summer of 1969 La Junta underwent a mitosis
of its own. The newest splinter group, MALO (Mexican-American Low-riders Association, acronym
spells "bad" in Spanish), was formed by some of the
original members of the Berets, who had become
members of La Junta and now are MALO.

It is worth noting that all of these organizations
have their roots in attempts to unify the gang and
car club Chicanos. Despite their expressed intent,
however, all of the organizations develop a life of
their own, an exclusiveness, an in-group and a "we-
they" dichotomy. The consequent relationships are
usually of a new rival in the field, rather than a
unifying force.

Although the proliferation of groups to reform cholos has not done much for organizational unity it has been effective in another way. What we may be seeing is the reconstitution of all of the old gangs, but with political content and strong emphases on Mexican-American identity and community problems. This in itself would be somewhat of a revolution. Despite inter-group rivalry, there has been a marked decline in the number of deaths and injuries resulting from the old type gang "rumbles."

Splinter Groups

Despite the growing number of splinter groups, the Berets remain the most formidable. Perhaps with a more flexible and existential organizational framework they can avoid, in the future, further splintering off of potential leaders into potent rivals.

Meanwhile they are making a place for themselves in the organizational spectrum of Mexican-American groups. The spectrum itself does not follow the left to right and class caste patterning of Anglo social and political groups. It follows an age and educational level patterning on a scale of politicization with a dimension of ideologies.

If machismo on an interorganizational level is measured by inclusion in planning councils, notoriety, and controversy, then the Berets have succeeded in establishing machismo both within the interorganizational framework and with the larger Anglo community. Some people have said that the Brown Berets are "just a gang" but if this is so it is the only gang in town with its own newspaper, free clinic, and national reputation.

The aforementioned categories (vendido, distant father, and machismo) relate to the patterns of interaction within the Mexican-American community. This is the area within which the "we-they" framework operates. As yet, there is no real pattern development for interaction with Anglo and Black organizations.

The relationships between the Berets and organizations outside of the Mexican-American population may be subject to considerable confusion, and is, with the exception of the Black Power groups, so limited as to be uni-dimensional, preferably only on a single specific, one-shot basis.

When the Berets' major activity was finding issues around which to organize themselves, and actions which would legitimize their existence as something other than a barrio gang or a car club, they began their meetings with the leaders of the Black Panthers and other militant Black Power people. The personal childhood experiences of several of the leaders mandated a priority to stopping the gang fights between Blacks and Browns. Additionally, they admired and identified with the Black Power line. As one of them had stated, "The Blacks didn't have anything either until they started burning down Watts, and Newark and Detroit, and then they had to be listened to—the man had to start being careful with how they treated them." Rap Brown, Stokely Carmichael and later Eldridge Cleaver and Huey Newton became heroes to these young men who were, then, not particularly knowledgeable about their own identity nor cause-specifics. In February, 1968, when Tijerina, Carmichael and H. Rap Brown jointly addressed an audience at the Los Angeles Sports Arena, the Berets were able to officially acknowledge the Black-Brown coalition. This never became a popular cause among the Mexican-American population generally.

Most of the major leaders of the Black Power movement who spoke in Los Angeles during 1968 either met with or spoke to rallys sponsored by the Brown Berets. When Panthers were killed by police actions, Berets acted as pall bearers. When Martin Luther King was assassinated, Berets took part in the "watch night" ceremonial in Los Angeles. When the school blowouts occurred in East Los Angeles, a Black high school walked out in sympathy. But the Beret constituency had difficulty accepting this coalition. The Beret office was attacked several times with epithets of "nigger lovers." The Berets seemed then to feel that it was not "too cool" to keep pushing coalition. Also, they and the Panthers had discovered that neither organization really had the strength to protect members of each other's race who were being attacked by their own. This seemed to suggest that both organizations have only so much power as they derive from avoiding opposition to the street mores of their societies.

Despite continuing cordial relationships between the Berets and the Black militants, the Berets have begun to soft pedal the coalition idea in their rap lines. However, in April of 1968, while hopes were still high, the Beret Prime Minister spoke of Black and Brown coalition on a radio interview:

> I'd just like to say that the man, the establishment has been dividing Black and Brown people just too long. They've been divided by publicity whenever there's an incident. Like over in Watts it seems a Chicano kid shotgunned a Negro, a Black rather, and they blew it up real big. They play games with the poverty programs, the Blacks go to the poverty programs and get told that the Mexicans are getting everything, and then you have the Mexicans going to the poverty programs and they're told that the Blacks are getting everything ... But the Black and Brown people will continue to get together.
> One thing we have in common with Chicanos and Blacks is that we are both fighters. We learned to be fighters from growing up in this environment. The man knows this and puts us in Vietnam to fight the Viet Cong, also our brothers. We figure that since Chicanos came down through the Bering Straits part Oriental, and then that honkie, what's his name? Cortez, came across over and raped our women, so we're half mongoloid and half caucasoid, that makes the Viet Cong our brothers.

Less than three months later, in late July, several Berets went to a liquor store in the Black area of Pasadena, to refill the party supplies, and narrowly avoided a gun battle with some Black militants who had no knowledge of coalitions nor symbols, and felt threatened by the Beret symbol.

The Brown Berets have seldom had official relationships with white radical or liberal groups. The basic reasons for this are mistrust and divergence of goals. The SDS, for instance, is regarded as being Communist co-opters who "will use you for their own purposes." In public statements they veil this mistrust behind statements like: "They have their own priorities and we have ours. It dilutes our cause when they use it for their purposes."

In the quest for legal aid, the Berets have been involved with both the ACLU and the Committee for the Defense of the Bill of Rights.

211

The experience with ACLU antedates others:

> About two years ago we had an alert patrol.
> After three months of this we had the ACLU
> come in and they said 'we have a police mal-
> practice complaint center in Watts, drop your
> alert patrol and we'll set up a center to serve
> the purpose.' It really hasn't acted as any kind
> of pressure group.
> It would be much more meaningful to get some
> money to set up some lawyers in our own
> community, Chicanos for the defense. That
> would be much more meaningful than working
> through ACLU. We're trying to get our own
> lawyers who live in the community and we
> feel they would have to try just a little harder
> because they would have to come back and
> face the guys from the people and put up with
> the reaction.[9]

The ACLU did rise in stature in the Berets' eyes in
June, 1968. This is because of the activities of A. L.
Wirin, ACLU constitutional lawyer, who made the
motions for bail reductions at the arraignment of
the "Chicano Thirteen." One year later when a new
round of grand jury indictments were handed down
Wirin responded in like manner.

The Committee for the Defense of the Bill of
Rights (formerly known as the Committee for the
Defense of the Foreign Born) were hosts for a series
of receptions for Tijerina in February, 1968. After
one reception on Mulholland Drive at which Cuban-
made movies about the war in Vietnam were fea-
tured, the Berets identified the group as "either C.P.
or Communist Front." The Committee had been
securing legal counsel for the Berets at no cost to
them. However, the lawyers frequently called in at
the last possible moment and were usually unprepared to effectively handle the charges. Identification with this organization led later to charges of
Communist Influence by one very conservative
news commentator and a newspaper.[10]

After the mis-handling of an early case by the
Committee the Berets began developing their own
legal resources preparatory to disassociation with
both the Committee and the adult Chicano "leader"
who had enlisted their services. The Berets, with
their concern for purity, are just as leary of dealing
with any organization suspected of Communist

leanings, as they are with the usually more conservative "vendidos."

Although the Berets frequently appear for "rap sessions" and speeches at meetings of Anglo liberal groups, the only on-going relationship they sustained with any such group has been with the Los Angeles Psychologists for Social Action. The Psychologists' group undertook co-sponsorship with the Berets of the East Los Angeles Free Clinic. This relationship was always a tenuous one. It was sustained essentially by the authors and a small committee of LAPSA.

Previous to the opening of the clinic, when the committee met with Berets there was often friction and occasionally more serious emotional repercussion. The Berets made it very clear that any cooperation would have to be on a basis of the Berets handling the interactions with the Mexican-American community. The psychologists were to function only to draw outside help, professional and financial, into the project. Much to the consternation of the authors, some of the psychologists over-stepped this well defined line. The problems centered about housing the clinic. The Berets had been unable to find a landlord who would provide either free or very low rent facilities. The psychologists wanted to broaden the base of community support by bringing "community leaders" into the planning and getting them to secure the housing. The Berets wanted no other community organization or agency involved in the project.

When the clinic was finally established, the grant had been made on a basis of co-sponsorship by the professional group. For the first two months of clinic operation, the co-sponsorship idea functioned well. However, at the first meeting of the professional staff, on July 31st, the Prime Minister of the Berets stated that he did not want any kind of organizational co-sponsorship. LAPSA, which had lent its name to the clinic only for funding purposes, happily withdrew its name. Individual professionals of that group continue to do volunteer service at the clinic.

Mexican-Americans in East Los Angeles may affiliate with any of a variety of formal and informal groups. The groups range from relatively informal gangs, to car clubs to social clubs and political and social organizations. The years 1967-68 witnessed an increase in the numbers and variety of Chicano organizations—particularly those oriented to youth and young adults. There is some competition for active membership and relatively few groups survive to reach a level of organization to be reckoned as a force within the community. The mortality rate of these groups and the inability of any group or coalition of groups to present a united community front have presented puzzles and questions to the many social scientists who have grappled with them.

The interactions of the Brown Berets within the world of organizations are indicative of the behaviors which result in this organizational quandary. While some aspects of the Beret's uniqueness present specific positive and negative valences in the organization of Mexican-Americans, many other behaviors are clearly a product of traditional status implications within the context of the Mexican-American in Los Angeles.

The most obvious element in the relationships of the Berets to other organizations is the Beret quest for purity. In this they share the concern of young radicals as described by Cohen and Hale:

> Traditional political thought has always held that the most effective response to frustration among large numbers of people is collective action toward changing the institutional structure of society. Few on the left would dispute that, in theory. But collective action implies alliances, whereas the student who sees rebellion as a private act usually decorates his world view with extremely militant and exclusive moral imperatives. Morality and politics seem to be incompatible. Translated into tactics, this attitude often takes on the appearance of hostility toward the adult world, and has led many observers to interpret the student movement as one more manifestation of the conflict between the generations. But it is something more than hostility toward adults qua adults. The fear of distasteful alliances—of "selling out"—is partly a fear that, in spite of everything, the student will eventually be co-opted by Suburbia. And for much of the new left, that means the end of a decent human existence.[11]

The Berets have additional reason for suspicion because there have been various attempts to subvert, co-opt, infiltrate and manipulate their organization. Because of these experiences they have developed a very guarded stance which they verbalize and rationalize on a basis of "strength through organizational purity."

Brown Beret relationships with other organizations and other leaders within the Chicano community may be behaviorally categorized as "vendido," "distant father" or "machismo." Some relationships are conglomerates but evolve into a more specific category in the course of time.

Most of the Mexican-Americans over thirty-five who have some claim to political success or business and professional achievement are classified as vendidos. There are two categories of vendido— those who have deliberately "sold out" for personal profit, and those who are "being used by the establishment" as "tokens" or "puppets." So far as the Berets are concerned, neither are to be trusted nor dealt with for any reason. Instead they are to be "exposed" as "enemies of their people."

"Distant fathers" are those leaders who are geographically distant and have developed ideologies of Chicano power. These include Corky Gonzales, Cesar Chavez and Reies Tijerina.

Machismo, a truncated adolescent assertion of masculine identity involves a grappling for status. The consequent role behaviors are evidenced in relationships with organizations of age peers and to some extent, with older, less militant organizations within the community.

The Beret involvement with non-Chicano groups seems to depend on several pivotal points. They relate with individuals rather than with a group. If there is trust and mutual respect with these individuals, there is little reluctance to enter a specific cooperative action. The "mutual" respect must include specific safeguards to organizational integrity for the Berets. This requirement becomes difficult to achieve because the Berets' perception of their condition of integrity is strongly flavored by "feedback." If the press or other Chicano organizations and individuals challenge the Berets' affiliation, that affiliation will likely be severed.

For instance, the events leading up to severance of clinic co-sponsorship consisted of an article in a neighborhood newspaper which emphasized the role of the professional organizations in administering the clinic; several "rap sessions" with groups of Chicano college students at which the Berets' opposition to the "Anglo establishment" was challenged on the basis of co-sponsorship; resentment by the Brown Beret leader of the inefficiency of his members in meeting the work demands of clinic responsibilities in contrast with the apparent efficiency of the professional organizations.

At this juncture in the development of ethnic pride and militancy, any appearance of dependency is apt to be considered eventually as "co-option."

It is becoming increasingly difficult for social scientists to be participants in, or students of, the internal dynamics of ethnic movements. Even when the social scientist is himself a member of the particular ethnic group in question, he is often denied access to the inner life of the group. He is suspect on the basis of his educational level, if nothing else.

Possibly, the only way a social scientist can study such groups is through involvement with them in a particular action project or program in which he serves as a "resource" person to the group. In such cases, that which the social scientist "gets" is approximately proportional to what he "gives."

FOOTNOTES

1. Paul M. Sheldon, "Community Participation and the Emerging Middle Class," in *La Raza: Forgotten Americans*, edited by Julian Samora (Notre Dame, Indiana: University of Notre Dame Press, 1966), pp. 137-138.
2. *Ibid.*
3. *Ibid.*
4. *Ibid.*, p. 144.
5. Erik H. Erikson, *Childhood and Society* (2d ed.; New York: W. W. Norton, Inc., 1963), p. 235.
6. *La Vida Nueva*, March 12, 1969. p. 3.
7. Los Angeles Times, February 12, 1968, CC S Part II. Don Munson, "America's Brown Beret Revolution," *Saga*, August, 1968, p. 38.
8. Sheldon, *op. cit.*, p. 145.
9. Joe Razo at Colloquiem, U.S.C. April 12, 1968.

10. George Putnam and the *Los Angeles Herald-Examiner*, October, 1968.

11. Mitchell Cohen and Dennis Hale (eds.), *The New Student Left* (2d ed. rev.; Boston: Beacon Press, 1967), p. xxii.

'BROWN POWER' UNITY SEEN BEHIND SCHOOL DISORDERS

Dial Torgerson

"We want to walk out," a group of students at Lincoln
High School told teacher Sal Castro last September. "Help
us."
    The students, like Castro, were Mexican-Americans --
at a mostly Mexican-American school deep in the belt of
east-of-downtown districts which together comprise the
United States' most populous Mexican-American community.
"Don't walk out," Castro told them. "Organize."
And -- as has now been seen -- they did.
    What resulted was a week-and-a-half of walkouts,
speeches, sporadic lawbreaking, arrests, demands, picketing,
sympathy demonstrations, sit-ins, police tactical alerts
and emergency sessions of the school board.
    It was, some say, the beginning of a revolution -- the
Mexican-American revolution of 1968.
    In the midst of massive walkouts and police alerts, Dr.
Julian Nava, only Mexican-American on the Los Angeles Board
of Education, turned to Supt. of Schools Jack Crowther.
"Jack," said Nava, "This is BC and AD. The schools will not
be the same hereafter." "Yes," said Crowther, "I know."

FIRST MASS MILITANCY

    And, in the vast Mexican-American districts of the city
and county of Los Angeles -- the "barrios" (neighborhoods)
where 800,000 people with Spanish names make their homes --
leaders of a movement to unite what they call "La Raza"
swear the barrios will never be the same, either.
    Since World War II the Mexican-American community has
had leaders calling for unity, change, better education,
civil rights, economic opportunity and an end to what they
called second-class citizenship. But the community never
backed them up. Except for a few instances of picketing,
nothing happened. Then came the school walkouts, the first
act of mass militancy by Mexican-Americans in Southern California. "Viva la Revolucion," the youngsters' signs read.
"Viva la Raza." (Raza translates "race" but is used in a
sense of "our people.") And, surprisingly to some, stunning
ly to others, the community backed them up.
    The men and women of the once-conservative older gener-
ation jammed school board and civic meetings, shouting their
approval of what their children had done. Parents of student

218

arrested during demonstrations even staged a sit-in in the
Hall of Justice. "The people are with us, now," one young
leader says.

Observers within the community say it heralds the entry
of a powerful new force on the American scene: a new united
Mexican-American movement drawing a nationalistic, brown-
power fervor from 4.5 million people in five Southwestern
states. With underground newspapers, cooperation with Negro
groups, plans for political action and economic boycotts,
leaders say they will show the country a new type of Mexican-American: one proud of his language, his culture, his
raza, ready to take his share of U.S. prosperity. But
there's no doubt at the grassroots levels, where earlier
pleas for unity never reached before -- in the minds of the
younger men and women on the streets of the barrios, from
East Los Angeles to Pico Rivera, from the fringes of Watts
north deep into the San Gabriel Valley.

Listen to the voices there of La Raza -- and the message
observers say these voices bring to the Anglo world:
...the scene is a rainy sidewalk outside East Los Angeles Junior College. A white panel truck halts and four young
men in brown berets and mixed, cast-off Army fatigues and
boots jump out, craning their heads left and right to see if
they are pursued, and then file into the campus for a meeting. They are members of the Brown Berets, the most militant
of East Los Angeles Mexican-American groups. They have been
accused of inciting high school students to riot, using nar-
cotics, being Communists. There are several hundred of them
here and in the Fresno area, their leaders say.

FRANKLY ADMIRING STUDENTS

"The deputies and the cops have really been harassing
us," said David Sanchez, a college student who dropped out
to be chairman of the Berets. "Sixty-five Brown Berets
have been arrested in the past month. There are warrants
out now for five of us because of the school walkouts."

The four sit on a concrete bench and speak in quiet
voices to a newsman, glancing at times down the wet, wind-
swept walkway toward the street, nodding in reply to greet-
ings from frankly admiring students with the slightly superior air of young men slightly past 20, slightly revolutionary, and slightly wanted.

"Communism? That's a white thing," said Carlos Montes,
mustachioed minister of public relations for the Berets.
"It's their trip, not ours," said husky Ralph Ramirez, minister of discipline. Added Montes: "It's pretty hard to
mix Communists and Mexican-Americans. Che (Che Guevara,
the late Cuban revolutionary some Berets seem to seek to
resemble) doesn't mean a thing to the guy on the street.
He's got his own problems." Despite their vaguely ominous
look, the Berets claim wide community support. "A lot of
mothers' clubs help us with contributions," said Sanchez.
"Men's clubs, too. They're happy to see there is finally
a militant effort in the community. And they like what
we're doing with the gangs."

In each barrio there are kids' gangs (The Avenues, the Clovers, the White Fence, Dog Town, Happy Valley) which have long shot up each other, and whole neighborhoods, in senseless warfare. "Gang fights are going out," said Montes. "We're getting kids from the the different gangs into the Brown Berets. It's going to be one big barrio, one big gang. We try to teach our people not to fight with each other, and not to fight with our blood brothers to the south."

Police say the Berets were among the "outside agitators" who helped cause the student disturbances. "The Chicano students were the main action group," said Sanchez. (Chicano is a term for Mexican-Americans which members of the community use in describing themselves.) "We were at the walkouts to protect our younger people. When they (law officers) started hitting with sticks, we went in, did our business, and got out." What's "our business"? "We put ourselves between the police and the kids, and took the beating," Sanchez said.

SIGNIFICANCE EXPLORED

What significance lies behind the militant movement? "They've given these people a real revolutionary experience," said Dr. Ralph Guzman, a professor of political science at Cal State Los Angeles. "No Marxist could do better. They're making rebels. When they see police clubbing them, it's the final evidence that society is against them--that existing within the system won't work." "I don't know what's going to happen. I'm worried. I think there will be violence. I'm not predicting it. But from what I've seen--I saw riots in South America and India when I was with the Peace Corps--I think we all have a potential for violence."

...the scene is Cleland House, a community meeting hall in East Los Angeles. Two hundred people, most of them adults, jam the hall, facing representatives of police and the sheriff's and district attorney's office invited there by a civic group.

STUDENT GIVES VERSION

"We were at the alley, just breaking out, when the cops charged at us," said Robert Sanchez, 17, a student at Roosevelt High. "If I could be allowed to express myself with dignity, I'd do so. But if they're grabbing me, or hitting me, and there's a rock or a brick there, I'd throw it." "The only reported injury," said Police Inspector Jack Collins, head of the patrol division, calmly, "was a police officer hit in the eye with a bottle..." "Parents got beat up too!" yelled a man's voice. "Now try to get out of that one!" shouted Sanchez.

In an office, later, Lincoln High teacher Castro explained the walkouts:

"It started with the kids from Lincoln." said Castro, 34,
a social studies and government teacher who himself grew
up in the East Los Angeles barrios. "They wanted things
changed at the school. They wanted to hold what they call
a 'blowout'--a walkout. I stopped them. I said, 'Blow
out now and everyone will think it's because you want short
skirts and long hair. Organize. What do you need?' They
said they needed some help in making signs, printing up
demands, things like that. We got them help from college
kids--mostly from the United Mexican-American Students at
the different colleges. A blowout committee was established
at each of the four East L.A. schools. And there was one
committee with kids from each school.

ORIGINAL PLAN

"The original plan was to go before the Board of Education and propose a set of changes, without walking out--
to hold that back to get what they wanted. Then, at Wilson
High Friday (March 1), the principal canceled a play they
were going to do ("Barefoot in the Park")as unfit, and the
Wilson kids blew out. It was spontaneous. Then Roosevelt
and Lincoln wanted to blow, too. Garfield, too. Later on
(March 8) Belmont, which was never in on the original plan,
came in, too.
"These blowouts in the other schools, like Venice and
Jefferson, weren't connected with the Chicano blowouts, but
they may have been in sympathy. Some of the kids from
schools uptown asked us to send representatives to tell them
how to organize. What do you think of that! The Anglo
schools asking the Chicano kids to help them organize. They
should've told them 'Ask your dads how they organized to
oppress us all these years.'"

SIGNIFICANCE WEIGHED

And what significance lies behind the sudden surge of
student activism?
"These things weren't thought up by the kids," said
Philip Montez, western program director for the U.S. Commission on Civil Rights. "Eight years ago the Council on
Mexican-American Affairs was asking for bi-cultural education, one of the things the youngsters want now. But
all attempts to move the community were abortive. Movements would start and peter out. We could never get a
commitment. We were dealing with older people, conservative,
with livings to make, kids to raise. Up 'til now the
Mexican-American community hasn't had the sophistication
for organization or movement. But things are different
now. The kids are close to being anglicized and middle
class--which is apparently what it takes to bring them
closer to being able to work a system. That's why they're
the leaders.

221

IDENTITY-SEEKING

"Tied in with it is an identity-seeking process. These kids say proudly: 'I'm a Mexican, and I want to learn about my culture.' It used to be, when I was a kid, we'd play it pretty cool about that Mexican thing. Someone would say 'Are you a Mexican?' and you'd say, 'Well, y'know...' and change the subject, or make a joke. But the society has changed, too. Always before in the Mexican-American community there was a faith and belief in the Democratic society, that through good graces you'd achieve success. Be conservative. Family-oriented. Know God is on our side. But they don't believe it any longer. There's a higher level of sophistication. They don't want to sit around and wait. They see they've got to make it work. That you've got to grease the wheels of democracy.

"That's what the kids were doing when they walked out-- and it caught the imagination of the adults. Now, for the first time, the community is behind them. And the adults are asking: 'Why did the kids have to show us why we make mistakes?"

...the scene is Belmont High School, on the other side of the Civic Center from the East Los Angeles barrios. Only one-third of the students there have Spanish names, as compared with 90% at some Eastside schools. Yet Belmont, too, joined the demonstrations.

"I was arrested," said Frances Spector, 16, an A12 at Belmont who was charged with disturbing the peace. She has light brown hair and blue eyes, but feels strongly about the demonstrations--and what happened to her. "I was told to go home by a school official, and police stopped me on the street and put me in the police car. They said they were taking me home. But we went to the police station." (Ten of the 15 persons arrested during the demonstrations were picked up during the Belmont walk-out, in which police say outsiders played a large role: of the 10 arrested, 9 were nonstudents.)

VIEW ON DEMANDS

How does she feel about the student demands? "At Belmont," said Frances, "you look at the industrial arts classes, and it's all Chicano and black. You look at the college preparatory classes, and it's all Anglos and Asians. That can't be the way they really fit! They can't be getting the right counseling. They're just putting people where they think they belong because of what color they are."

Is there any significance to students' complaints that Mexican-Americans are being pushed into shop courses, and discouraged from taking academic courses? "I was graduated from Roosevelt High in 1945," said Dr. Nava, now 40, who got his Ph.D. from Harvard in history. "I was told to take auto shop. And I did. I did as I was told. Then I went into the Navy--and I wasn't a Mexican anymore, I was just Julian. It opened my eyes. But, then, in the Navy I was

222

an auto mechanic--so I can't say that the advice was all
bad. A lot of those decisions were based on what the high
school counselors considered 'a realistic assessment of the
chances of success.' They realized the chances, then of a
Mexican-American getting through college.
    "I'm just worried for fear they're still making those
'realistic assessments.' I just wonder how many other
Julians have ended up in an auto shop, somewhere. And
stayed there."
    "They had me believing my oldest kid, Hector, wasn't
too bright," said Charles Ericksen, whose wife came from
Mexico and whose children went to East Los Angeles schools
before he became a public relations man in Sacramento. "All
he could get were Cs. The counselor told me Cs were fine,
all we could expect. They said he had no leadership potential. He never had any homework. Then we moved to
Sacramento, and he went into a school where he's the only
Mexican-American. They call him 'Taco.' And he gets all
As and Bs and is president of his class."
    "It's wrong when people say, 'We have a terrible school
system,'" said Dr. Guzman. "All in all, it has an excellent reputation in our country. But it may not be effective
in certain corners of society. The policy is established
downtown for all the areas and all the schools. But, in
some areas, such as the Mexican-American areas, they find
that somehow these rules don't apply. Their tests don't
work. And they wonder why. You know why? They don't
understand our people. They're not trying to."

SCENE AT UCLA

    ... the scene is UCLA, where, late last month, hundreds
of delegates from 25 different Mexican-American groups
gathered at a symposium sponsored by the Associated Students
of UCLA and the United Mexican American Students.
    "Integration is an empty bag," said Rudolfo (Corky)
Gonzales, of Denver, head of the Crusade for Justice, a
Colorado civil rights group he says numbers 1,800. "It's
like getting up out of the small end of the funnel. One
may make it, but the rest of the people stay at the bottom.
Our young people reject politics. All the new leaders we
developed a year ago are now working for the poverty
program. They were bought out. They are not provoking a
revolution. They're putting water on fire. Young leaders!
Don't spend your time trying to educate a racist majority.
Teach your own people. Tell them to be proud of their
names, their values, and their culture. Ask them if they're
willing to fight for their rights and dignity. And ask
them: are they willing to die for it?"
    "The violence in New Mexico was the moment of awakening
for La Raza," said another speaker, Reies Tijerina--"El
Tigre," the Tiger, leader of the militant Alianza (Alliance)
of Indio-Spanish peoples of northern New Mexico. (Because
their ancestors date to Spanish conquistador days, before
there was a Mexico, Tijerina's followers prefer Indio-Spa-

nish to Mexican-American. Often, in Colorado, New Mexico
and Texas the term "Spanish-American" is used.)

Tijerina came to the symposium while free on appeal
bond for his conviction on charges of aiding and abetting
an assault on two federal officers--forest rangers held
by Alianza members when they invaded a national forest in
October, 1966. Last June raiders shot up the courthouse
at Tierra Amarilla, N.M. and Tijerina is charged with numerous counts on which trial is still pending.

"Since Tierra Amarilla," said Tijerina in Los Angeles
"there has been a closer association. People realize the
need for closer cooperation in different parts of the Southwest. As we get closer to danger, the brotherhood tightens
in closer. I myself am not a violent man. I don't believe in outright violence. But in dealing with our
government, we find it urgent and natural to make our demands in a different way from 30 to 40 years ago."

Bert Corona, head of the Mexican-American Political
Assn., urged the Mexican-American community to fight for
power politically--but the militancy of the meeting, which
primed much of the young Chicano leadership for the demonstrations of March, was best illustrated by Luis Valdez:
"We're in the belly of the shark," said young Valdez. "In
occupied California."

He worked for a time helping efforts of Cesar Chavez,
leader of the United Farm Workers Organizing Committee, in
Delano. Chavez achieved notable success in unionizing
Mexican-American farm workers in the San Joaquin Valley--
and then, disturbed by threats of violence by some Mexican-
Americans he said were "seeking a short-cut to victory,"
went on a highly publicized 25-day fast to dramatize his
nonviolent approach.

He had been scheduled to speak at the UCLA symposium,
but couldn't because of his fast. That same week Tijerina
was making numerous appearances in the Los Angeles area,
flanked by Brown Beret bodyguards, embracing and praising
Black Nationalist leaders, and stirring young militants
with hints at violence and calls for valor and a willingness to die, if need be, for La Causa--the cause.

Valdez, wearing a Che Guevara type costume, attacked
the "gabachos"--a Mexican-American term for Anglos--and
showed a militancy more characteristic of Tijerina than
Chavez: "It's time for a new Mexican revolution," he
said. "And which Chicanos are going to lead the next
revolution? The ones in the belly of shark! Nosotros!
We're going to lead that revolution! We've got to stand
up and talk straight to the gabachos--say, hell, no, I
won't go, to their whole lousy system. I won't go to your
suburban barrio. I won't talk your language. I won't eat
your food!" Amid cheers, he added: "Support Tijerina!
And Viva la Raza!"

Has this revolution, as some say, already started?
Were the New Mexico raids and the San Joaquin Valley
strikes a prelude to the beginning of a real grass-roots
movement in Los Angeles? "These things sometimes appear

in a flash," said Dr. Leo Grebler, an economist who is
chairman of the committee for the Mexican-American Study
now underway at UCLA. "And, then, they disappear in a
flash. Since it is so new, it's hard to tell. I don't
know of any criteria to predict if it will be a permanent
force. In the past, attempts to unite, to draw in other
Spanish-speaking people, have been flashes. I maintain an
attitude of skepticism. I have to think in my terms, and
my terms are skeptical, based on past performances."

"But, then, the Mexican-American population is younger
than the rest of us (50% of the community is under 20),
and youth feels the social issues more severely than the
older leaders. Numerically, the importance of the young
will stay with us for at least this generation. The young
are here, and they'll stay with us. What they'll do with
their power we'll have to wait and see. I'd like to take
a look, say about 1970 or 71, and see what changes occurred.
But we can't predict it. All we can do is wait, and see,
and then record it."

At the end of the week the Brown Power movement had
achieved one objective--the school board had agreed to
meet in East Los Angeles. Will it all end there? In the
barrios they say no. Next, they predict, will come economic boycotts, political drives, perhaps more demonstrations.

The history Dr. Grebler plans to write is already
under way, they say. Because history, say Southern
California's young Chicanos, is something which is happening
now.